The Underdog in American Politics

The Underdog in American Politics

The Democratic Party and Liberal Values

Karl G. Trautman

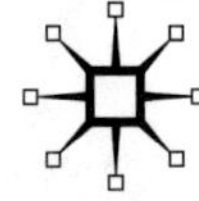

THE UNDERDOG IN AMERICAN POLITICS
Copyright © Karl G. Trautman, 2010.

First published in 2010 by
PALGRAVE MACMILLAN®
in the United States—a division of St. Martin's Press LLC,
175 Fifth Avenue, New York, NY 10010.

Where this book is distributed in the UK, Europe and the rest of the world,
this is by Palgrave Macmillan, a division of Macmillan Publishers Limited,
registered in England, company number 785998, of Houndmills,
Basingstoke, Hampshire RG21 6XS.

Palgrave Macmillan is the global academic imprint of the above companies
and has companies and representatives throughout the world.

Palgrave® and Macmillan® are registered trademarks in the United States,
the United Kingdom, Europe and other countries.

ISBN: 978–0–230–10274–3

Library of Congress Cataloging-in-Publication Data

Trautman, Karl G., 1960–
     The underdog in American politics : the democratic party and liberal
  values / Karl G. Trautman.
        p. cm.
     ISBN 978–0–230–10274–3 (alk. paper)
       1. Democratic Party (U.S.)—History. 2. Liberalism—United States—
  History. 3. United States—Politics and government. I. Title.

JK2316.T73 2009
324.2736—dc22   2009039553

A catalogue record of the book is available from the British Library.

Design by Newgen Imaging Systems (P) Ltd., Chennai, India.

First edition: June 2010

10 9 8 7 6 5 4 3 2 1

Printed in the United States of America.

Contents

Figures

Preface

Thanks go out to many people: my colleagues who read various parts of my writing over the last several years, Amy Zesbaugh who provided invaluable assistance in helping the book come to completion, and my wife Deb for realizing how important this book is to me.

It is difficult to pinpoint exactly when my passion for the underdog began. The easy explanation is that I am a redhead. I realized very early on in my life that there was a characteristic I had that I could not hide from anyone. I understood from a very early age how it felt to be different. It seemed to me that I had to try harder than anyone just to be part of the crowd; or equal. That is the curse. The blessing is much stronger; I sought out other people who were somehow different and began to understand what they went through.

The comparatively mild form of discrimination I received when I was young is actually extraordinarily trivial; it cannot in any way be equated with the harsh examples that individuals and groups have experienced in the past (and still feel today). However I still remember it, or part of me does. The feelings of injustice that it brought forth in me is one of the links I have with underdogs.

Perhaps it began because of when I grew up; I have vague memories of underdog struggles from my childhood. They include the 1967 season of the Boston Red Sox, the Impossible Dream song from the play *Man of La Mancha* and the assassination of Bobby Kennedy. What do all of these have in common? They all involve tremendous struggles of long shots that, ultimately, come up short.

Wherever it began, I have been rooting for underdogs all my life. I hope this book helps you understand why.

CHAPTER 1

Introduction

The Intent of the Book

The purpose of this book is to explain and analyze the historical and ideological links of the Democratic Party to underdogs. It is my hope that the reader will understand how the concept of the underdog has shaped, and continues to shape, the politics of Democrats. This book may be used as a tool to harness the power of the underdog for continued progressive political change.

Why Underdogs? Why Democrats?

It seems that everyone wants to be seen as the underdog. Romantics, idealists, and do-gooders are drawn to the defense of them. Individuals who stand up for them are considered heroic. Organizations that represent them are acclaimed. Nations that fight for their interests are praised. Culture is shaped by how underdog stories are incorporated into its fabric.

The underdog has a particular appeal to Americans. American society is defined and influenced by concerns about equality and fairness. It is also troubled by discrimination, persecution, and injustice—persistent reminders that many core American ideals fall short of reality. This unease is expressed through sympathy and empathy and is often played out on the stage of American politics.

Moreover, there is a process appeal of underdogs as well; Americans love a good game. Rooting for the team, person, party, or company that is perceived to be behind in a contest is exciting. If ideals interrelate with the contest, all the better: thought and emotion combine to produce political dramas.

The reader may ask: Why the Democratic Party? I believe, as a party, it best represents the history, culture, and interests of underdogs in American politics. The ideology of the majority of Democrats is still some strand of liberalism, however hidden by employing the linguistic turn of "progressive." Liberals have historically fought for the "little guy" (no sexism intended)—the person who does not have much money, power, or resources to better his or her lot in life. Democrats have also stood up for groups that have been historically discriminated against in law and practice: most notably, the poor, women, racial and ethnic minorities, gays and the disabled.

While there is a story to be written about the Republican Party and underdogs, it deserves a distinct focus and comprehensive analysis that is beyond the scope of this book.

What Is an Underdog?

Even though underdogs have an endearing appeal for so many, the definition of the word is ambiguous. *Webster's* gives three definitions, one being "a person who is handicapped or at a disadvantage because of injustice, discrimination, etc."[1] The *Scholastic Pocket Dictionary* defines the word as a "person, team, or group that is expected to be the loser in a game, a race, an election, or other contest."[2]

On Wikipedia, there is a section labeled "Sympathy for the Underdog." Some of the words in that section capture a core component of the idea: "a social or ethnic group which suffers from discrimination, persecution and/or economic disability and which on that base gains the sympathy of public opinion in its own or other countries."[3] Thus it seems that almost everyone, or anything, could be considered an underdog at some point in time.

Some people believe that the term came from nineteenth-century dog fighting: the winner of the contest was the top dog while the loser of the contest was the underdog.[4] There was even a familiar nineteenth-century song and poem by David Barker titled "The Under Dog in the Fight." Its lyrics describe the sentiment many feel when two participants with unequal power battle each other:

> I know that the world, the great big world,
> From the peasant up to the king,
> Has a different tale from the tale I tell,
> And a different song to sing.
> But for me—and I care not a single fig
> If they say I am wrong or right wrong,
> I shall always go for the *weaker* dog,
> For the under dog in the fight.
> I know that the world, that the great big world,
> Will never a moment stop.
> To see which dog may be in the fault,

But will shout for the dog on top.
But for me I shall never pause to ask
Which dog may be in the right
For my heart will beat, while it beats at all.
For the under dog in the fight.
Perchance what I've said I had better not said,
Or 'twere better I had said it incog.
But with my heart and with glass filled up to the brim
Here is luck to the *under* dog.[5]

As applied in this book, the general contours of an underdog are as follows:

1. A paramount concern with equality and fairness.
2. The description of a person, group, or nation that is disadvantaged because of injustice, persecution, or discrimination.
3. The description of a person, group, nation, or idea that is expected to lose.
4. An overriding concern with empathy and sympathy.

These contours are diagrammed on figure 1.1.

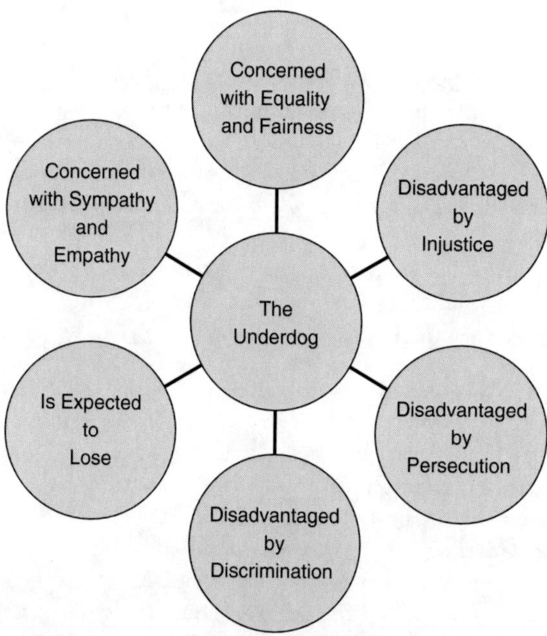

Figure 1.1   The structure, scope, and methodology of the book

The Structure, Scope, and Methodology of the Book

How will I illustrate the underdog concept? The concept will be elucidated in chapter 2 by how it is represented in different cultural discourses. Chapter 3 continues this approach by examining the relationship between the political culture of the Democratic Party and the underdogs. The chapter concludes with an examination of the links between Democratic political ideology and underdogs.

Chapters 4 through 8 are the core of the book and focus on how the underdog concept correlates with specific Democratic presidential candidates and presidents. Many remarkable people have chosen to try and represent the Democratic Party to the nation as its presidential candidate. I have selected a sample of them as the primary focus of my analysis. Some of them were successful and became the nominee, while others fell short of that goal.

Presidential candidates were chosen because of both symbolism (they become the national emblem of the party) and substance (the policies they wish to enact are associated with the ideological identity of the party). Every four years this ritual is repeated, as candidates try to reinforce, contest, or redefine the symbolism and substance of the party to the nation.

Generally, I analyze these politicians by focusing on process, image, and substance:

- **Process:** Was the candidate perceived as an underdog in their political contests? Which ones: Nomination contests or general election? Why were they expected to lose?
- **Image:** Did the candidate represent themselves as an underdog? Was it part of their biography? How did the media help create their image as an underdog?
- **Substance:** What political ideals did the candidate want to champion? How would they have helped underdogs? If they became president, what specific policies did they try and enact?

More specifically, I use biography, ideology, campaign dynamics, and public policies (if they became president) as my methodologies to exemplify the correlations between them and the underdog concept, with selected illustrative examples to show vital correlations.

How these analytical methods interact with the definitional components of the underdog concept are diagrammed in figure 1.2.

Underdog concepts associated with Democratic presidential candidates are as follows: a concern for equality and fairness is the

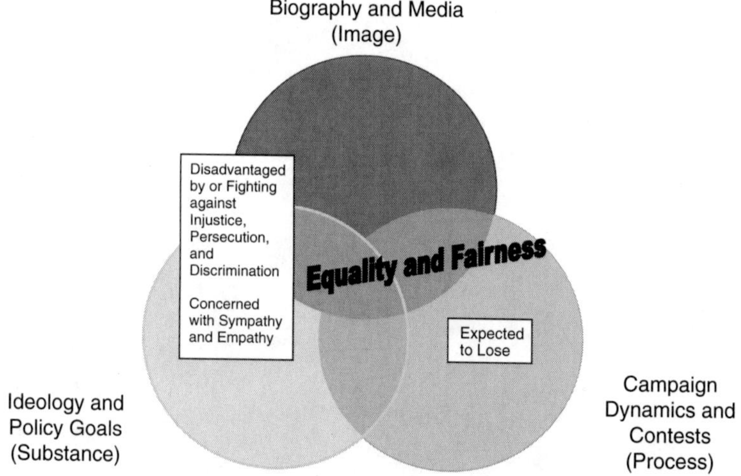

Figure 1.2 Interaction of analytical methods and definitional components of the underdog concept

fundamental component; it is part of the process, image, and substance. The candidate, issue, or cause is expected to lose; that is the process. Disadvantaged by or fighting against injustice, persecution, and discrimination and a concern with sympathy and empathy are part of the image of the candidate and the ideology and policy goals they fight for forms the substance.

In particular, chapter 4 analyzes Thomas Jefferson and Andrew Jackson, the founders of the Democratic Party, and William Jennings Bryan for his strong analytical links with underdogs. Chapter 5 surveys the party's Glory Days, and I examine selected underdog characteristics associated with Franklin D. Roosevelt, Harry Truman, John F. Kennedy, Lyndon Johnson, Eugene McCarthy, Bobby Kennedy, and Hubert Humphrey.

Chapter 6 narrows the focus to two decades: the 1970s and 1980s. George McGovern, Jimmy Carter, Gary Hart, and Jesse Jackson are analyzed in this chapter. Chapter 7 focuses on three Democrats: Bill Clinton, Al Gore, and Howard Dean. The final chapter examines Barack Obama and the future of the party.

The link between culture and underdogs is where my analysis begins. That is the subject of chapter 2.

CHAPTER 2

Culture and Underdogs: The Endearing Appeal

I have chosen culture as a way to introduce the reader to underdogs because of its analytical links to fundamental ideas and activities that American society and politics is based on. Some of these ideas are faith, fairness, equality, and freedom. Some of these activities involve sports and entertainment. Both traditional and popular culture play key roles in helping Americans understand their nation.

American culture is full of religious, political, economic, and social ideals. Their significance is in their linkage to deeply held American beliefs and practices. Analyzing American politics without understanding the link to culture is impossible, as historian Stanley K. Schultz observes: "Americans are a people who, from their national birth pangs onward, have told themselves as well as the rest of the world that they have built a classless society based on human equality, freedom of boundless opportunity, and reward for individual initiative. How could such a people's politics and political institutions ever stand separate from their everyday cultural activities and aspirations?"[1]

This chapter specifically analyzes the link between underdogs and religion, early American political history, business, baseball, and film. The first place is foundational: religion.

The Underdog in Religion

Christianity

To some, the life and story of Jesus Christ relate strongly to underdogs. In *Jesus the Radical: A Portrait of the Man They Crucified*, R. T. France writes, "He always seemed to take a delight in reversing the standards most people accepted. One of his famous slogans was, 'The first shall be last and the last first.' He had no time for the barriers of convention and privilege which people erect between themselves to boost their self-importance. He was always the champion of the underdog."[2]

There are sections in the Bible that reveal the importance of the poor to the faith. From Deuteronomy 15:11: "For the poor will never cease out of the land: therefore I command thee, saying, Thou shalt surely open thy hand unto thy brother, to thy needy, and to thy poor, in thy land."[3] From the New Testament, Matthew 25:35–45: "When I was hungry, you gave me something to eat, and when I was thirsty and you gave me drink…and when I was naked, you gave me clothes to wear…. 'Whenever you failed to help any of my people, no matter how unimportant they seemed, you failed to do it for me.' "[4]

In 1995, Phillip Yancey wrote in *The Jesus I Never Knew*, "Growing up, Jesus' sensibilities were affected most deeply by the poor, the powerless, the oppressed—in short, the underdogs. Today, theologians debate the aptness of the phrase 'God's preferential option for the poor' as a way of describing God's concern for the underdog."[5]

Liberation theology has a clear link to underdogs. One of its core concepts is a "preferential option for the poor."[6] Former Catholic worker Jason Rowe observes that this phrase "contended that God does not remain neutral in the face of social situations where the poor are exploited, but rather 'opts for' or takes the side of the poor in their struggle for justice."[7]

The main focus of liberation theology has been in Latin America, where it has intermingled with Marxist theories to produce strategies to combat inequality and poverty.[8] Love and social justice are key aspects of this theology, as religious scholar Leo G. Perdue wrote in 2005: "Liberation for the downtrodden is the actualization of the commandments of God to love and care for the neighbor. Love is actualized in solidarity with the oppressed, in experiencing their lot, and in capturing their vision of both life with God (spirituality) and the divine reign (social justice)."[9]

This has been a controversial interpretation of Christianity[10] that still resonates with many Catholics today, including the U.S. ambassador to the Vatican, Miguel Diaz. The former theology professor is a Cuban American who has included in his writings two major figures from liberation theology: Ignacio Ellacuría and Gustavo Gutíerrez.[11] When he was chosen for the post, College of Saint Benedict President MaryAnn Baenninger, commented that "Miguel is a highly-respected theologian and scholar…. Most importantly, he has a deep commitment to Catholic social justice and to inclusiveness in the Catholic Church."[12]

Christian socialism is also related to the concept of the underdog. It seeks to unite religious faith and political ideology by emphasizing what they have in common. According to Wikipedia, "Christian socialists draw parallels between what some have characterized as the egalitarian message of Jesus, who—according to Christian Gospel—spoke against the religious authorities of his time, and the egalitarian, anti-establishment, and sometimes anti-clerical message of most contemporary socialisms."[13]

Historically, many American politicians have linked their Christian faith to political action that supported the cause of economic underdogs. One prominent example is Norman Thomas. Before World War I, he was a Presbyterian minister in New York City. In the 1920s through the 1940s, he also was an active socialist who ran for mayor of New York City, governor of New York, and president of the United States.[14] Another example is Frank P. Zeidler. During the Depression, Zeidler read socialist literature. He was the Socialist mayor of Milwaukee from 1948 to 1960. He ran for president as a socialist in 1976. His Lutheran faith spurred his activity on behalf of socialism.[15]

Judaism

Ancient Jewish history is full of stories of more powerful societies conquering Jewish population and forcing them into exile; the Assyrians were victorious over the Jews in 721 BC while the Babylonians defeated them in Judah in 586 BC. It was the Romans, however, who brought the biggest anguish to the Jews. In AD 70, they conquered Judea and burned Jerusalem. Eventually, in AD 135, they made the study and observance of the Bible illegal. The death penalty was the consequence of breaking that law. Many Jews would not let go of their God and became martyrs.[16] This is a classic case of the underdog.

There are many tales of the underdog found in the Hebrew Bible. As Susan Nidtich explains in *A Prelude to Biblical Folklore: Underdogs and Tricksters*, "The underdog is the poor relative, the youngest son, the exile, the ex-prince, the soldier of the defeated army—the person, in short, who is least likely to succeed and yet does." Nidtich links them to us; this gives the concept its power: "The underdog evokes our sympathies; we root for underdogs because of the underdog aspect of our lives, our insecurities real or imagined, and when they succeed we succeed."[17]

Historically, the Jewish view of the world is one that is seen from the point of view of those with many disadvantages. This perspective neatly divides the world into binary opposites, as author Alain Finkielkraut explains: "the world was divided into torturers and victims, I belonged to the camp of the oppressed. I had no need of consciousness raising or of a dose of reality . . . an instinctive and unconditional solidarity united me with all the earth's damned."[18]

Jews have been discriminated against by many societies. In the Middle Ages in Europe, they were not allowed to enter into professional occupations and not allowed to own land. They were believed to be evil and forced to live in ghettos. Historically, it was not that long ago (the 1930s and 1940s) when six million of them were killed by Hitler's regime.[19]

For some people, discrimination against Jews can be rationalized by conjuring up negative stereotypes of them. In the 1983 book, *Anti-Semitism in America*, Harold E. Quinley and Charles Y. Glock analyzed six images of Jews to try and determine the degree of anti-Semitism in the United States at the time. These images were the Jew as Monied, the Jew as Pushy and Intrusive, the Jew as Power-Hungry, the Jew as Prideful and Conceited, the Jew as Clannish, and the Jew as Dishonest and Unethical. This analysis, based on surveys taken in the 1960s, found anti-Semitism feelings to be only a small minority in America. The fact that these questions were asked and studied reveals the staying power of past prejudice and discrimination in American society.[20]

Perhaps the most well-known example of a Jewish underdog is the biblical story of David and Goliath.[21] The story of the young shepherd boy challenging the giant soldier continues to have a great appeal to Americans today and is used for political advantage. Lee Atwater, the late Republican political strategist, once remarked, "David is still getting good PR for beating Goliath."[22]

The Underdog in Early American Political History

In one sense, the underdog is the history of America. Some settlers came for religious freedom. Others came for political freedom. Economic freedom and the ability to keep more of the fruits of one's labor were the dominating motivations for immigration for many others.

Could America have been destined to be the home of the persecuted? In 1776, Thomas Paine wrote that this was possible, maybe even probable: "The reformation was preceded by the discovery of America, as if the Almighty graciously meant to open a sanctuary to the Persecuted in future years, when home should afford neither friendship nor safety."[23] Injustice was inevitable, if the colonies did not become independent: "it is not in the power of Britain to do this continent justice: The business of it will soon be too weighty, and intricate, to be managed with any tolerable degree of convenience, by a power so distant from us, and so very ignorant of us."[24]

There is a widespread view that America was founded on the political victory of the underdog. The American Revolution is often portrayed as the rising of the weaker colonists and the defeat of the mighty British Empire by them. For example, Samuel Adams of Massachusetts was affiliated with the Country Party that later became the better-known Sons of Liberty. According to the Samuel Adams Heritage Society, the party was an "underdog on Boston's political scene. As the opposition party in the Massachusetts assembly and town meetings the Country Party was a perfect platform for criticizing the established order."[25]

The military victory of General George Washington in the Revolutionary War was also a victory of the underdog. As political pundit Chris Matthews writes, "In 1778, the British forces included fifty thousand regular troops and more than thirty thousand German mercenaries. George Washington never had more than twenty thousand men under his command."[26] Washington had fewer troops than the British and was up against an empire. He led an insurgency. His option was a lucid one: "The choice for the underdog is literally, 'death or victory.' . . . before the battle of Long Island, George Washington told his rag-tag Continental Army, 'we must resolve to conquer or to die.' "[27]

The 1787–1788 debates over the ratification of the Constitution can also be linked to the concept of the underdog. To set up a workable national government, while still keeping the freedom of the inhabitants of the new nation intact, was itself an underdog *position*. Some of the antifederalists feared that history showed that a widespread republic would eventually, and inevitably, decay into oppression. For example, Brutus wrote to the citizens of New York that "History furnished no example of a free republic, any thing like the extent of the United States. The Grecian republics were of small extent; so also was that of the Romans. Both of these, it is true, in process of time, extended their conquests over large territories of country; and the consequence was, that their governments were changed from that of free governments to those of the most tyrannical that ever existed in the world."[28]

The odds were that the republic would not last; history was against the idea that the United States would retain its form of government. Benjamin Franklin expressed a similar concern when he was asked, at the conclusion of the Constitutional Convention, what the result was: "A republic, if you can keep it."[29]

There are others who claim that the dreams of freedom that drove many white European underdogs to come to America were satisfied only on the backs of the less powerful. For example, Native Americans can argue that they are the true underdogs in American society. Their culture, traditions, and economic system were trampled over by the dominant European immigrants through assimilation, regulation, or extermination.[30]

African Americans can point to the cruelty of slavery and its debilitating repercussions as proof that they are the true underdogs in America. It is not necessary to ascertain if this is an accurate claim; its significance lies mostly in the dominant cultural perception. As author Cornel West writes, society is "content to see blacks remain the permanent underdog."[31] That societal perception has been complicated by the election of Barack Obama as U.S. president in 2008.

Of course, there are plausible claims made by women and other groups that they can be thought of as underdogs as well. Unfortunately, that list is a long one, comprised of (but not limited to) both defacto and dejure instances of discrimination of women and racial, ethnic, and sexual minorities.

Organizations can also be perceived as underdogs. Businesses can evoke sympathy and decry inequality and unfairness. Precisely how they do this depends on the purported discrepancy between their situation and the dynamics of free-market based capitalism.

The Underdog in Business

A good example of the perception of businesses as underdogs occurred during the period after the Civil War. Many small businesses began to claim that they were being treated unfairly because of the growth of the corporation. From the 1870s through the first decade of the twentieth century, the economic trusts were the central target of this criticism. Small businesses complained that they had little power to resist the dictates of the giant corporations and trusts that had formed during this era.

John D. Rockefeller and Standard Oil are prominent examples of this dominating trend. Standard Oil came to dominate the refining, transporting, and marketing of oil in the United States after the Civil War. Many underdogs were created as a result of how the Standard Empire was run. The tactics used by Standard to destroy their competition were efficient, as chronicled by writers Peter Collier and David Horowitz. A good example was George Rice, a small refiner from Ohio, who

> had been selling a modest amount of oil in the South for many years when the Standard's marketing affiliate there, Chess, Carley and Company, was given the word to rub him out. Knowing that he was involved in a

dubious battle, Rice decided nonetheless to fight back. He lowered his prices, assuming that the usual rules of a price war obtained. But the dealers who had bought his oil for years stopped their orders even though his prices were lower than those of Standard products. One dealer told Rice that he couldn't afford to defy Chess, Carley and Company because he knew the firm had been authorized by the Standard to spend up to $10,000 to break anyone selling Rice's oil.[32]

Journalist Ida M. Tarbell chronicled Rockefeller's business practices in a series of magazine articles in the 1890s and an influential 1904 book, *The History of the Standard Oil Company* that exposed how he attained his power.

When Tarbell was growing up, she experienced personally how Rockefeller's tactics wounded people. Her father was in the oil business in Pennsylvania in the 1860s, the place where oil was first discovered in the United States. He took the side of the independent oil producers who refused to be compelled into Rockefeller's burgeoning empire in 1872. Tarbell's family's life would never be the same.

Author Daniel Yergin describes how it affected Ida: "She remembered the agonies and financial difficulties her father had endured—the mortgaged house, the sense of failure, the apparent helplessness against the Octopus, the bitterness and divisions between those who did and those who did not come to terms with Standard Oil."[33] Tarbell's father, like countless others, had become underdogs—people who had lost their competitive struggles to more powerful forces.

The unfairness of the methods Rockefeller used to build his empire was the key to Tarbell's criticism. She claimed that he "has systematically played with loaded dice, and it is doubtful if there has been a time since 1872 when he has run a race with a competitor and started fair."[34] Tarbell's father, and others like him, must have experienced a deep sense of injustice due to the unfairness of the competition.

The power of large corporations to create underdogs is not just history. Even today many businesses feel that they are truly underdogs; that they are objectively at a competitive disadvantage to other companies. Size is the most obvious disadvantage. Small firms do not have the economies of scale that larger ones have. Unequal access to technology, financial resources, and political influence can also produce disadvantages. Some handicaps are structural while others are primarily temporal.

For example, many existing businesses cannot compete with companies such as Wal-Mart over price because of the price discounts it receives, or demands, from suppliers. As a result, many lose sales.[35]

Although it is impossible to prove a direct causative relationship between a business closing and the geographical proximity of a Wal-Mart, it is difficult to deny that there is a perceptual *correlation*.

It may be more than a perceptual correlation. In April 2006, Wal-Mart began to offer assistance to its competitors. The *New York Times* reported that Wal-Mart "announced a wide-ranging effort...to support small businesses near its new urban stores, including the hardware stores, dress shops and bakeries with which it competes....Wal-Mart said it would offer those businesses financial grants, training on how to survive with Wal-Mart in town and even free advertising within a Wal-Mart store."[36] The headline on Jim Gilliam's blog read "Wal-Mart admits it destroys small business." According to Gilliam, small business can compete only by "accept(ing) Wal-Mart's training and blood money."[37]

There is another perspective, however, on what Wal-Mart has done. It is a natural part of capitalism that the strong survive and the weak die. Wal-Mart's presence forces the surviving stores to change in a positive, consumer-friendly way. Moreover, the increased economic activity that Wal-Mart can bring to a community can also help create a business climate where new stores are started.[38]

It is also possible to conceive of Wal-Mart as a champion of the underdog. In the beginning stages of its growth, Wal-Mart challenged the economic dominance of Main Street-type businesses over small towns. *Looked at from a consumer point of view, the shopping public was the underdog.* Consumers were paying too much money (unnecessarily, because of the lack of competition) for goods and services before Wal-Mart came along. In a market-based economy, consumers were disadvantaged, financially gouged by stores that often used tradition and sentiment to mask their greed. Wal-Mart's founder, Sam Walton was not defensive about what he did: "You bet I closed that mom-and-pop store on Main Street, those fine folks who've been charging you a 40 percent mark-up for the past 25 years!"[39]

Wal-Mart also portrays itself as an underdog in the marketing of its history. As writer Liza Featherstone notes, "The Wal-Mart Visitors' Center, on the Bentonville town square on the site of the first Wal-Mart, features the original shabby storefront....At every turn, the Visitors' Center presents Wal-Mart as the underdog who 'proved the doubter's wrong,' Walton himself is shown in plain work clothes and a shabby cap-rarely in a suit-and is constantly referred to as a man who 'never turned his back on his roots.'"[40] In this way, the people of Bentonville, Arkansas (and rural America in general), are assumed to be underdogs—not as advantaged as people from metropolitan areas.

Still, what Wal-Mart has been doing to change the economies of states and nations bothers many people. The fundamental problem is its size and scope: it is huge and constantly growing in different directions. *Anything that is not as big and smart as Wal-Mart is an underdog: ordinary people, unions, local communities, distributors, smaller businesses, and any governmental body that dares not play its game.*

But sometimes communities do successfully challenge Wal-Mart. For example, Greenfield, Massachusetts, in 1993 rejected proposals that would have allowed Wal-Mart into their town.[41] In 2005, the voters in Lorain, Ohio, rejected a Wal-Mart proposal. A lawyer for the Ohio preservation group described that battle in the following way: "It's a great day for the underdog."[42] Sheet Metal Workers Union business agent Joe Thayer remarked that "[t]hey did about a dozen expensive glossy mass mailings, with cover letters from sellout 'leaders.' They did 'push-poll' phone banks and paid hundreds of folks $8 an hour to work all the polling places. Wal-Mart even called City Hall 40 times the day before election. All we had was the people!"[43] In both cases, it is estimated that Wal-Mart significantly outspent their opponents in those political battles.[44]

Passionately rooting for the team that has been outspent is something that many sports fans do. The link between underdogs and baseball further illustrates the power of the concept.

The Underdog in Baseball

The language of sports is filled with references to surprising comebacks and miraculous victories. In order for there to be a surprise or miracle, however, there first needs to be some inequality between the competitors. The inequality, whether it is in ability or experience, produces the basic ingredients for the eventual contest. The game, or match, then creates excitement for the spectator because no one can be sure who the eventual winner will be. The need for excitement produces what Jimmy Frazier and Eldon Snyder refer to as "an emotional marketplace" for fans. Rooting for the underdog satisfies emotional needs by both experiencing a thrill and protecting oneself from trauma. As Frazier and Snyder write, "If the underdog should win, the emotional investment is repaid with a good deal of excitement and emotional reward. If on the other hand the underdog loses, the spectator probably will not be particularly surprised and should not especially feel the loss. After all, the spectator knew he or she was rooting for an underdog."[45]

The emotional needs are closely linked to equality. How one perceives the legitimacy of inequality in American society could be related to what team, or individual, you root for in a sporting contest. If you value the underdog, then you might want them to win, or at least be satisfied with them coming close to winning. This would increase the prestige of the underdog, and some aspect of inequality is lessened.[46] These relationships are diagrammed in figure 2.1.

A recent example of this phenomenon is the Boston Red Sox World Series championship of 2004. The Red Sox produced a tremendous amount of underdog excitement in the playoffs that year. There were two emotional thrills produced for Red Sox fans. One was the miraculous comeback win over the New York Yankees in the American League Championship Series. The other was winning the World Series, a feat that had not been accomplished in eighty-six years.

The premise of any Yankees-Red Sox game is the inequality between the two teams. This inequality can be interpreted in a number of ways. One is the amount of World Series titles at the time: the Yankees had won twenty-six, the Red Sox seven. Adding to this numerical disparity was when the titles were won: the Yankees last victory was in 2000 while that of the Red Sox was in 1918.[47]

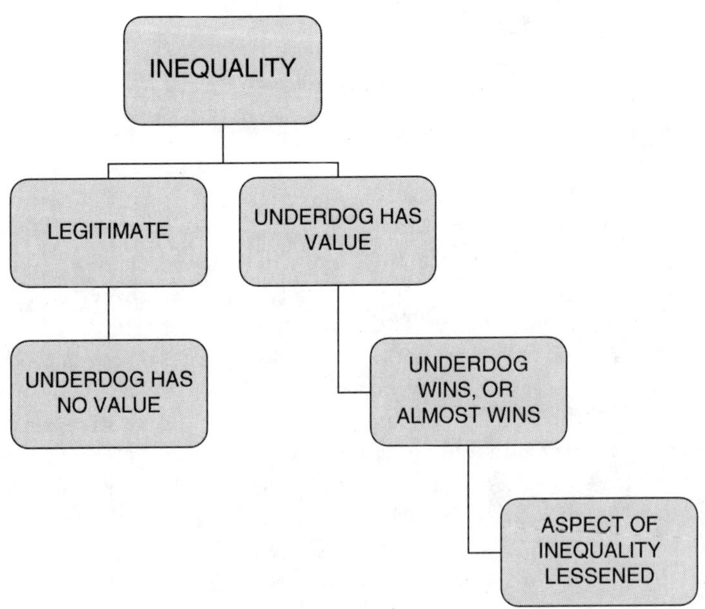

Figure 2.1 Perceptions of the legitimacy of inequality as it relates to sports

The other aspect of inequality is money. The Yankees have the reputation of being unafraid, and unashamed, of spending as much money as necessary to win. In late 2008, they spent heavily for several free agents: multiyear contracts were signed by infielder Mark Texeria and pitchers C. C. Sabathia and A. J. Burnett. Their contracts are worth more than $423 million.[48] Regarding the Red Sox-Yankees rivalry, former Major League Baseball Commissioner Fay Vincent's words probably reflect the sentiments of many fans: "I can't root for Yankees because of the payroll and Steinbrenner...I'd rather root for the underdog. If the Yankees don't win it's a mistake. They ought to win every year, they have so much money, and they buy all the great players."[49]

In the American League Championship Series of 2004, the Red Sox were behind three games to none before they won four straight. This was a tremendous underdog achievement for the Red Sox as they "became the first team in Major League Baseball history to win a seven-game postseason series after losing the first three games and only the 3rd in North American professional sports history (to do so)."[50]

Compared to the Yankees, the Red Sox are still the financial underdogs, even with their 2007 World Series championship. Starting off the 2009 season, they had a $121.7 million payroll. This was far behind the Yankees $201.4 million.[51] Moreover, the Red Sox franchise as of April 2009 was worth "only" $833 million, far below the Yankees $1.5 billion.[52]

However, it is difficult to consider the Red Sox as underdogs if they are compared to the team they beat in the 2007 World Series: the Colorado Rockies. In April 2007, the Red Sox had $146 million in player expenses and were worth $724 million.[53] This contrasts with the Rockies $63 million in player expenses and team value of $317 million.[54]

If one really believes that wide amounts of inequality are illegitimate, particularly if the inequality has been broadened by the power of financial wealth, what baseball teams would he or she root for? If it is the inequity in the current value of teams, the favorites would be the Florida Marlins and the Pittsburgh Pirates. As of April 2009, they have the lowest (Florida) and the second lowest (Pittsburgh) value of all major league teams.[55]

One of the most compelling underdog stories in recent baseball history was that of the 2008 Tampa Bay Rays. Despite the fact that they had the lowest payroll, they won the American League pennant. This was totally unexpected, in that they had finished last in the American League East Division nine out of the ten previous years.[56] Moreover, they defeated the Red Sox in a seven game series. Compared to the

Rays, the Red Sox could no longer genuinely play the role of the underdog. Their 2008 payroll was $90 million above the Rays.[57] The Red Sox had also won two World Series titles in four years.

Writer Mike Lopresti described the 2008 Rays as "the underdog's underdog." Why? Because their pennant-winning season should not have happened: "They are the contradiction to nearly every chapter and verse of what a team supposedly needs to thrive in modern baseball.... You need money. You need stars. You need experience.... The Tampa Bay Rays have none of the above."[58]

The Rays eventually lost the 2008 World Series to the Philadelphia Phillies. The Phillies, however, can also be conceived as underdogs. They were established in 1883 and have won exactly two World Series: 1980 and 2008.[59] If there is a gross inequity in the amount of championships a team has won, compared to the length of time the franchise has been around, an underdog has been created. Moreover, if the team *has not moved from their geographic location*, their underdog identity deepens. Looked at this way, the Philadelphia Phillies are underdogs. But the biggest baseball underdog is the Chicago Cubs. Because of their history, everyone expects the team, eventually, to fall short of winning the top prize. The Cubs were started in 1902 and have won only two World Series titles: 1907 and 1908.[60]

The link between sports and underdogs has been captured by many films. In more recent film history, there is *Rocky* (1976), *The Karate Kid* (1984), *Jerry McGuire* (1996), *Seabiscuit* (2003), and *Cinderella Man* (2005).[61] The story of the underdog in films is more universal than sports.

The Underdog in Film

One of the most significant American filmmakers to champion the underdog was Frank Capra. The most noteworthy of his films were made in, or portrayed, America in the 1930s and 1940s. They portray people who are struggling against tremendous forces. Some of these struggles are both personal and financial. They can also be political and societal struggles. The best known is *It's a Wonderful Life* (1946).

There are three other films of Capra that also illustrate the power of the underdog in American culture. They are *Mr. Deeds Goes to Town*, *Mr. Smith Goes to Washington*, and *Meet John Doe*. These were made in the mid-1930s and early 1940s. This was a time when the United States was struggling with the Great Depression and beginning to feel anxious about growing world political threats. These films fit the time period, as author

Lance Morrow explains, in that "the nation's popular culture had evolved an elaborately moving self-mythology of the American Underdog."[62]

In *Mr. Deeds Goes to Town*, Gary Cooper plays Longfellow Deeds, a simple Vermont man, who inherits $20 million. He decides to take his money and spend it on farms, so that the homeless can work on them. This ultraistic act lands him in court, as his mental capacity is questioned by his dishonest lawyer and remote relatives who want his money. In the end, he is declared sane.[63]

On one level, the application of the underdog theme is fairly straightforward: the homeless are the underdogs and Deeds is trying to help them. His courtroom remarks illustrate this:

> From what I can see, no matter what system of government we have, there will always be leaders and always be followers. It's like the road out in front of my house. It's on a steep hill. Every day I watch the cars climbing up. Some go lickety-split up that hill on high, some have to shift into second, and some sputter and shake and slip back to the bottom again. Same cars, same gasoline, yet some make it and some don't. And I say the fellas who can make the hill on high should stop once in a while and help those who can't. That's all I'm trying to do with this money. Help the fellas who can't make the hill on high.[64]

On another level, Deeds symbolizes the *individual as underdog* in the modern world. The grand meaning of the film, as Capra writes in his autobiography, is "the rebellious cry of the individual against being trampled to an ort by massiveness-mass production, mass thought, mass education, mass politics, mass wealth, mass conformity." In the end, the power of individualism prevails and a "simple, honest man, driven into a corner by predatory sophisticates, can, if he will, reach deep down into his God-given resources and come up with the necessary handfuls of courage, wit, and love to triumph over his environment."[65]

In *Mr. Smith Goes to Washington*, the underdog theme is even more explicit. Jimmy Stewart plays Jefferson Smith, a newly appointed U.S. Senator. He was chosen by Joseph Paine, a political hero and friend of his father. Paine is also, unknown to him, a corrupt political boss. Smith is chosen because of his inexperience. He is not expected to challenge the established, and sleazy, congressional power structure. Smith realizes the corruption, crushing his political idealism.

Eventually, he rebels. Smith tries a filibuster to publicize, and thus stop, the corruption. Paine tries to stop Smith's rebellion by both censoring newspaper accounts of his resistance and manipulating information about him.[66] Smith fights back with desperate sincerity. His words are a classic expression of the centrality of the underdog struggle to the human spirit: "I guess this is just another lost cause, Mr. Paine. All you people don't know about the lost causes. Mr. Paine does. He said once they were the only causes worth fighting for. And he fought for them once, for the only reason that any man ever fights for them. Because of just one plain simple rule: 'Love thy neighbor.'"[67]

In *Meet John Doe*, the underdog is the common man. In the film, Gary Cooper stars in the title role. The plot revolves around Long John Willoughby, a homeless baseball pitcher who is used by a newspaper columnist in an attempt to save her job. Her job is in danger because the paper was recently sold to a publisher named D. B. Norton, who is intent on driving up circulation. She writes a letter to the editor and attributes it to a fictional person named "John Doe." The letter deals with not only his own unemployment, but also with broader forces at work in American society: the inhumanity, greed, and hypocrisy (and other ill treatments) that badly affect the poor. His protest will be to commit suicide on Christmas Eve by jumping off the roof of city hall.[68]

The letter is a huge success, as tremendous interest is created in the plight of John Doe. Willoughby finally speaks in front of a large audience, addressing the feelings that the letter released in many people. He urges the common man to band together and stop pitying themselves: "I know a lot of you are saying, 'What can I do? I'm just a little punk. I don't count.' Well, you're dead wrong. The little punks have always counted because in the long run, the character of a country is the sum total of the character of its little punks."[69]

The speech is a triumph, as he is mobbed by well-wishers. John Doe clubs spring up across the nation. People begin to get to know their neighbors, but the new publisher of the newspaper wants to cynically use these clubs as a vehicle to become president. Willoughby eventually realizes this and plans to expose Norton's plot. Norton reacts by threatening to use the media to destroy the John Doe movement. Willoughby responds with disbelief:

> You mean to tell me you'd try to kill the John Doe movement if you can't use it to get what you want?...Well, that certainly is a new low. I guess I've seen everything now...You...think of deliberately killing an idea that's made millions of people a little bit happier....Why, your type's as old as history—if you can't lay your dirty fingers on a decent idea and twist it and squeeze it and stuff it into your own pockets, you slap it down....Well, you go ahead and try. You couldn't do it in a million years with all your radio stations and all your power, because it's bigger

than whether I'm a fake, it's bigger than your ambitions, and it's bigger than all the bracelets and fur coats in the world.[70]

Eventually, Norton uses the media to expose Willoughby. The people turn on Willoughby. He shows up at city hall on Christmas Eve. About to commit suicide, he changes his mind after persuasion from the columnist and some of his supporters. Interestingly, Norton and his supporters are also there. The key persuasive line comes from the columnist: "The John Doe movement isn't dead yet. You see, John, it isn't dead or they [Norton's group] wouldn't be here. It's alive in them. They kept it alive by being afraid. That's why they came up here."[71]

The common people are expected to lose, like all underdogs. However, in *Meet John Doe,* they never lose because the battle never ends. Whether it is revealed in religion, referenced by American history, created by business practices, attached to baseball, or enjoyed through film, the power of the underdog is formidable.

How does the concept relate to American politics? One major party, the Democrats, has consciously identified itself with underdogs. The next chapter begins by analyzing the relationship between the political culture of Democrats and underdogs and concludes by examining the links between Democratic political ideology and underdogs. It is to these themes we go next.

CHAPTER 3

The Political Culture and Core Ideals of Democrats

This chapter begins with an exploration of Democratic political culture, focusing on how power functions within the culture and how it relates to artists. Next, we examine the correlation between Democratic political ideology and underdogs, by analyzing liberalism and the core party ideals of reform, sympathy, social progress, empathy, justice, fairness, and equality.

Political Culture

According to political scientist Jo Freeman, there are underlying differences between the Republican and Democratic Party that are critical in understanding other differences: "The first one is structural: in the Democratic party power flows upward, and in the Republican party power flows downward. The second is attitudinal: Republicans perceive themselves as insiders even when they are out of power, and Democrats perceive themselves as outsiders even when they are in power."[1]

Since power flows upward, it is crucial for Democrats that access remains open to as many people as possible. Losers are entitled to access. Everyone in the party should be listened to and represented by leaders.[2]

This conception of Democratic Party political culture correlates with an aspect of the moralistic political culture, as theorized by political scientist Daniel Elazar: Everyone should be able to participate in politics, according to moralistic political culture—not just the elite or professionals.[3] Although the definitions of access and participation are not the same, access can be viewed as a prerequisite to participation.

Since losers are entitled to access, and underdogs usually lose, then *how* losers are included in the party is critical to party identity. Many believe that it is simply not culturally legitimate for the winner of a Democratic nomination fight to publicly snub who he or she defeated. The core impulse is that Democrats embrace those left behind, including defeated candidates of their own party.[4]

For example, it would have been culturally illegitimate for Barack Obama to have given the cold shoulder to Hillary Clinton supporters once he became the presumptive Democratic presidential nominee in 2008. What right, *as a Democrat*, would he have had to dismiss the millions of voters who supported her in the primaries and caucuses? Instead, he was gracious in praising her at a joint appearance on June 27, 2008. The event took place in Unity, New Hampshire. The symbolism was perfect in representing the political culture of the party: not only was the name of the town fitting, but both candidates had garnered the same number of votes in the January primary.[5] Writer Carla Marinucci described the imagery of the event: "their show…was so carefully coordinated that even their clothing matched: he in a sky-blue tie, she in a sky-blue blazer."[6]

The outsider viewpoint can be related to underdogs in many ways. The world view of Democrats and Republicans are different, in that Democrats observe society from the periphery, while Republicans perceive the center as who they represent. The essence of the insider/outsider contrast is important, as Freeman explains: "Since Republicans as individuals control most of the major private institutions, particularly economic ones, a strong central government is seen as a threat to their power. The Democratic periphery feels a strong government is necessary in order to counterbalance private economic domination. Indeed, they feel that the state's primary function *ought* to be a check on private economic power."[7]

Artists

Underdogs are on the periphery of society—that is what helps to make them underdogs. Since artists are usually not in the mainstream, most of them are Democrats. According to Garrison Keillor, "There's a reason why 95% of people in the arts are Democrats. An artistic gift is dropped on you by God and if you attend to the gift and are true to it, you will sometimes be in serious need of a helping hand.…Artists…are drawn toward stories of failure, know that satire is always in behalf of the underdog and the outnumbered."[8]

Examples of contemporary American art that portray underdog struggles can be found in many forms, including country music. Even though country music is usually associated with Republicans, some people believe that link is way off base. As songwriter Bobby Braddock wrote in the Music Row Democrats blog, "Country music is the music of everyday people. Why would we NOT belong to the party that sympathizes with the underdog? Country music is the music about families and mommas and babies. Why would we NOT belong to the party that cares about health care for seniors and children?"[9] Music Row Democrats were formed in December 2003. Less than three years later, they were purported to have more than 1,300 members, including Emmylou Harris, Rodney Crowell, Nanci Griffith, and Beth Nielson-Chapman.[10]

The well-known controversy associated with the Dixie Chicks' statements about President Bush and the Iraq war can also be linked to the support of the underdog. While playing in London on March 10, 2003, their lead singer Natalie Maines criticized the looming war. "Just so you know, we're ashamed that the President of the United States is from Texas."[11] Later, she issued the following politically correct statement: "As a concerned American citizen, I apologize to President Bush because my remark was disrespectful. I feel that whoever holds that office should be treated with the utmost respect. I just want to see every possible alternative exhausted before children and American soldiers' lives are lost. I love my country. I am a proud American."[12]

It is obvious that Maines, like millions of others around the world, felt powerless to stop President Bush from invading Iraq. She was frustrated. The people who were against the Iraq invasion were underdogs, in that they expected to lose. President Bush was going to invade Iraq regardless of expressions of public opposition and doubts about the action.

Many musicians become involved in elections by using their fame and talents to help candidates. For example, many of them supported Democrat John Kerry in the 2004 presidential election. There was a tour titled "Vote for Change" that featured concerts that were scheduled to include performances by Bruce Springsteen, John Mellencamp, Dave Matthews, Bonnie Rait, James Taylor, and the Dixie Chicks as well as others. This endeavor was presented by the liberal political action committee, MoveOn.org. The article about this in the *New York Times* was titled "Underdog Anthems on a Patriotic Theme."[13]

The top contenders for the 2008 Democratic presidential nomination attracted many musicians to their campaigns. Examples include the following:

- The remaining members of The Grateful Dead performed a concert for Barack Obama on February 4, 2008, in San Francisco.[14]
- In February 2008, the Black Eyed Peas posted two videos on YouTube that backed Barack Obama.[15]

- Elvis Costello played at a fundraiser for Hillary Clinton in October 2007.[16]
- Jackson Browne and Bonnie Rait played for John Edwards in New Hampshire and Iowa in 2007.[17]

Folk music has a long history of being linked to underdog and progressive causes in America. For example, backers of 1876 Democratic presidential candidate Samuel Tilden used the song " 'Hold the Fort" in support of him. The song was slightly modified and used by people supporting the Greenback Party four years later.[18]

There was a strong connection between folk music and support for underdog causes in the 1930s and early 1940s. As political scientist Betty Zisk writes, these dealt with "a variety of *common causes*; violence and injustice in labor organizing ('Joe Hill,' 'Which Side Are You On?'), tales of the Spanish Revolution ('Jarama Valley,' 'Viva la Quince Brigada') . . . [and] racial injustice ('Strange Fruit')."[19] In the early 1960s, Bob Dylan sang many songs of underdogs, including "Blowin' in the Wind" from his album *The Feeewheelin'*. "Blowin' in the Wind" was an adaptation of "No More Auction Block," the black spiritual that originated in Canada after slavery was abolished there. It was a huge hit for Peter, Paul, and Mary in the summer of 1963.[20] The song was popular in the antiwar and civil rights movements of the 1960s.[21]

In 1978, the Library of Congress compiled a bibliography of labor and industrial folksongs. The breadth of the list reveals the rich history of the link between folk music and American underdog struggles. For example, *Death in the Dark: A Collection of Factual Ballads of American Mine Disasters*, *Working Women's Music: The Songs and Struggles of Women in the Cotton Mills, Textile Plants and Needle Trades* and *Hard Hitting Songs for Hard-Hit People*.[22]

A more recent example of how folk music can be linked to underdogs is centered on musician Pete Seeger. A day before Barack Obama's 2009 inauguration, Seeger and other musicians played at the Lincoln Memorial in Washington, DC. The classic 1940 folk song, "This Land Is Your Land"[23] was performed. However, Seeger sang stanzas that most Americans had never heard before; stanzas that dealt with poverty around the Depression and feelings of protest.[24] Writing in the late fall of 2009, musician Peter Yarrow believes the song is appropriate for health care reform because

[t]o my mind, the most important focus that we, those of long determination and commitment to a just and equitable society, need to maintain

in song and in spirit, is an observance of our gratitude for what is good and is so exciting that is re-emerging in our country.[25]

Many people in the film industry sympathize with underdogs. In 2006, actor George Clooney won an Academy Award for *Syriana*. In his acceptance speech, he proudly boasted of the motion picture industry's outsider role in American society: "We are a little bit out of touch in Hollywood every once in a while. We were the ones who talked about AIDS when it was being whispered. We talked about civil rights when it wasn't really popular. I'm proud to be part of this Academy.... I'm proud to be out-of-touch."[26]

Slumdog Millionaire won the Academy Award for the best picture of 2008. The story is about a poor Indian boy from Mumbai who won money on a popular game show in India.[27] It was a controversial film; some objected to the portrayal of the poverty of Indian children. Others thought the title was humiliating.[28] Director Danny Boyle defended the title by invoking the spirit of the underdog: "Basically [the title] is a hybrid of the word 'underdog'—and everything that means in terms of rooting for the underdog and validating his triumph—and the fact that he obviously comes from the slums."[29]

Artists are drawn to seeking truths, many of them uncomfortable for the society they live in. A productive way to channel their discoveries is to push for liberal reforms based on sympathy.

Liberalism, Democrats, Reform, Sympathy, and Underdogs

At what point did the Democratic Party become associated with liberalism? The answer to that question depends on what is meant by liberalism. I use liberalism in how the concept is used in the political discourse of today, not its classical definition. This is similar to how cognitive linguist George Lakoff used the term in his book *Moral Politics: How Liberals and Conservatives Think*. To Lakoff, political liberalism "characterizes the cluster of political positions supported by people called 'liberals' in our everyday political discourse: support for social programs, environmentalism; public education; equal rights for women; gays, and ethnic minorities; affirmative action; the pro-choice position on abortion; and so on."[30]

In other words, the intellectual theories of Adam Smith and John Locke are not as useful to my analysis as the rhetoric and public policies of George McGovern and Barack Obama are. It is impossible, of course, to dismiss political philosophy as unimportant. Political ideals compel most politicians to get "into the game" in the first place. However, how ideals interact with the underdog concept is my primary focus.

In the twentieth century, liberalism became part of the national political discourse and acquired political significance during the 1930s.[31] Franklin D. Roosevelt wrote that the "liberal party...is a party which believes that, as new conditions and problems arise beyond the power of men and women to meet as individuals, it becomes the duty of the Government itself to find new remedies with which to meet them."[32]

Contemporary liberalism can be characterized in the following ways:

- "(it)...embraces a larger role for government in protecting and ensuring equal opportunity, such as affirmative action....(it) places a premium on civil liberties and counsels against government intrusion in private matters of personal and moral choice."[33]
- "The essence of liberalism consists of a genuine respect and concern for the thoughts and feelings of the common people. Liberalism is opposed to special privileges for the rich and powerful and committed to freedom, justice and peace" (political scientist Jeff Taylor).[34]
- A liberal is "a person who generally supports governmental action to promote equality (such as welfare and public education), favors governmental intervention in the economy, and supports environmental issues" (political scientists Daniel M. Shea, Joanne Connor Green and Christopher E. Smith).[35]
- "Liberals are those that believe in institutions that limit inequality and injustice" (economist and writer Paul Krugman).[36]

The base of a political party is a critical component of its strength. According to news commentator Daniel Shore, a base is "that solid core of political supporters who will stick with you through electoral thick and thin as long as you are perceived as advancing their principles."[37] Democrats are linked to liberals because liberals are the base of the party. They have been since at least FDR. Even with the Monica Lewinsky scandal, liberals stuck with Bill Clinton. Thus Democrats owe their base gratitude and respect. Why? Without their base, they would be like a rudderless ship drifting on the political sea—or perhaps a car without a functioning steering wheel.

How does a party appreciate an ideology when it is so difficult to explain? In 2008, writer Eric Alterman observed that "one reason liberals today find themselves vulnerable to vituperation from so many quarters simultaneously is the difficulty they face in explaining, even in the most rudimentary terms, their basic philosophical beliefs."[38]

Why is it so difficult to explain liberalism's fundamental philosophical beliefs? *Because the core of liberalism is in its application.* According to historian Arthur Schlesinger, Jr., "Liberalism in America has been a party of social progress rather than of intellectual doctrine, committed to ends, rather than to methods."[39] The crux of the problem is that liberalism's philosophical nucleus is difficult to consistently define with much precision over a long period. Social progress has a distinct look every time it is realized in different historical eras. As Schlesinger wrote, "When a laissez-faire policy seemed best calculated to achieve the liberal objective of equality of opportunity for all—as it did in the time of Jefferson-liberals believed, in the Jeffersonian phrase, that government is best which governs least. But when the growing complexity of industrial conditions required increasing government intervention in order to assure more equal opportunities, the liberal tradition, faithful to the goal rather than to the dogma, altered its view of the state."[40]

Advocating social progress in the United States usually means fighting for reform. In 1993, former Democratic Senator and presidential candidate Gary Hart wrote that the American political reformer "is practically unique in the world of modern Western democracy. He has no real counterpart in sister industrialized cultures. . . . He does not want to move left; he wants to move forward. He is not a rigid ideologue; he is a pragmatic progressive."[41]

Both reform and social progress have distinct looks in different eras. So how does one know what liberalism looks like when it changes its stripes so often? Look for who is siding with society's underdogs.

Liberal reformers side with underdogs; they want to see more and deeper equality, less discrimination, persecution, and injustice and a society that rewards fairness more. They also want to skewer special interests and upset the establishment. This is difficult to achieve. As Machiavelli stated, "the reformer has enemies in all those who would profit by the old order, and only lukewarm defenders in all those who would profit by the new order, this lukewarmness arising partly from fear of their adversaries . . . and partly from the incredulity of mankind, who do not truly believe in anything new until they have had actual experience of it."[42]

Sympathy and reform have important links. Writing in 1913, sociologist Lester Frank Ward, observed that sympathy "is a real though representative feeling, usually painful, and consists of a 'realizing sense' of suffering in another being."[43] According to the *Collins Essential English Dictionary,* one definition of sympathy is an "understanding of other people's problems; compassion," while another one means "feelings of loyalty or support for an idea or a cause."[44] Successful reform is linked to sympathy in the following way, according to sociologist Charles Abram Ellwood: "conscious changes for the better in human society can be satisfactorily brought about only by the enlistment of the feelings upon the side of the change; for it is feeling which sanctions the new adjustment upon its individual or organic side.... sympathetic feelings are obviously those which can be most easily enlisted on the side of changes advantageous to the group.... In any reform movement in human society... there must be a constant appeal to sympathetic emotions, if the movement is to be successful."[45] *Rational* sympathy, according to Ellwood, is the preferred type of sympathy that forms the basis for social progress.[46]

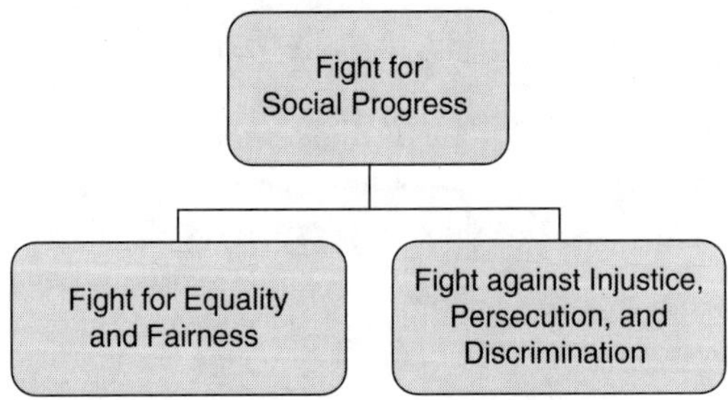

Figure 3.1   Liberalism and the underdog concept: Social progress

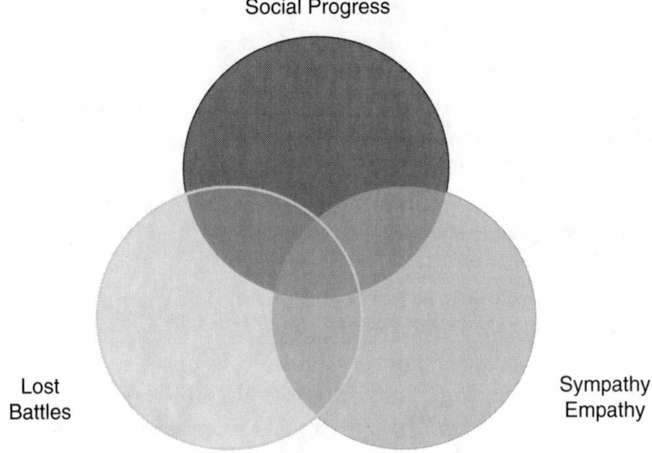

Figure 3.2   Liberalism and the underdog concept: Goals, usual results, and emotions

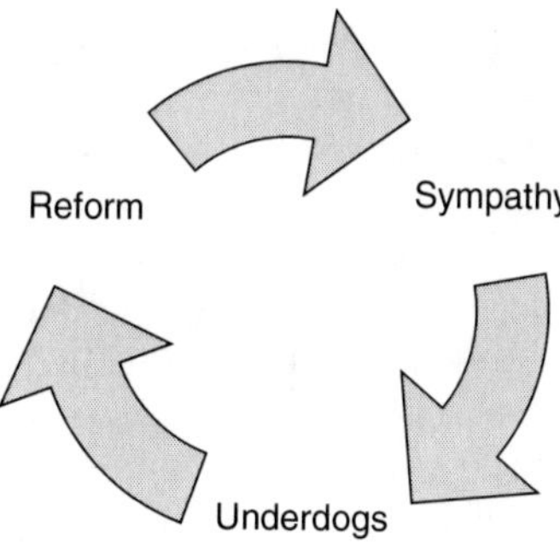

Figure 3.3   Sympathy, underdogs, and reform

Essential Ideals: Empathy, Fairness, and Equality

One of the most original interpretations of how liberalism applies to contemporary American politics was formulated by George Lakoff. Using conceptual metaphors, Lakoff theorizes that liberals and conservatives morality differ because of distinct notions of family models. The morality of liberals is established on the nurturant parent model, while the morality of conservatives is centered on the strict father model.[47] He describes the nurturant parent model in the following way: "The principal goal of nurturance is for children to be fulfilled and happy in their lives and to become nurturant themselves. A fulfilling life is assumed to be, in significant part, a nurturant life, one committed to family and community responsibility. Self-fulfillment and the nurturance of others are seen as inseparable. What children need to learn most is empathy for others, the capacity for nurturance, cooperation, and the maintenance of social ties, which cannot be done without the strength, respect, self-discipline, and self-reliance that comes through being cared for and caring."[48]

The model parental traits that children would copy, in order to help produce liberal morality in themselves, include the following: fairness, creativity, empathy, responsibility, and basic happiness.[49] Liberal morality, however, cannot flourish without receptivity: "the world must be as nurturant as possible and respond positively to nurturance. It must be a world that encourages people to develop their potential and provides help when necessary. . . . It must be a world governed maximally by empathy, where the weak who need help get it from the strong."[50]

Just how could a world be governed, to the maximum possible extent, by empathy? Political systems could be structured, and maintained, so that empathy is encouraged to be demonstrated by the people who participate in them. Public policies could be crafted so that empathy is contained in their substance. Leaders could be chosen, at least partially, on the basis of their empathy.

What would such a world look like? It would contain many of the core characteristics of the underdog concept. Empathy and fairness would prevail as the powerful would help out the feeble. It would have a lot in common with the conceptual folkheim of Sweden's Social Democratic Party, as articulated by Per Albin Hansson in 1928:

> The basis of the home is togetherness and common feeling. The good home does not consider anyone as privileged or unappreciated; it knows no special favourites and no stepchildren. There no one looks down upon anyone else, there no one tries to gain advantage at another's expense, and the stronger do not suppress and plunder the weaker. In the good home, equality, consideration, co-operation, and helpfulness prevail. Applied to the great people's and citizens' home this would mean the breaking down of all the social and economic barriers that now divide citizens into the privileged and the unfortunate, into rulers and subjects, into rich and poor, the glutted and the destitute, the plunderers and the plundered.[51]

This world would also have a lot in common with the idealized conception of Democrats that Garrison Keillor writes about in *Homegrown Democrat*. In the book, the author and radio personality illuminates some of the bedrock principles of the party: "I am a Democrat, which was nothing I decided for myself but simply the way I was brought up, starting with the idea of *Do unto others as you would have them do unto you*, which is the basis of the simple social compact by which we live."[52]

Does a place actually exist where no one knowingly discriminates and commits unjust acts? Does a place exist where nobody is consciously involved with an organization that either is structured, or acts, for injustice or discrimination? In short, is there a place where people not only believe in the social compact, but also consistently act upon it?

In a material sense, that ideal place exists *only* in the minds of writers and philosophers. However, that does not mean that the social compact cannot be strived for; individuals, governments, and organizations can operate as much as possible with an ethic of reciprocity. Democrats who attempt to create a society based on the social compact have many examples from religion and philosophy to help their cause:

- "What you wish your neighbors to be to you, such be also to them." Sextus the Pythagorean

- "What thou avoidest suffering thyself seek not to impose on others." Epictetus
- "Never impose on others what you would not choose for yourself." Confucius
- "Hurt no one so that no one may hurt you." Muhammad[53]

It would be very controversial for a Democratic politician to publicly explain his or her ideals and policy goals with a specific religious justification. It could be more acceptable to use Greek or Chinese philosophers. If either one was *actually* used it would also be rare. However, the Golden Rule does influence American politics. The presence and power of the American religious and cultural infrastructure give politicians an incentive to at least imply that the Golden Rule should be followed more.

Keillor also hints at equality: *"You are not so different from other people so don't give yourself airs."*[54] Democrats stand for core equality; an ideal that helps anchor the ideological nucleus of the American political system. In his study of party ideologies in America, political scientist John Gerring listed equality as the Democratic Party's persistent theme from 1828 to 1992 (the end date of his comprehensive analysis).[55] If one could drill down and see the roots of *every* human being, the similarities would overwhelm the differences. Elitism is thus incompatible with Keillor's vision of Democrats.

In what *context* does equality, nurturance, fairness, sympathy, and the Golden Rule thrive? Metaphorically, the context is the family. One of the most famous uses of the word by a Democrat came from former New York Governor Mario Cuomo in his keynote address to the 1984 Democratic National Convention. His speech was filled with family themes, like this: "We believe in a single fundamental idea that describes better than most textbooks and any speech that I could write what a proper government should be: the idea of family, mutuality, the sharing of benefits and burdens for the good of all, feeling one another's pain, sharing one another's blessings—reasonably, honestly, fairly, without respect to race, or sex, or geography, or political affiliation."[56]

The use of the family metaphor is not without risk for Democrats. Author Robert Kuttner believes that its use was a disguise that functioned to conceal (sometimes not very successfully) what is essentially a social-democratic ideology. As he states in his 1987 book, *The Life of the Party,* "The family metaphor is an honorable attempt to temper the crude individualism of the laissez-faire creed—to find some new basis for civic empathy and social solidarity that Americans will instinctively view as legitimate. But it is a very tricky image, because most Americans don't like either the implicit confinement of their own family of origin, or the implication that a national family must take care of other people's bastard children."[57]

Do most Americans really want to feed, shelter, and love the bastard children of others? Put in that way, probably not. However, if people recognized a part of themselves in these "bastard children," then they would be more open to helping them. As Keillor writes, "We don't let people lie in the ditch and drive past and pretend not to see them dying.... The logical extension of this spirit is social welfare and the myriad of government programs with long dry names all very uninteresting to you until you suddenly need one and then you turn into a Democrat."[58]

Liberalism, Underdogs, Economic Inequality, and Justice

Fairness and equality are two more concepts where the underdog idea and Lakoff's understanding of liberalism interconnect. He states that "fairness is about the equitable distribution of objects of value (either positive or negative value) according to some accepted standard."[59] To Lakoff, there are multiple fairness models, including equality of distribution, equality of opportunity, procedural distribution, rights-based fairness, need-based fairness, scalar distribution, contractual distribution, equal distribution of responsibility, scalar distribution of responsibility, and equal distribution of power.[60]

To theoretically unpack each of these models of fairness is beyond the scope of this analysis. Examining a few of these, however, illustrates some of the links between liberalism and the underdog concept.

The scalar distribution of responsibility can be defined as "the greater your abilities, the greater your responsibilities." Need-based fairness can be defined as "the more you need, the more you have a right to." Putting these two models together produces the slogan associated with Karl Marx: "From each according to his abilities, to each according to his needs."[61] Marx's famous phrase is contained within his *Critique of the Gotha Programme*, written in 1875:

> In a higher phase of communist society, after the enslaving subordination of the individual to the division of labor, and therewith also the antithesis between mental and physical labor, has vanished; after labor has become not only a means of life but life's prime want; after the productive forces have also increased with the all-around development of the

individual, and all the springs of co-operative wealth flow more abundantly—only then can the narrow horizon of bourgeois right be crossed in its entirety and society inscribe on its banners: From each according to his ability, to each according to his needs![62]

The ideological basis of that phrase can be traced back to earlier sources besides Marx. One is the French philosopher Morelly, who wrote *The Code of Nature* in 1755.[63] Former Yale University President Theodore D. Woolsey's *Communism and Socialism in Their Theory and History* described some of Morelly's basic laws of society: "*First.* That nothing in society shall belong separately or in proprietorship to any one, except those things that are in daily use, either for his wants, his pleasures, or his daily labor. . . . *Second.* That every citizen shall be a public man, sustained, maintained, and employed at the public expense. . . . *Third.* That every citizen, for his part, shall contribute to the benefit of the public, according to his strength, talents, and age. On this principle, his duties shall be adjusted according to distributive laws."[64]

According to Lakoff, the key questions related to Marx's famous phrase, centers on morality: "Is need-based distribution moral? And is the scalar distribution of responsibility moral?"[65] The answers to these questions are complex, but one's ideology and degree of sympathy felt for the underdog suggest some.

Wealth Redistribution, Public Opinion, and Ideology

The scalar distribution of responsibility can be related to the philosophy behind progressive taxes. For example, abilities of an individual can be measured by how much income one makes. The more income, the more responsibility owed to society, and thus a higher percentage of one's income should be paid to the government. Essentially, this is government redistribution of wealth.

This philosophy is supported by a majority of Americans, according to an April 2009 poll by the Tax Foundation: 52 percent would back a larger tax on high-income earners for redistributing wealth, while 31 percent would be against it. When ideology is considered, the support for the idea diverges: 74 percent of liberals would support it, while 57 percent of conservatives would be against it.[66] Crudely translated: Liberals believe the scalar distribution of responsibility is moral, while conservatives do not.

Additional results from the Tax Foundation poll revealed that liberals are more willing to raise taxes and increase services (23 percent) than conservatives (3 percent). One way to pay for services is through the federal income tax. The poll found that 44 percent of liberals thought that their federal tax burden was too high, compared to 66 percent of conservatives.[67]

An earlier poll supported the notion that Americans are *not* in favor of the redistribution of wealth. A June 2008 Gallup survey asked Americans about the approach government should take to fix the economy. The survey found that 84 percent of Americans did not support "steps to distribute wealth more evenly" while only 13 percent did. Among Democrats, the wealth redistribution choice rose to only 19 percent. What the 84 percent supported was the government focusing on a more general method: "take steps to improve overall economic conditions and the jobs situation."[68]

Why the divergence? Most likely it was the timing of the poll: the economy had weakened substantially from June 2008 until April 2009. However, it still helps reveal a broader point: Americans favor particular government programs, yet not necessarily the usually unstated, macrolevel effect of them (that is redistribution of wealth). In 1964, political scientists Lloyd Free and Hadley Cantril judged most Americans as ideological conservatives, yet operational liberals. Kuttner found this predictable "since the essence of the American Constitution is a series of ingenious restraints on government, and liberalism in the American experience has been as much a rejection of radicalism as an alternative to feudalism."[69]

Although these poll results reveal ideological and partisan differences, they may obscure the level of overall societal *agreement* on these general issues. Political scientists Benjamin I. Page and Lawrence R. Jacobs have updated, and illuminated, Americans beliefs about economic inequality in their 2009 book, *Class War?* According to them, a number of surveys conclude that the "evidence demonstrates that majorities or pluralities of Democrats and Republicans, and of upper-, middle-, and low-income earners, mostly *agree*...that taxes are necessary to fund essential government programs, that higher taxes should be accepted when needed, and that the better-off should pay more."[70]

Page and Jacobs also conclude that "about six out of ten Americans have consistently favored having money and wealth 'more evenly distributed' and have rejected the proposition that it was already fairly distributed." This was not just a possibly unrepresentative snapshot of public opinion either; it came from polling carried out over thirteen years, between 1984 and 2007.[71]

How does all of this correlate with sympathy or empathy? To empathize with the needy is to understand their hardships. To sympathize with them is to be open to supporting policies that would alleviate their condition. Taxing the rich higher and increasing services could accomplish that goal.

Do Americans have a consistent view on government redistribution of wealth? It is difficult to say. However how they feel about the subject is probably related to how they conceive what is an *essential* government program, when higher taxes are actually *needed* and who constitutes the *better-off*.

What is also clear is that the use of the word "government" is not an ideal way to build support for public action. It seems that most Americans want more fairness, recognize the need for communal action to realize a fairer society, but cannot admit (or allow politicians to articulate) that it is the government that must take steps to make it happen.

Thus any battle for wealth redistribution by government is an underdog battle, if it is couched *in those terms*. Why? Because it will most likely lose. However, if "wealth distribution by government" is replaced by "middle class," "equality of opportunity," or specific government policies aimed at particular problems, then public policies that actually help underdogs could have a better chance of actually being enacted.

Why are crude appeals to wealth distribution by government usually unsuccessful? It is because Americans have a moral uncertainty toward wealth. As political scientist Samuel Huntington observes, " 'Equality' in American thinking has rarely been interpreted as economic equality in terms of wealth and income, but rather as equality of opportunity." Morality and power are linked in the following way, according to Huntington: "money becomes evil not when it is used to buy goods but when it is used to buy power.... [and] economic inequalities become evil when they are translated into political inequalities."[72]

Wealth Redistribution and Justice

Underdogs fight against injustice. Is there justice in government redistribution of wealth? Justice is a complicated concept, with varying definitions based on how one measures it, what scope is involved, and the time frame under consideration. The analysis becomes a little more manageable if a particular aspect of it is considered. Distributive justice seems to be the most relevant component of justice in considering government redistribution of wealth.

There are a variety of principles of distributive justice. According to the Stanford Encyclopedia of Philosophy, they can differ "in what is subject to distribution...in the nature of the subjects of the distribution . . . and on what basis distribution should be made."[73] The basis of the distribution "of the benefits and burdens of economic activity among individuals in a society "[74] is the core philosophical principle in analyzing government redistribution of wealth.

Strict egalitarianism is one method of distribution. Equal respect for people guides the belief that the same level of services and goods are owed to every person.[75] Another method of distribution is offered by political philosopher John Rawls. Among other aspects of justice, Rawls suggests that "social and economic inequalities are to satisfy two conditions: first, they are to be attached to positions and offices open to all under conditions of fair equality of opportunity; and second, they are to be to the greatest benefit of the least advantaged members of society."[76] The justification for social and economic inequality on the basis that they are to be the greatest benefit of the least advantaged members of society is the difference principle.[77] How might the difference principle point legislators in the right direction? According to philosophy professor Peter S. Wenz, they "can pass laws that have the effect of reducing disparities in income and wealth between rich and poor."[78]

The difference principle has been criticized from many different outlooks. For example, it is not acceptable for supporters of strict equality; common criticisms involve the *inequality of materialism*—how it contributes to power differentials and how it affects the expressions of equality.[79]

Justice and equality, two principle concerns of the underdog, are thus linked together in the concept of government redistribution of wealth. Does fighting for the underdog mean not being satisfied with *any* inequality of materialism? Or does fighting for the underdog mean pushing society to *continually* try to meet Rawls' conditions? Either fight is always met with resistance from powerful forces. The centrality of the power dimension is critical, as Aristotle observed many years ago: "the weaker are always anxious of equality and justice. The stronger pay no heed to either."[80]

Underdogs, Fairness, Consumers, and Free-Market Capitalism

"Defending the powerless is a basic task of government, an article of faith in the America I grew up in. . . . The government is there to do battle with those who would sell you cars that are firebombs or TV sets that cause cancer in small children or vitamins that make hair sprout on your palms or hamburgers made from deceased springer spaniels."[81]

Those are Garrison Keillor's words from *Homegrown Democrat*. They also generally correlate with how most Americans view the relationship between the role of government and the free market. According to a 2009 Pew Research Center for the People & the Press poll, 62 percent of Americans believe that a "free market economy needs regulation to best serve public interest." Opinions diverge based on party identification: 75 percent of Democrats agreed with the statement while only 48 percent of Republicans did.[82]

The partisan divide reappears when people were asked if "government regulation of business does more harm than good." While 54 percent of all respondents agreed with the statement, only 41 percent of Democrats did. This contrasts with 75 percent of Republicans who agreed. When ideology is included, the gap is even greater: 29 percent of liberal Democrats agreed with the statement, while 81 percent of conservative Republicans did.[83]

In the theoretical free market, consumers are viewed as powerful actors. If a product or service is either overpriced or inadequate in any way, the consumer simply does not have to purchase it again. A free market with perfect information and ease of entry and exit creates an environment where the consumer is king.

However, in actuality, the consumer can be permanently harmed by dangerous products and services. A person who was crippled by a defective steering mechanism will probably find little satisfaction boycotting any future purchases from that automobile company. Finding out that extended exposure to a product that has been in one's household for years causes cancer does little good to the person who comes down with the disease twenty-five years later.

The link between fairness and consumers is vital to understanding how the underdog concept applies to critiques of free-market capitalism. Consumers are not being treated fairly by businesses when they are unaware of the harmful effects of products they purchased. Without effective regulation, businesses are free to pursue their own financial interest, no matter how unfair it is to consumers, without much fear of being stopped. A good illustration of this is evidence revealed in the criminal investigation of the tobacco industry in the 1990s. The investigation eventually led to a 1998 multibillion dollar settlement with forty-six states.

Documents uncovered in the investigation suggested fraud was committed by the industry. Labeled "Smoking Howitzers" by Lowell Bergman and Orlana Zill, the memos and other papers was a factor in making known the idea of the covering-up of evidence, the control of scientific research, and the improper use of attorney-client privilege by tobacco industry lawyers.[84]

It was a Democrat from Mississippi who is credited with starting the movement that eventually led to a $246 billion settlement paid by 13 tobacco companies to the 46 states. Michael Moore was the Mississippi Attorney General for 16 years, starting in 1988 and ending in 2004. He helped persuade other state attorney generals to join him in trying to make the companies be held liable for Medicaid expenses related to caring for smokers.[85]

Even though Moore is a self-styled conservative Democrat, he believes people ought to be treated fairly and with justice.[86] His 1998 characterization of tobacco companies left little doubt of what he thought of the morality of their business practices: "I believe they're the most corrupt and evil corporate animal that has ever been created in this country's history. They sell the drug, they make a drug, and they sell it knowing that it's addictive. They market it to our children, who they know will become addicts and they know that they will die from the causes of—of this tribute tobacco related disease."[87]

Moore's fight against the tobacco industry was an *underdog fight*: almost everyone thought that he would lose the struggle. As he recalled in a 1998 interview: "in retrospect, it was the—the biggest challenge, the biggest legal challenge in history. If we could climb this mountain, so to speak, then there would never be one larger than this. No challenge greater. Nobody have [*sic*] ever beaten the tobacco industry before."[88]

Democrats are open to government regulation of business because they know the private sector can abuse economic freedom. Even though Americans believe deeply in economic freedom, their faith is tempered by an understanding of human nature. Ultimately, businesses are run by, and answerable to, people. Americans instinctively realize the power, and inevitability, of greed; whether it is in the ruthlessness that is sometimes associated with profit maximization, or the heartlessness that is too often a result of attempts to maximize shareholder value.

Greed helps produces unjust outcomes. Injustice creates underdogs. Government works to address and diminish injustice. Democrats, more often than not, are the party of government activism.

Fighting for the underdog can take many different forms. It means protecting Americans from the inevitable excesses of the economic marketplace. It also means vigorously pushing for more equal opportunity to be realized, rather than simply idealized. Economic and social inequality is acceptable, as long as there seems to be progress toward reducing it. Of course, the difficulties arise not only in measurement and scope, but also in language: how is *progress* defined? What does *vigorously* pushing for equal opportunity actually look like?

Although many Democrats have fought tirelessly for these ideals, it is their presidential candidates that most people remember. Throughout its long history, the Democratic Party has nominated many candidates who have, to varying degrees, fought for underdogs. The next part of the analysis begins with the three men who have helped define what the modern party stands for: Thomas Jefferson, Andrew Jackson, and William Jennings Bryan. They are the subject of chapter 4.

CHAPTER 4

The Founders and the Great Commoner: Jefferson, Jackson, and Bryan

There is a good historical reason why every year many state Democratic parties label their annual social gathering and fundraiser the Jefferson-Jackson dinner: Thomas Jefferson and Andrew Jackson are considered the founders of the party. William Jennings Bryan was nominated three times as the Democratic standard bearer from 1896 to 1908. His influence on what the party stands for still reverberates today.

Thomas Jefferson

Jefferson is associated with the underdog concept in many ways, given the complexity and depth of his life and mind. I have chosen to focus on his early writings against the British, his stance on the Alien and Sedition Acts, and the presidential election of 1800.

Early Writings against the British

In the early 1770s, Jefferson wrote *A Summary View of the Rights of British America*. It was published in 1774. This early piece of writing lists complaints that serve to illustrate how the colonists were underdogs to the British; discriminated against and treated unfairly and unjustly. Writer Fawn Brodie classifies and characterizes some of the grievances: "*You do not listen to us*—Of all our petitions 'to none of which was ever even an answer condescended' . . . *You are cheating us*—You 'have raised their commodities called for in America to double and treble of what they sold for before such exclusive privileges were given' . . . *You are unfair*—'Justice is not the same thing in America as in Britain' . . . *You play favorites*—You sacrifice 'the rights of one part of the empire to the inordinate desires of another.' "[1]

Jefferson concluded *A Summary View of the Rights of British America* with a sweeping condemnation of British actions: "Scarcely have our minds been able to emerge from the astonishment into which one stroke of parliamentary thunder had involved us, before another more heavy, and more alarming, is fallen upon us. Single acts of tyranny may be ascribed to the accidental opinion of the day; but a series of oppressions begun at a distinguished period, and pursued, unalterably through every change of ministers, too plainly prove a deliberate and systematical plan of reducing us to slavery."[2]

In 1901, author Henry Childs Merwin labeled the work "in reality a political essay... [where] he went to the root of the matter, and with one or two generalizations as bold and original as if they had been made by Rousseau, he cut the Gordian knot, and severed America from the Parliament of Great Britain."[3] These generalizations began his work of sympathetically portraying the colonists as disadvantaged by injustice.

Jefferson's most famous work is the Declaration of Independence. Essentially, the document makes a compelling case for an underdog *concept*; that a democratic form of government based on liberty should exist: "We hold these truths to be self-evident, that all men are created equal, that they are endowed by their Creator with certain unalienable Rights, that among these are Life, Liberty and the pursuit of Happiness.... That to secure these rights, Governments are instituted among Men, deriving their just powers from the consent of the governed."[4]

The United States of America was an underdog concept because a government based on democracy was not considered within the bounds of orthodox political discourse at the time.[5] Moreover, broad opinion in Europe at the time thought that it would probably fail.[6]

Elsewhere in the document, Jefferson listed offenses that King George III had committed against the colonists. These offenses aimed to elicit sympathy. He started off with the past: "the history of the present King of Great Britain [George III] is a history of repeated injuries and usurpations, all having in direct object the establishment of an absolute Tyranny over these States."[7]

Jefferson then enumerated the specific offenses. Some of the offenses are ambiguous: "he has refused his Assent to Laws, the most wholesome and necessary for the public good." Others were more particular: "He has called together legislative bodies at places unusual, uncomfortable, and distant from the depositary of their public Records, for the sole purpose of fatiguing them into compliance with his measures." Others were lethal: "He has abdicated Government here, by declaring us out of his Protection and waging War against us...He has plundered our seas, ravaged our Coasts, burnt our towns, and destroyed the lives of our people."[8]

The colonists were sympathetically portrayed by Jefferson; almost as hapless victims to the cruelty of King George III. Reading Jefferson's text, one could almost believe that the colonists were being emasculated, and then slaughtered, by the British. They were also portrayed as being persecuted: "He has kept among us, in times of peace, Standing Armies without the consent of our legislatures...He has affected to render the Military independent of and superior to the Civil power."[9] This description makes King George III look like a bully; and bullies help create underdogs by the way of persecution.

The view of Americans as underdogs and Brits as oppressors is a powerful image that still resonates in modern times, as author Ted Nace observes: "Even today, when our military forces encircle the world, we still cast ourselves as the scrappy underdog-the wisecracking GI defying Hitler's war machine, the gladiator leading a slave revolt against Caesar, the towheaded farmboy going one-on-one against Darth Vader. Those are quintessentially *American* heroes. Even if the movie is set in Ancient Rome or in a 'galaxy far, far away,' the villains are easy to spot by their upper-class British accents."[10]

His Stance on the Alien and Sedition Acts

Jefferson's party was the object of discrimination with the passage of the Alien and Sedition Acts of 1798. These acts were passed during the time of the French Revolution and the resulting hope and fear that it spread around the world. The president could authorize the imprisonment or deportation of aliens considered "dangerous to the peace and safety of the United States," speech critical of the government could be restricted, and the residency requirement for American citizenship was increased from five to fourteen years.[11] Historian Noble Cunningham described Jefferson's reactions to them: "[He] saw the alien and sedition laws as an attempt to silence Republican newspapers, to drive Republican-minded aliens from the country, and as 'an experiment on the American mind to see how far it will bear an avowed violation of the constitution.' "[12]

In some areas of the United States, these actions created sympathy for the targets of these laws. Thus the Federalists contributed to the depiction of Jefferson's ideological allies as underdogs; political victims of a federal government that was totally controlled (with the huge exception of Jefferson as vice president) by the Federalist Party.[13]

Evidence of how the Sedition Act in particular contributed to the link between the underdog concept and Jefferson's ideological allies is found in "Sedition Act of 1798: A Brief History of Arrests, Indictments, Mistreatment & Abuse," a report by Gordon T. Belt of the First Amendment Center.[14] Several of the words used in the title elicit sympathy in and of themselves: mistreatment and abuse. The case of James Thomas Callender illustrates how sympathy can be created by government action that is seen as unjust, unfair, or unequal.

Callender was a journalist from Scotland who later became a naturalized American citizen. He criticized the administration of John Adams in print voraciously as "one continued tempest of malignant passions. As President he has never opened his lips, or lifted his pen without threatening and scolding; the grand object of his administration has been to exasperate the rage of contending parties, to calumniate and destroy every man who differs from his opinions."[15] His words left no doubt as to his choice in the upcoming election of 1800: "between Adams, war and beggary, and Jefferson, peace and competency."[16]

While working in Virginia, Callender was indicted. Eventually he was ordered by Supreme Court Justice Samuel Chase to pay $200 and sentenced to nine months in jail. Callender continued to publish negative remarks about Adams while in jail.[17]

Democrats James Madison, James Monroe, and Thomas Jefferson backed Callender's writings. Jefferson gave money to him. It was Federalist marshals who chose the Federalist jurors who convicted him under the authority of the Federalist Supreme Court Justice Chase. Historian Edward John Larson describes what happened next: "The conviction backfired.... The Republicans [current-day Democrats] turned Chase's bullying tactics at Callender's trial into an effective campaign issue. 'The judges spoke of Mr. Callender in the most contemptuous manner,' one partisan newspaper reported, 'and made many remarks which proved that he was much better qualified to act as a *prosecutor* than to act as an impartial judge.'"[18]

Historian Joseph J. Ellis describes what happened after the Sedition Act began to be enforced: "as soon as the Federalists launched their prosecutions of Republican [Democratic] editors and writers...it became clear that the prosecutions were generally regarded as persecutions. Most of the defendants became local heroes and public martyrs."[19]

Persecution can lead to empathy and sympathy; both are essential ingredients in the creation of the underdog concept.

The Presidential Election of 1800

The election was a critical turning point for the United States. George Washington had served his two terms. Federalist John Adams wanted a second term. Thomas Jefferson was ready to deny him that. While John Adams received only sixty-five electoral votes, Aaron Burr and Jefferson each had seventy-three electoral votes.[20] This occurred even though Jefferson was the party's presidential candidate. James Horn of the Thomas Jefferson Foundation summarizes the intrigue associated with the election: "consequently the sitting House of Representatives, still dominated by Federalists, was called upon to break the deadlock. The opportunity for defeated Federalists to prevent Jefferson from gaining the presidency by voting for Burr, or at the very least to extract concessions from the Republicans in return for voting for Jefferson was too hard to resist. Early in the new year rumors began circulating that Burr would be elected, or that the Federalists intended to throw things into confusion by defeating an election altogether, and making a President...by act of Congress."[21]

What precisely did some Federalists have in mind? According to author Fawn Brodie, "Federalists in the House were planning, should there be a tie vote between Jefferson and Burr on the floor, to declare an interim president, preferably the newly appointed Chief Justice, John Marshall."[22] Jefferson and his allies refused to go along with this for one simple reason: it would become a model. As Jefferson stated, "that precedent once set, it would be artificially reproduced, and would soon end in a dictator."[23] Popular democracy would be doomed.

There were rumblings of secession, violence, and civil war. Some southern states threatened to resort to arms if Jefferson did not triumph. Maryland's Joseph Nicholson cautioned that "Virginia would instantly proclaim herself out of the union" unless the Federalists backed down.[24] The Democratic Party's leader in the House of Representatives at the time was Albert Gallatin.[25] He admitted that "it was threatened that if any man should be thus appointed President by law and accept the office, he would instantaneously be put to death."[26] According to historian John Edward Larson, "word spread that Governors McKean and Monroe would dispatch their state militias to suppress any Federalist coup and that the Republican [current-day Democratic] states would join in forming a new government under a revised constitution." The feeling was mutual for many of their political opponents: "some Federalists spoke of their states responding in kind, raising the specter of disunion or civil war."[27]

Governor McKean and Governor Monroe represented Pennsylvania and Virginia. If they left the union, the new country would have been split in half. Nevertheless, Jefferson was firm in his belief that any attempt by the Federalists to maintain their power was usurpation, and thus should be resisted. Jefferson even tried to intimidate his political opponents with an appeal for a new Constitutional Convention.[28]

Eventually after thirty-six ballots, Jefferson prevailed over Burr in the Electoral College tally. Something quite notable had just happened: a nonviolent change in political power for one branch of the federal government (the executive) had been sanctioned by another branch (the legislative). However imperfect some of the rules were (the twelfth amendment to the constitution would be adopted in 1804),[29] in the end the elites respected the political institutions that they helped create.

Jefferson's election as president in 1800 was a victory of what was then an underdog concept; that a government would *allow itself* to be voted out of office. The administration of John Adams did not use the military to stop Jefferson from taking power. Instead, a peaceful transfer of power from one political party to another in the new United States occurred. In March 1801, Jefferson wrote that "We can no longer say there is nothing new under the sun. For this whole chapter in the history of man is new.... The order and good sense displayed in this recovery from delusion, and in the momentous crisis which lately arose, really bespeak a strength of character in our nation which augurs well for the duration of our Republic."[30]

In retrospect, his election was remarkable. In 1819, Jefferson recalled that the "revolution of 1800 ... was as real a revolution in the principles of our government as that of 1776 was in its form; not effected indeed by the sword, as that, but by the rational and peaceable instrument of reform, the suffrage of the people."[31]

In more general ways, Jefferson can be linked to the underdog concept by the following:

• Many of Jefferson's *constituents* lived in small towns and were tied to the land. They can be interpreted as underdogs because there were influential elements in American society that were poised to deny power to them. These elements consisted of Federalists and their allies. The sway of habit and the pull of memory was part of that power. According to political scientist Jeff Taylor, "having been only recently freed from the yoke of a king, possessing political leaders who had lived under royal rule for most of their lives, and operating under a newly created system of government, Americans feared that Federalist leaders might try to restore monarchy."[32]

- Jefferson's deep commitment to *reform* can be interpreted as an underdog concept in that reform is usually unsuccessful. Even though he once advocated a revolution every nineteen years in a letter he wrote in 1789 to James Madison,[33] the core concept involves the appropriateness of recurring civic change. Gary Hart concluded that "Jefferson wished to thwart any kind of permanent aristocracy—the predictable social and political aristocracies of wealth and power—by institutionalizing reform, by keeping alive the spirit of revolution in the hearts of future generations of Americans."[34]

- Sympathy was connected to democracy for Jefferson. Sympathy was not a romantic sentiment; instead, as historian Andrew Burstein describes, his democracy was "a radical movement based on sympathy for the people at large." Jefferson "aligned himself with the emotional health of the 'corporeal inhabitants' of 'this corporeal globe.'" His influence is still felt today: dedication to humanitarian improvements as an instrument of modern public policy is part of contemporary American politics.[35]

Some Republicans claim that Jefferson would be aligned with their party if he was alive today. His commitment to a small central government gives that claim credence. Others, however, believe that he would be a Democrat because of the political culture of the party. In 1977, historian Robert Kelley wrote "if Thomas Jefferson were to be brought back to life today, he would have little difficulty seeing where he belonged. The Democratic party is still the party of outsiders, of the ethnic minorities who are relatively low in cultural and economic status or who in other ways have been made to feel excluded by the host culture."[36]

Andrew Jackson

Andrew Jackson's tragic early years would easily put him in the category of underdog—one who is expected to lose and has significant disadvantages. His formative years coincided with the American Revolution. His father died before he was born. From the time the Declaration of Independence was signed, until the victory at Yorktown, Jackson experienced a great deal of excitement. He helped the American side and was taken prisoner by the British. However, he also experienced a great deal of loss. His brother had died after a battle and his mother died near the end of the war. He had become an orphan before the age of fifteen.[37] Author Robert V. Remini describes how this time affected Jackson: "The American Revolution was one long agony for Andrew Jackson. Perhaps there were moments when he felt like a patriot and hero, but most of the time he experienced hardship, pain, disease, multiple wounds of the head and fingers, and grief arising from the annihilation of his immediate family.... He saw himself as a participant 'in the struggle for our liberties' and he never forgot the price that he and others had paid to secure them."[38]

Jackson was also associated with underdogs in other ways, including through his military service at the Battle of New Orleans in 1815, the elections of 1824 and 1828, his hatred of the Second Bank of the United States, and his Indian removal policy.

The Battle of New Orleans

Jackson's image as an underdog hero was born with the Battle of New Orleans. In one of the last battles of the War of 1812, American military forces fought the British on January 8, 1815. Jackson led the battle. The Americans were outnumbered by the British, with 7,500 British attackers versus 5,000 American troops. The Americans won the battle. Incredibly, only 13 Americans were killed that day, while approximately 2,000 British lost their lives. Adding to the legend of Jackson was the fear that a much larger British army and fleet was coming to support their existing forces.[39]

In the overall context of the war, the battle was not decisive. A peace treaty had been signed (but was not yet in effect) in late December 1811. It was the image of Jackson's victory, however, which cemented his connection to the underdog.

The battle's effect on how the War of 1812 was remembered is described by the historian Donald Hickey: "If it was a defining moment in American history, it was...because it boosted American self-confidence and enabled Republicans to forge the myth of American victory. In the wake of this battle, the war could hardly be mentioned in public in the United States without evoking proud memories of how a motley American army had decisively defeated the very troops who had ended the great Napoleon's reign in Europe."[40] Jackson's underdog triumph at New Orleans would be reinserted into the cultural memories of twentieth-century Americans with the number one hit of 1959, "Battle of New Orleans," by Johnny Horton.[41]

The Elections of 1824 and 1828

No candidate received a majority of the Electoral College vote in the 1824 presidential election. Consequently, the outcome was decided by the U.S. House of Representatives. John Quincy Adams was elected president even though Jackson had gained more popular votes. Jackson received 41.4 percent of the popular vote while Adams received 30.9 percent.[42]

Even though it was a legal win for Adams, it was felt by many that the result was somehow unjust. That feeling was fueled by the "corrupt bargain" alleged to have taken place between Speaker of the House Henry Clay and Adams: Clay was named Secretary of State in exchange for his successful maneuvering to round up votes for Adams in the House of Representatives.[43]

Majority rule by the people was the underdog concept after this result. The following questions may have been asked by Americans then: Wasn't it always the case that an elite group of people had the final authority to determine who would gain political power? Did it really make a difference that these were, in this case, members of Congress? Andrew Jackson did not like where he thought his country was heading, as writer Jon Meacham states: "that the election unfolded according to the letter of the Constitution did not matter to Jackson. The way he saw it, the son of a president, Adams, had struck a deal with the Speaker of the House, Clay." The whiff of an undemocratic dynasty was strong: "he thought the country was watching the founding of a dynastic line that could perpetuate itself despite the wishes of the people."[44]

Moreover, wasn't the spirit of the American Revolution being violated—that of believing that the people *could* be trusted with making their own decision about whom they wanted to govern them? Even though the Constitution placed the Electoral College as a potential barrier between majority rule and the election of the president, hadn't American democracy *evolved* since 1787?

A basic issue in viewing the American political experiment as an underdog concept is whether aristocracy or democracy will actually prevail when a change of regime is near. French writer Alex de Tocqueville recognized how this related to political parties when he wrote, "I *am* saying that aristocratic or democratic passions can easily be found at the bottom of all parties, and that though they may slip out of sight there, they are, as it were, the nerve and soul of the matter."[45] It would not be an exaggeration to view democratic passions as the "nerve and soul" of the Democratic Party.

In 1828, this core impulse of the party would be released, and satisfied, with Jackson's election as president. Jackson received 56 percent of the popular vote to Adams's 43.6 percent.[46] The differences between the 1824 and 1828 elections were stark, as writer Kenneth T. Walsh points out: "It was the first time that all the states except Delaware and South Carolina chose their electors by popular vote, a sign that the elites who had run the country, such as the state legislators and landed gentry, were losing power. In addition, most states, by reducing or abolishing property requirements, had made it easier for citizens to cast ballots. The total vote rose from nearly 357,000 in 1824 to more than 1.1 million in 1828."[47]

One of Jackson's top priorities, as historian H. R. Brands reports, "was repairing the damage done to American liberty by the foes of democracy. Such, at any rate, was how Jackson viewed his mission. His election...turned the American political world on its head. Not since Jefferson's victory in 1800 had there been a hostile takeover of the presidency."[48]

At least in historical memory, the unreceptive takeover of the presidency is the place where Jefferson and Jackson are linked in the minds of Americans as underdogs. Both had to struggle over the status quo, entrenched interests, and the unwillingness of the powerful to let go of control. Both succeeded in this fight. This is a foundational core of the Democratic Party.

Jackson directly associated his personal life struggle with the political battle between aristocracy and democracy that was developing in the United States at the time. As author Sean Wilentz notes, "By defeating Adams and winning the presidency, he had taken his continuing search for vindication to a new level, becoming the first man of lowly birth to occupy the presidency despite the numerous obstacles that fortune had placed in his way.... he had also, in his own mind, defeated the forces of privilege that threatened to destroy the basic principles of the American Revolution and restore British-style, aristocratic corruption."[49]

Hatred of the Second Bank of the United States

The Second Bank of the United States was charted in 1816 to stabilize American currency.[50] Jackson saw the bank as a symbol of aristocratic privilege—thus, by definition, opposed to the interests of the common man. The common man was linked to democracy, and democracy was the underdog to aristocracy. Jackson had a lot to say on the bank. The ideological core of his objection to the bank concerned equality and justice:

"Distinctions in society will always exist under every just government. Equality of talents, of education, or of wealth can not be produced by human institutions. . . . When the laws undertake to *add* to these natural and just advantages . . . to make the rich richer and the potent more powerful, the humble members of society-the farmers, mechanics, and laborers—who have neither the time nor the means of securing like favors to themselves, have a right to complain of the injustices of their Government."[51]

The common people, like all underdogs, would lose in their struggle with the privileged classes because they did not have the time, money, and education to effectively lobby the government. As political scientist Joseph White observes, "Jacksonian Democrats thought the economy worked pretty well, and government could only inject favoritism into the system, using some people's money to favor others."[52] Moreover, publicizing the unfairness of laws that have been created by the rich and the powerful is a staple for underdogs.

Another reason Jackson was against the bank was that it would have meant a stronger central government. A stronger central government (as opposed to state government) would have favored the political and financial establishment and thus discriminated against the rural areas of the south and west. According to author David S. Reynolds, "for Jackson, the bank, which had twenty-nine branches and controlled a third of the nation's bank deposits, stole money from average Americans and handed it over to wealthy stockholders, a large percentage of whom were northeasterners or foreigners."[53]

The establishment, at least in how it was perceived in culture and used by politicians, was the cities of the Northeast and their financial institutions. Jackson and his party's ideological conceptions of the bank (not necessarily how it would actually affect public policy) are the links to the underdog concept. Where is the *justice* in having the government giving a bank, essentially, a license to steal? Where is the *fairness* in having stockholders (a minority of the population) make money off the majority (who do not own stock)? Aren't the south, west, and the rural areas in general being *discriminated* against by the financially more powerful northeast?

Indian Removal Policy

It is easy to characterize Native Americans as underdogs—people who are expected to lose, are discriminated against and are persecuted by the powerful. Unfortunately, a great deal of early American history confirms the veracity of this characterization. It can be argued that Andrew Jackson's actions as president helped create this role for them. The most significant of these was his signing of the Indian Removal Act of 1830.[54]

The act allowed Jackson to grant land west of the Mississippi River to Native American tribes in exchange for them giving up their land in the eastern United States.[55] The intent was to remove them from the eastern states. The methodology used is described succinctly by the office of the historian in the U.S. State Department: "As incentives, the law allowed the Indians financial and material assistance to travel to their new locations and start new lives and guaranteed that the Indians would live on their new property under the protection of the United States government forever. With the Act in place, Jackson and his followers were free to persuade, bribe, and threaten tribes into signing removal treaties and leaving the southeast."[56]

The act was successful. By the end of the Jackson presidency, more than 45,000 Native Americans were relocated to land west of the Mississippi River.[57] The success was accompanied by tragedy. One of the tribes who resisted Jackson was the Cherokees. They were forced to march west by 7,000 federal troops. It was an ugly sight, as historian Robert V. Remini notes: "The militiamen sent into the Cherokee country were not disposed to treat the Indians kindly. With rifles and bayonets, they flushed the Indians out of house and cabin and locked them in stockades specially erected for the purpose.... When the captured Cherokees turned for one last look at their homes they saw them in flames, set ablaze by the lawless rabble who followed the soldiers. These outlaws looted and raped and desecrated graves.... By the thousands the Indians were herded into stockades where many sickened and died."[58]

Apologists for Jackson's Native American policies might argue that he thought the best way he could help these underdogs was to protect them, like the "Great White Father" role that many U.S. presidents had with Native American chiefs in early U.S. history.[59] Even though he was an Indian fighter earlier in his life, there is evidence to suggest Jackson cared about them. The caring was paternalistic, as his message to Congress on December 8, 1830, illustrates:

> And is it supposed that the wandering savage has a stronger attachment to his home than the settled, civilized Christian? Is it more afflicting to him to leave the graves of his fathers than it is to our brothers and

children? Rightly considered, the policy of the General Government toward the red man is not only liberal, but generous. He is unwilling to submit to the laws of the States and mingle with their population. To save him from this alternative, or perhaps utter annihilation, the General Government kindly offers him a new home, and proposes to pay the whole expense of his removal and settlement.[60]

How can a party that fights for underdogs bring about a supreme injustice toward a whole group of people? New Jersey Whig Senator Theodore Frelinghuysen spoke for six hours against Jackson's Indian Removal Act. He linked injustice and race to the policy: "Do the obligations of justice change with the color of the skin? Is it one of the moral prerogatives of the white man, that he may disregard the dictates of moral principles, when an Indian shall be concerned?"[61]

The Party's Decline

It is easy to suggest today that Jackson's Native American policies were simply racist, and that he created a new class of underdogs, rather than protecting them. If this was true, it might call into question his role as a Democrat. How could a founder of the party act this way and still be a Democrat? Easily.

Slavery and racism were consistent themes for Democratic presidential candidates then, as political scientist John Gerring explains:

Greater continuity can be found in the Democrats' position on matters of race than historians have generally acknowledged. Douglas's principal slogan...was "popular sovereignty"—a term that referred to the rights of states to decide political matters by democratic choice rather than by the...intervention of the federal government. This same principle, labeled "local sovereignty" by Lewis Cass, the Democratic standard-bearer in 1848, was just another way of expressing the party's traditional stance of "states' rights." From the 1830s on, it was considered critical to select as the party's presidential candidate a northern leader who was "safe" on the slavery issue—a "northern man with southern principles," as the phrase went.[62]

The issue of slavery became increasingly divisive for the party from the mid-1830s to 1860. The intensity of the divisiveness was related to the expansion of the country; would slavery be legal in the new states of the west? National power, war, and racism merged in a way that called into question the party's commitment to helping underdogs.

Although Democrats won four of the six presidential elections from 1836 to 1856,[63] the issue eventually tore the party apart. The party was on the wrong side of the most important issue in nineteenth-century American politics. From 1860 to 1932, only two Democrats occupied the White House. It was a long purgatory for the nation's oldest political party.

During this time, some national Democrats did fight for the underdog. The most prominent representative of this fight was Nebraskan William Jennings Bryan.

William Jennings Bryan

Known as the Great Commoner, William Jennings Bryan was the main symbol of the Democratic Party around the turn of the twentieth century. Bryan was the Democratic nominee for president in 1896, 1900, and 1908. He lost every contest. Even though he was unsuccessful in reaching the White House, his fiery rhetoric in defense of underdogs helped shape the modern ideological core of the Democratic Party.[64] In addition, significant public policies that he had championed in his career were eventually enacted.[65] Many of these reforms helped underdogs.

The Election of 1896

How did Bryan come to capture the Democratic Party? The key factor was his ability to connect emotionally with the millions of Americans who felt anxiety about the profound economic and social changes that had been occurring since the end of the Civil War. He addressed fears that many ordinary Americans had sensed, but might not have been able to articulate, about the future. These fears were associated with the economic and social uncertainty that had been created as a result of the nation's transformation from a primarily agricultural nation to one that was increasingly industrial. This was the broader historical context in which Bryan and his followers took over the Democratic Party.

The key symbol in the national political debate was currency: would it be based on gold or bimetallism? Since 1792, the United States had adopted a policy of bimetallism.[66] In 1873, however, the United States adopted the Gold Standard and demonetized silver.[67] This coincided with the Panic of 1873 that caused severe economic pain for many Americans. Between 1873 and 1875, 18,000 businesses failed, and 89 out of 364 railroads went bankrupt. Real estate values went down, corporate profits disappeared, and wages dropped. In 1876, unemployment was at 14 percent.[68]

To Bryan and many others, the demonetization of silver was the core policy change that needed to be corrected. In 1878, Congress put silver back into distribution with the Bland-Allison Act, which required that the federal government put silver dollars (among other things) into circulation.[69] The act, however, did not affect the economy significantly since Republican President Rutherford B. Hayes did only the bare minimum to comply with the law.[70]

In 1890, Congress acted in favor of silver again with the Sherman Silver Purchase Act. Author Charles R. Geisst describes some of the economics and politics around this legislation that "required the Treasury to buy a specific amount of silver each month in order to maintain its price. This was Congress's bow to the Western mining states. Silver was used mostly for coins and for backing silver certificates. However, many people saw little use for it, and much was returned to Treasury vaults shortly after being placed in circulation."[71]

In 1893, another financial panic hit the United States. Business scholar Jerry W. Markham describes the aftermath of the panic: "some six hundred banks eventually failed...as well as some 15,000 businesses. Four million persons were left unemployed....A long depression...lasted from 1893 to 1897. Historians called this the 'Great Depression' until that title was taken by the depression that occurred in the 1930s."[72]

Did the currency changes have an actual economic effect on the financial turmoil during these times? On one level, that question is not central to the study of underdogs. Instead, the currency debate is important because it became *the social and political symbol* for millions of Americans trying to understand the dramatic changes that were occurring in the country. Gold was the culprit and silver was the answer.

Understanding the passion for silver is impossible without historical context, as historian Michael Kazin observes: "in the mid-1890s, most Americans assumed that wealth consisted largely of products that were tangible and visible-crops, livestock, iron, coal, textiles, real estate. When calamity struck, they naturally fell to arguing whether the fault lay in a surplus or shortage of the shiny commodities, or specie, on which their dollars were based." However, the passion for silver (even if it was misinformed or irrational) had to have enemies: people, regions, or institutions that persecuted common Americans. "Because creditors, industrialists, and the bank of England favored gold, ordinary Americans who resented their power, and often found it mystifying, rallied to the promise of free silver."[73] It was in this background in which Bryan sought to gain the Democratic presidential nomination in 1896.

Bryan faced many challenges to winning the nomination. First of all, he was not rich, and thus he could not help finance his campaign. Second, he came from a sparsely populated, and traditionally Republican, western state. Third, he was not well-known nationally. Fourth, establishment Democrats did not support him. Fifth, he was not a public official. Sixth, and last, he would be only thirty-six years old in November 1896.[74]

Even with these disadvantages, he prevailed. His underdog campaign succeeded because the Democratic Party was splintering. President Grover Cleveland's conservative economic policies had alienated many key parts of the party. Cleveland was weak and thus in no position to choose his successor as the party's next presidential nominee. Bryan's substantial oratory skills in elucidating core ideals of the party also helped him win. In August 1893, Bryan articulated them in a congressional speech: "To-day the Democratic party stands between two great forces, each inviting its support. On one side stand the corporate interests of the nation, its moneyed institutions, its aggregations of wealth and capital, imperious, arrogant, compassionless.... On the other side stands that unnumbered throng which gave a name to the Democratic party and for which it has assumed to speak. Work-worn and dust-begrimed, they make their sad appeal.... This army, vast and daily vaster growing, begs the party to be its champion in the present conflict."[75]

The links with underdogs are clear: if the corporate interests are compassionless, then they lack sympathy and empathy. A party that fights for underdogs cannot be on the side of compassionless interests. The depiction of a crowd of tired, dirty, and sad people evokes an image of people who might be expected to lose their next battle, whether the battle is for a job, food, or a place to sleep. What caused these people to be tired, dirty, and sad? Surely some injustice is to blame.

Bryan's most famous oration was the "Cross of Gold" speech he gave during the Democratic National Convention in 1896. Its rhetoric contained many moralistic allusions to underdogs. There is one underdog cause, however, that he believes particularly deserving to be fought for: the rural areas and farmers away from the Atlantic coast. He believes these interests have been neglected by the Democratic Party:

"Ah, my friends, we say not one word against those who live upon the Atlantic Coast; but those hardy pioneers who braved all the dangers of the wilderness... rearing their children near to nature's heart... where they have erected schoolhouses for the education of their children and churches where they praise their Creator, and the cemeteries where sleep the ashes of their dead- are as deserving of the consideration of this party as any people in this country. It is for these that we speak."[76]

This is a plea for the party *equality*—between regions of the country and between urban and rural interests. His link to underdogs is also revealed by implying that these interests (similar to Jefferson's description of the colonists 120 years previously) have been *persecuted* and *discriminated* against: "We have petitioned, and our petitions have been scorned. We have entreated, and our entreaties have been disregarded. We have begged, and they have mocked when our calamity came."[77]

Fundamentally, these rural interests are more important than cities: "You come to us and tell us that the great cities are in favor of the gold standard. I tell you that the great cities rest upon these broad and fertile prairies. Burn down your cities and leave our farms, and your cities will spring up again as if by magic. But destroy our farms and the grass will grow in the streets of every city in the country."[78]

Rural America and farmers were becoming underdogs during this time period. The significant price deflation that occurred between 1866 and 1896[79] hurt the ability of farmers to make a living. The plight of some of them was dreadful: "the forgotten farmers were caught on a treadmill. Despite unremitting toil, they operated year after year at a loss. In a vicious cycle, their farm machinery increased their output of grain, lowered the price, and drove them deeper into debt."[80]

Part of Bryan's political strategy was to capture the rural vote, no matter what party it came from. Thus, he also became the Populist Party and Silver Republican Party presidential nominee in 1896. The Populist Party and Bryan had a lot in common with each other; they wanted to challenge the status quo and supported broad reforms in American society. Bryan had even supported Populist presidential candidate James Weaver in 1892.[81] In that year, Weaver won 8.5 percent of the national vote and Kansas, Colorado, North Dakota, Idaho, and Nevada.[82] The states that Weaver won contained only *three* of the top 100 largest urban areas in the nation: Denver, Kansas City, Kansas, and Topeka, Kansas.[83] In 1894, Populists elected six senators and seven congressmen and captured more than 1.5 million votes.[84] There was substantial support for the Silver Republicans in the west.[85]

It was Bryan's explicit preference for rural underdogs that contributed to his defeat in the general election against Republican William McKinley. As political scientist James L. Sundquist observes, "He did not set class against class; he set rural against urban. When...he spoke of '*your* cities' and '*our* farms,' he cast out of his circle not just urban capital but urban labor too."[86]

It is not a fact that Bryan did not want the support of urban underdogs. It is just that he had to convince them that supporting their political ideals was more important than any possible price increases for necessities that might occur if Bryan's silver policies were enacted.[87]

Bryan was not successful in uniting urban and rural underdogs to win the election. McKinley won the 85 major American cities with a plurality of 464,000 votes. In 1892, the conservative Democrat Grover Cleveland had won them with a 162,000 vote plurality.[88] McKinley won the presidency with 51 percent of the national popular vote to Bryan's 46.7 percent.[89]

There are other parallels between the underdog concept, Bryan and the 1896 presidential election. They include the following:

- The Democratic Convention in Chicago drew supporters of causes who wanted more equality and rights for people who were being discriminated against. This included people and causes that backed woman's suffrage, wanted to allow Chinese immigrants to receive civil rights, and advocated for Christian and secular socialism. The convention also drew Democrats that differed from President Cleveland's economic policy.[90] What did these people have in common? They all, to some degree or another, felt like outsiders and represented groups that they believe had been persecuted or ideas (free silver) that had lost.
- Bryan was *a financial underdog* to McKinley. The Republicans had much more money to campaign on than the Democrats and Populists: it is estimated that they had an approximately 10–1 advantage.[91]
- McKinley's campaign used the American flag as a partisan tool to discredit Bryan. The flag was a symbol of the McKinley campaign.[92] The Democrats had been outmaneuvered, as historian Lawrence Goodwyn writes, "frustrated Democrats found it difficult to show proper respect for the national emblem without participating in some kind of public endorsement of McKinley."[93] If the flag was the symbol of patriotism, and McKinley was equated with the flag, then how could any patriotic American ever vote for Bryan? The result: Patriotism and McKinley win and rebellion and Bryan[94] lose; the usual result for an underdog.

Anti-Imperialism

Although Bryan was the Democratic nominee in 1900 and 1908, he never came as close to winning the presidency as he had in 1896.[95]

However, he regularly brought up critical issues that would help shape what the party stood for. The most significant one in 1900 was imperialism. The United States was fighting a distant war in the Philippines. The Filipinos wanted their sovereignty and independence, while the American government was unwilling to give it to them, at least at the time.[96] This conflict was part of the overall Spanish-American War that had ended in 1898 with the Treaty of Paris. The treaty gave Guam and Puerto Rico to the United States and Cuba its independence. It also permitted the United States to buy the Philippines from Spain.[97]

At this time, there was a feeling by many Americans that it was immoral to occupy the Philippines. The United States was acting more like a traditional European country, more concerned with power than with principles. Bryan believed that American national strength, derived from its historic commitment to standing up for underdog struggles for freedom, was being undermined because of our occupation. As an example, he brings up the Boer war that was occurring in South Africa, in which Britain was fighting Afrikaners for power in southern Africa:[98]

> Even now we are beginning to see the paralyzing influence of imperialism. Heretofore this nation has been prompt to express its sympathy with those who were fighting for civil liberty....In 1896, all parties manifested a lively interest in the success of the Cubans, but now when a war is in progress in South Africa, which must result in the extension of the monarchial idea, or in the triumph of the republic, the advocates of imperialism in this country dare not say a word in behalf of the Boers....Sympathy for the Boers...is due to the fact that...we believe in the principles of self-government...If this nation surrenders its belief in the universal application of the principles set forth in the Declaration of Independence, it will lose the prestige and influence which it has enjoyed among the nations as an exponent of popular government.[99]

Was Bryan correct? Does American influence and prestige depend upon universally applying such concepts as equality, justice, and fairness in international relations? Or can the United States maintain its strength by *selectively* fighting for the underdog, like supporting some struggles for national liberation and actively opposing others? These questions would be faced (although not necessarily framed in the same way) by other Democratic presidential candidates in the twentieth century; most notably Hubert Humphrey, Eugene McCarthy, Bobby Kennedy, and George McGovern's positions on the Vietnam War.

Anti-imperialism was not the only issue of the 1900 campaign for Bryan. He also mixed in criticisms of the trusts and reiterated his support for silver.[100] Journalist Henry Pringle believed that his over-all message just did not coagulate: "for all his magnetism . . . William Jennings Bryan always spoke for disorganized minorities. They did not seek some common end, they disagreed violently among themselves."[101] Minority causes are usually underdogs because of majority rule. They could triumph if they are organized enough to produce effective coalitions. This was not the case in 1900.

The broad correlations between underdog concepts and Bryan are numerous. They include the following:

- **His Christianity.** The most famous example is the end of his 1896 Cross of Gold speech. He makes an obvious parallel between his candidacy and the cruxification of Jesus Christ: "Having behind us the commercial interests and the laboring interests and all the toiling masses, we shall answer their demands for a gold standard by saying to them, you shall not press down the brow of labor this crown of thorns. You shall not crucify mankind upon a cross of gold."[102]
- **His embrace of struggle.** He was involved in a life-long exertion to battle for the causes he believed in. The titles of two books he wrote after his 1896 and 1900 electoral defeats reveal this dedication to his ideals: *The First Battle* and *The Second Battle or The New Declaration of Independence*. One must struggle for underdog causes because they are always under assault by more powerful societal forces.
- **Campaign finance reform.** Among other features, the 1908 Democratic platform called for individual contributions to be limited, publicity for contributions before elections and banning corporate contributions.[103] In 1924, the party platform appealed for "federal candidates to be furnished 'reasonable means of publicity at federal expense.'" This was proposed by Bryan.[104]

Bryan did, however, leave out one underdog group from the causes he supported: blacks. Bryan's views of the fundamental power divide in American politics did not include blacks. This is not surprising since he was a Democrat; the "solid south" was still the most reliable base of party support.[105] Arguably, he adjusted his views on equality to match the realities of American blacks. He claimed that southern blacks had equal protection under the law, except for majoritarian political rights.[106] According to historian Robert W. Cherney, this "must have soothed the conflict between Bryan's principles of equality and the attitudes of his southern supporters, but he must have had a difficult time ignoring the realities of discrimination and denial of rights everywhere in the south.

Indeed, he could only have believed what he said if he refused to look around himself when he and his family lived in Texas, North Carolina or Florida."[107]

Bryan was described by writer Herbert David Croly in 1911 as "best understood as a Democrat of both Jeffersonian and Jacksonian tendencies, who has been born a few generations too late."[108] While that may be accurate, he also provided a vital ideological link between the founders of the Democratic Party and the new challenges it faced in the modern age.

Americans today remember the party's historical link to underdogs more by Franklin D. Roosevelt than by Jefferson, Jackson, or Bryan. It is to him and other key Democrats in the party's glory days of the twentieth century where the analysis turns next.

CHAPTER 5

The Glory Days: FDR to Humphrey

Franklin Roosevelt

Franklin Roosevelt grew up in a wealthy and privileged family in New York. He did not personally experience much injustice, persecution or discrimination growing up. He was isolated from the poor and their daily struggles, though he did have some contact with the poor in his early life. While he attended Groton, a Massachusetts college preparatory school,[1] he joined their Missionary Society. As part of it, he helped an elderly black lady with her household tasks. He also worked at their summer camp in New Hampshire that was composed of poor boys from the Boston and New York slums.[2]

FDR was also exposed to the poor when he was engaged to Eleanor, who was involved in the Junior League in New York City. Eleanor opened his eyes to the poor: "she took him with her to visit a settlement house...One of the children was ill at school; Eleanor invited her fiancé to help her take the child home. After helping Eleanor take the girl into the dank, dark, foul-smelling tenement where she lived, he said...'My God, I didn't know anyone lived like that.'"[3]

New York State Senate

Roosevelt was an underdog when he ran for the New York State Senate in 1910; the last time the senate district he ran in had voted Democratic was 1884.[4] He prevailed on Election Day and won 15,708 votes to his Republican incumbent's 14,568.[5]

In Albany, FDR decided to take on another fight that most people assumed he would lose; he took on powerful Tammany Hall, widely known for its corrupt politics. Roosevelt led a band of Democratic insurgents who challenged the Tammany boss Charles Murphy. At that time, the state legislatures chose U.S. senators. Murphy wanted William Sheehan as U.S. senator. Roosevelt and his allies challenged him. Because of the resistance, Murphy was ultimately unsuccessful in getting Sheehan named to the seat. Instead, a compromise candidate was agreed on.[6] When the battle was over, FDR spoke before the New York City YMCA. His words illustrate his spirit in fighting for underdog causes: "I have just come from Albany and the close of a long fight which lasted sixty-four rounds…At the end of it was a free-for-all. Some got battered, but you can see by me that there were few scratches on the insurgents."[7]

He was not *unambiguously* on the side of underdogs with his reactions to the famous New York Triangle fire of March 25, 1911. Author Jean Kennedy Smith describes the horror and injustice: "The doors to the only stairwell were chained shut, ostensibly to prevent theft.…Forty-six employees fell or jumped to their deaths on the sidewalk below; one hundred perished in the inferno. All but fifteen were girls and young women between the ages of sixteen and thirty-five. In the trial that followed, the company was absolved of responsibility and collected $64,925 in insurance damages. Twenty-three families of the dead sued and received an overall total of $1,725. That amounted to $75 for each life lost."[8]

The fire symbolized greed and the atrocious working conditions that many industrial workers faced at the time.[9] As a result of the fire, bills that would reform labor conditions were considered in Albany. A key measure was a bill that would have limited children's and women's working hours. Roosevelt would not meet with a key supporter, Francis Perkins of the New York Consumers League. Perkins would later be his Secretary of Labor when he was president.

The measure passed, but FDR was not present at the vote. He voted for it in absentia. Later, he would inaccurately portray himself as one of the originators of the legislation.[10] According to author Conrad Black, "those who in later years would represent him as a radical champion of the left ignore how conservative, cautious, and at times ruthlessly opportunistic he was."[11]

Roosevelt's Paralytic Illness

Why did Roosevelt champion the underdog so vigorously throughout most of his political career? One reason is very simple: because he felt he was one himself because of his paralytic illness. For many years, it was thought to be polio, though a 2003 article in the *Journal of Medical*

Biography concluded that he most likely suffered from Guillan-Barre syndrome.[12] The precise nature of his illness is not the critical link to underdogs; instead it is how the sickness increased his awareness of others who were of a different socioeconomic class than he was.

Roosevelt developed polio at the age of thirty-nine, while on vacation in Canada. He fell into the cold Bay of Fundy on August 9, 1921. The next day he swam and jogged, but later felt tired and experienced chills. He was paralyzed from the waist down by August 13.[13] Roosevelt sought out medical experts and tried different rehabilitation techniques.[14] In 1924, Roosevelt visited Warms Springs, Georgia, for the first time. The therapeutic potential of the water appealed to Roosevelt.[15] After visiting, Roosevelt believed "that his six weeks in the waters of Warm Springs did more to improve his condition than any treatment he had received in the previous 3 years." He bought the center in 1926 after it had financial troubles.[16] More than two-thirds of his money went to the acquisition; it was the sole major personal financial gamble he ever took.[17] In 1927, the Georgia Warm Springs Foundation was formed.[18] From 1924 to 1945, he visited Warm Springs forty-one times.[19]

In the 1920s, handicapped people had many characteristics of underdogs. They were the subject of sympathy, disadvantaged by discrimination and generally considered defeated. As Hugh Gregory Gallagher notes, "the handicapped were kept at home, out of sight, in back bedrooms, by families who felt a mixture of embarrassment and shame about their presence." Not all were kept at home; some went to hospitals for their rehabilitation. There were relatively few of them, however, and the environment reinforced their status as societal outsiders: "these hospitals were often grim, depressing places—dark, gray piles indistinguishable from prisons and asylums. They had names such as House of St. Giles the Cripple, Children's House of the Home for Incurables, and the New York Society for the Relief of the Ruptured and Crippled."[20]

The atmosphere that Roosevelt helped create at Warm Springs was quite different. Instead of shame and exclusion, there was pride and inclusion. The key difference was in *broadening* the treatment that the patients received. Their medical care was not considered most important—the social and psychological characteristics of the handicapped were considered equally as important.[21] A pamphlet describing what the center does illustrates this: "to the special methods of treatment must be added the psychological effect of the group treatment, the stimulus caused by a number of people pursuing the same end, and each spurring the other on to more and better effort."[22]

Author Conrad Black describes FDR's personal involvement, and the effect it had on the patients: FDR "devised an exercise and water-therapy regime for each person...and infected almost everyone with his own determination and optimism. He personally led the exercises in the pool.... The combination of water, sun, exercise, companionship, and the inspiring manner of the leader did help most of those who attended." Economic discrimination was not a major factor at the center: "Roosevelt was not overly concerned about being paid for his services. Those who could afford to pay were expected to; those who couldn't were not."[23]

The rehabilitation center at Warm Springs was not the only place in Georgia where FDR developed a bond with underdogs. In the 1920s, he met many rural Georgians as he took drives in the countryside. He would understand the fears and problems of many of them during this time.[24] According to Roosevelt Institute President Emeritus Christopher Breiseth, FDR at Warm Springs "learned about class and race in the rural south and about pervasive poverty."[25]

How did Roosevelt's illness change him personally? Frances Perkins thought that the illness had a profound effect on him, as journalist Adam Cohen writes:

> Perkins, who knew him in his early years in New York society, and as a young legislator in Albany, had considered Roosevelt something of a prig. "His superficial feeling toward many people was that they were great bores, stupid and nonsensical," and he "didn't want to bother with them," she recalled. "After he was ill, flat, prostrated," he "had a total change of heart," she said. "Nobody was dull. Nobody was a great nuisance. Nobody made no sense. Nobody was good for nothing. Because they were human beings who could walk, and run, and exercise, they were all superior to him."[26]

According to Eleanor Roosevelt, FDR's illness affected his mentality: "anyone who has gone through great suffering is bound to have a greater sympathy and understanding of the problems of mankind."[27] His suffering allowed him to be able to personally connect to the sudden misfortunes that so many Americans experienced later in the Depression. As historian H. W. Brands observes, "Capricious calamity isn't part of the American Dream...Yet sometimes bad things *do* happen to people through no fault of their own. Roosevelt understood this in a way he hadn't before."[28] According to historian Paul Conklin, "Polio made an aristocratic Roosevelt into an underdog. For him it replaced the log cabin."[29]

New York Governor

Roosevelt ran against Republican opponent New York Attorney General Albert Ottinger in 1928.[30] He rhetorically fought for many underdogs in his campaign, including the handicapped, the elderly, and children and women industrial workers. He won a close race; out of more than 4.2 million votes cast, he beat Otinger by only 25,564 votes.[31]

FDR proposed many initiatives that could have helped society's underdogs:

- For the elderly poor, a commission to study economic security for senior citizens.
- To help reduce the price of electricity, an authority to operate, build, and finance facilities that would generate power. The private sector would transmit the power, but the state would own the facilities (unless there was overcharging, then the state could transmit the electricity).
- To help the sick, a bond for construction of hospitals.[32]

An economic slump started in the summer of 1929 and became a crisis with the stock market crash in October. What came next was widespread and harsh. As the late economist Nicholas Spulber wrote, "precipitous drops in prices, money supply, credits, investments, production, and employment, along with dramatic increases in bank failures, commercial and industrial bankruptcies, and farm mortgage foreclosures became everyday occurrences."[33] The Great Depression had begun.

Roosevelt began to address the economic situation in 1930. He recognized that unemployment was a serious concern and proposed some public works, job creation, and emergency relief.[34] In April 1930, he spoke to New York Democrats. Being a good party man, he brought up the legacy of the party's founder when he spoke out against concentration in American finance and industry: "If Thomas Jefferson were alive he would be the first to question this concentration of economic power."[35]

TERA, or the Temporary Emergency Relief Administration, is a good illustration of FDR's commitment to help the unemployed as governor of New York. TERA was started in 1931. The program, financed by modestly increasing income taxes, not only gave money to the unemployed but also required work for the recipients. It would be administered by Harry Hopkins, a social worker from Iowa.[36] The program, according to New York Attorney General John J. Bennett, was "the first enactment under which a State, as such, had accepted any liability for the support of its population, viewed not as wards but merely as men and women unable temporarily to accommodate themselves to the social scene, without at the same time placing such men and women in the position of recipients of a bounty or a dole [and] in such a manner as to preserve the self-respect of every beneficiary."[37]

New York, and the nation, was experiencing a clash between the long-established notions of opportunity and initiative and extensive unemployment. The core problem, as historian R. Alan Lawson observes, is "how to institutionalize compassion and still honor the tough-minded competitive initiative Americans thought they should follow."[38] Reconciling these two strong (and competing) ideals into at least a minimal level of societal acceptance is at the root of winning battles for economic underdogs. It is easier to act upon compassion if the cause of the disadvantaged condition is perceived to be *unrelated* to how hard one has tried to compete. There is no injustice if one does not try to get a job when there are employers offering them. In 1931 (and afterward), the problem was there were not enough jobs for the number of people who wanted them.

In the midst of his attempt to gain his party's nomination, FDR made a radio address on April 7, 1932 that clearly elucidated who the country should rely on to build the recovery: "These unhappy times call for the building of plans that rest upon the forgotten, the unorganized but the indispensable units of economic power...[and] that put their faith once more in the forgotten man at the bottom of the economic pyramid."[39] This rhetorical recognition of the poor is a sympathetic call for societal fairness. It is also a call to rebuild the economy from the bottom up, unlike the approach President Hoover was pursuing. This foreshadows the general approach of the New Deal.

His Presidency: Hope and Action for Underdogs

In 1932, the economic conditions in the nation were horrendous. Unemployment was estimated to be between 24 and 36 percent. The quantity of stock market and check transactions was 60 percent lower than they had been in 1929.[40] The pain that this produced was extensive. There were millions of losers in America now. Many were without jobs or hope. As author Nick Taylor describes, "Millions lost their homes, wore their clothes into rags, and had to forage like animals for food: city dwellers fought for scraps in garbage cans and dumps, while in the country, the hungry scratched for roots and weeds." But that was not the worst of it: "For all of the physical suffering, the greatest loss was to the spirit. People felt fear, shame, despair; the suicide rate soared, and the nation trembled at the prospect of a dark, uncertain future."[41]

Once Roosevelt became president, he moved quickly to alleviate the suffering of many Americans. He had three goals, as historian Alan Brinkley writes, "devise policies to end the Great Depression...create programs to help the millions in distress weather hard times until prosperity returned. And...to frame lasting reforms that would prevent a similar crisis from occurring again."[42]

FDR's first 100 days in office were a whirlwind of legislative activity designed to get the country moving again. He inundated Congress with a great deal of legislation, among these were farm relief and credit, unemployment aid to the states, the creation of the Tennessee Valley Authority and the Federal Deposit Insurance Corporation, and reform of the railroads.[43] Roosevelt supported economic underdogs with these programs.

Technically, the goal of his proposals was to help the economic conditions of Americans so that there would be fewer underdogs. If one was out of a job, they might be stereotyped as losers by society. More important, people might internalize their economic failure in a way that diminishes their self-confidence. Self-confidence is not only critical to success, but it is also a prerequisite for survival. As historian William E. Leuchtenburg notes, "To be unemployed in an industrial society is the equivalent of banishment and excommunication. A job established a man's identity—not only what other men thought of him but how he viewed himself; the loss of his job shattered his self-esteem."[44] FDR's first inaugural speech directly addressed this confidence gap: "This is preeminently the time to speak the truth, the whole truth, frankly and boldly. Nor need we shrink from honestly facing conditions in our country today. This great Nation will endure as it has endured, will revive and will prosper. So, first of all, let me assert my firm belief that the only thing we have to fear is fear itself—nameless, unreasoning, unjustified terror which paralyzes needed efforts to convert retreat into advance."[45]

As the economic downturn had lasted so long, many Americans felt that they were not likely to get a job, in contrast to what had occurred in previous cycles. Simply put, many Americans expected to keep on losing: income, employment, stability, and ultimately hope. FDR's fireside chats were important in helping stabilize the country because they helped make people feel less alone in their troubles. His speech of May 7, 1933, was full of references to underdogs:

- One was the nation itself: "Two months ago we were facing serious economic problems. The country was dying by inches."[46] A country that is dying is losing-losing its ability to economically survive.
- Another underdog was the jobless with families. He talked about how creating the Civilian Conservation Corps would help them: "we are giving opportunity of employment to one-quarter of a million of the unemployed, especially the young men who have dependents, to go into the forestry and flood protection work....we are relieving an appreciable amount of actual distress."[47]
- Industrial labor was another underdog: "well-considered and conservative measures will likewise be proposed which will attempt to give to the industrial workers...a more fair wage return, prevent cutthroat competition and unduly long hours for labor."[48]

In 1935, the Rural Electrification Administration (REA) was created.[49] It is another example of a New Deal program designed to help underdogs. There was a tremendous inequality between rural and urban people regarding electrification. During the 1930s, only 10 percent of rural people had electricity while 90 percent of city people did. Most rural areas were not electrified because the private utility companies refused to build the lines. They claimed it was too expensive and farmers could not afford electricity.[50]

Without electricity, rural people could not share equally in the economic and social benefits of modern society. Without refrigeration, for example, it was not practical to eat fresh meat except a few months of the year.[51] William E. Leuchtenburg describes the plight of some rural women: "farm wives, who enviously eyed pictures in the *Saturday Evening Post* of city women with washing machines, refrigerators, and vacuum cleaners, performed their backbreaking chores like peasant women in a preindustrial age."[52]

By 1939, 25 percent of rural areas had electricity.[53] By the mid-1950s, electricity had come to just about every American farm.[54] Life was made easier for many Americans as a result; one could work inside the house at night. Moreover, the sense of rural isolation was diminished because of radio.[55] The significance of having, and not having, electricity is recounted by Arkansas physics teacher JoAnne Sears Rife, who grew up in the Depression: "the REA...became a much revered institution in our family, almost as sacred as church or the county Extension Service. . . . I remember life before REA. It was not dreadful, but it was not equal."[56]

Roosevelt had limited success in fixing the national economy in the first few years of his first term. And he was making enemies: "businessmen and bankers were turning more and more against Roosevelt's New Deal program. They feared his experiments, were appalled because he had taken the Nation off the gold standard and allowed deficits in the budget, and disliked the concessions to labor." He still continued to push for change: "Roosevelt responded with a new program of reform: Social Security, heavier taxes on the wealthy, new controls over banks and public utilities, and an enormous work relief program for the unemployed."[57]

FDR's second inaugural speech in 1937 straightforwardly addressed the economic underdogs of the nation:

In this nation I see tens of millions of its citizens—a substantial part of its whole population—who at this very moment are denied the greater part of what the very lowest standards of today call the necessities of life. I see millions of families trying to live on incomes so meager that the pall of family disaster hangs over them day by day. I see millions whose daily lives in city and on farm continue under conditions labeled indecent by a so-called polite society half a century ago. I see millions denied education, recreation, and the opportunity to better their lot and the lot of their children. I see millions lacking the means to buy the products of farm and factory and by their poverty denying work and productiveness to many other millions. I see one-third of a nation ill-housed, ill-clad, ill-nourished.[58]

Although Roosevelt did not completely succeed in alleviating the needs of the economic underdogs, his presidency gave hope to them. According to author Dexter Perkins, his connection to underdogs was an ideal match for what was needed in his time: "Roosevelt as an individual bulked large in the events of his epoch. The central reason for this fact lies in the gusto, the optimism, and the feeling for the underdog which he brought to a period of change."[59] Roosevelt's leadership abilities were recognized by Winston Churchill. Churchill admired his "generous sympathy for the underdog . . . [and] his intense desire for a nearer approach to social justice."[60]

The liberal legacy of FDR toward helping underdogs is extensive; it included his creation of the Social Security system (that eventually guaranteed that the elderly would have at least a minimum level of economic security) and his support for organized labor (that would give unions the legal backing they needed to grow). There were areas, however, where Roosevelt did not stand up for underdogs. Two of these involve Japanese Americans and African Americans.

Japanese Americans

Many people of Japanese ethnicity in the western United States became classic underdogs after the attack on Pearl Harbor. At least 110,000 of them were rounded up and put in detention camps. 70 percent of them were American citizens. The internments began with Executive Order Number 9066, signed in February 1942.[61] The way they were treated was shameful, as author Conrad Black writes: "the designated targets of this measure were given one week to dispose of their property as they wished, were rounded up in racetracks and fairgrounds and such places, and spent idle days and nights constantly interrupted by searchlights behind watchtowers and barbed wire."[62]

Although the United States was also at war with Germany and Italy during this time, the Japanese were treated worse than the Germans or the Italians. Compared to their total population, Japanese were arrested in disproportionate numbers.[63] Moreover, as author Brian Maso Hayashi states, "a Western Defense Command officer admitted that Japanese-Americans were initially interned on far slimmer evidence than German Americans." In addition, "on October 19, 1942 . . . some 52,000 California Italians without U.S. citizenship [were removed] from the status of 'enemy alien,' because as President Franklin Roosevelt said, they were not a security threat but 'a bunch of opera singers.'"[64]

The internments were justified because of "military necessity."[65] This included not only the traditional military defense of the homeland, but also the reality of racial hostility.[66] The atmosphere in the United States after Pearl Harbor (and the Japanese military victories in early 1942) created a space where the persecution of Japanese Americans flourished, as author Robert N. Rosen writes: "Citizens on the West Coast had become hysterical about the Japanese living in their midst. Some claimed they saw signals and strange lights sent or set up by Japanese Americans. Racial hatred and fear of the Japanese exploded. Law enforcement officials, politicians, the governor, California attorney general Earl Warren, the army general in charge of the West Coast, and Secretary Stimson all clamored for action."[67]

Executive Order Number 9066 also created a fresh gateway for economic discrimination against Japanese Americans. Although economic discrimination was not a new experience to them,[68] the sheer audacity of some of the racism is striking: a representative of the California Grower-Shipper Vegetable Association remarked, "We're charged with wanting to get rid of the Japs for selfish reasons...We might as well be honest. It's a question of whether the white man lives on the Pacific coast or the brown man."[69]

The situation that many Japanese Americans faced after their release was bleak. Internee Riichi Satow said, "Our things were all gone by the time we got back home...Nothing was left...everything had been stolen."[70] The aggregate economic losses to Japanese Americans were tremendous: an estimated $1.2 to 3.1 million (1983) dollars.[71]

The justification for Roosevelt's decision was that he had to do anything to win the war.[72] Eleanor Roosevelt differed from her husband on the issue. According to historian Doris Kearns Goodwin, "To her mind, the guarantees of the Bill of Rights must never be surrendered, even in the face of national disaster."[73] On December 16, 1941, she wrote in her newspaper column that respecting the rights of Japanese Americans was a "challenge of fairness to our citizens of every nationality."[74] However, she could not dissuade FDR from his decision.[75]

African Americans

For any Democrat to get elected as president after the Civil War, they had to first win the south. This was an easy task for most Democrats, as southerners were not inclined to support the party of Lincoln. Or more precisely, *white* southerners. But that was not a problem because they disproportionately dominated the southern electorate. Literacy tests, poll taxes, and understanding clauses were used throughout the south to disenfranchise African Americans after the Civil War.[76]

Part of the reason why Roosevelt was successful in getting much of his legislation passed through Congress was because he *didn't* challenge the racial status quo in the south. As historian Alan Brinkley observes, "he was never willing to challenge the central institutions of racial oppression in American life, fearful that to do so would damage the Democratic party in the South and lose him the critical support of powerful southerners in Congress."[77]

A good illustration of Roosevelt's relationship with African American issues was how he responded to lynchings. Unfortunately, victims of lynchings share many characteristics of underdogs; inequality, injustice, and discrimination. For example, in 1900, there were 115 lynchings; 106 of the victims were black. In 1915, 56 of the 69 lynchings were done to blacks. In 1923, there were 33 lynchings in the United States; 29 of them black victims. In 1933, 24 of the 26 lynchings were black victims.[78] Most of the lynchings occurred in border and southern states.[79] Robert A. Gibson writes that "the causes assigned by whites in justification or explanation of lynching Black people include everything from major crimes to minor offenses. In many cases, Blacks were lynched for no reason at all other than race prejudice."[80]

Federal anti-lynching bills were proposed by Democratic U.S. Senator Robert F. Wagner during the mid-1930s. His 1937 bill was filibustered to death in the Senate and never passed. Roosevelt's leadership skills were not used to make passage a priority.[81] His 1940 bill also died in the Senate.[82]

By not prioritizing anti-lynching legislation, Roosevelt resisted pressure from many sources, including his wife Eleanor, his mother Sara, and the NAACP (National Association for the Advancement of Colored People) Executive Secretary Walter White.[83] The nation would have to wait until 1968 before the first federal anti-lynching bill became law.[84]

Nonetheless, beginning in 1936, blacks became an integral part of the Roosevelt coalition. They voted Democratic for the first time in more than 70 years because of his relief programs, with 71 percent supporting FDR.[85] FDR's general coalition of liberals, urban blacks, southern Protestants, radicals, northern Jews, Catholics, small farmers, and union members would dominate the party until 1966.[86] The party would never be the same, as Alan Brinkley observed: "Franklin Roosevelt's creation of a new and vastly more powerful Democratic coalition shattered the South's grip on the party. No longer could the region hold Democratic presidential candidates hostage to its conservative demands.... and no longer could southern Democrats impose their racial views on the party as a whole."[87]

Harry Truman

One of the most significant links between Harry Truman and underdogs is civil rights. As a senator and president, Truman took many courageous steps in defense of civil rights. As a U.S. senator he was relatively liberal on civil rights issues.[88] Specifically, in 1938 he voted to end a filibuster over an anti-lynching bill. The filibuster succeeded and the anti-lynching bill did not pass then.[89] He made some speeches as a senator that supported political equality for African Americans. For example, in Sedalia, Missouri, on June 15, 1940, he said, "I believe in the brotherhood of man; not merely the brotherhood of white men; but the brotherhood of all men before the law. I believe in the Constitution and the Declaration of Independence. In giving to the Negroes the rights that are theirs, we are only acting in accord with ideas of a true democracy."[90]

As president from 1945 to 1953, he would both influence his party and the nation on civil rights. In September 1945, Truman called for the Fair Employment Practices Committee (FEPC) to be extended. Defense industries and government agencies hiring practices were watched for discrimination against blacks by this committee.[91]

In December 1946, the President's Committee on Civil Rights was appointed. In October 1947, the report was released.[92] The committee tried to answer some fundamental questions about America and civil rights: these concerned the goal, progress (or lack of), government responsibility, and needed action.[93] For instance, the committee enumerated areas where the right to physical security and safety was not being met: these included involuntary servitude, police brutality, administration of justice, and lynching. The denial of rights was not only for African Americans, but affected other minorities as well.[94] In addition, the committee detailed how African Americans were denied the right to vote through the white primary: "until 1944, the white primary, by which participation in the Democratic primary is limited to white citizens, was used in Texas, Alabama, Arkansas, Georgia, Louisiana, and Mississippi as the most effective modern 'legal' device for disfranchising Negroes. While some southern Negroes succeeded in spite of various obstacles in voting in general elections, almost none voted in the Democratic primaries. Since the Democratic primary is the only election of any significance, the device of the white primary resulted in exclusion of Negroes from government in these states."[95]

The report also examined discrimination in public schools. It found "separate but equal" did not exist in reality: "whatever test is used— expenditure per pupil, teachers' salaries, the number of pupils per teacher, transportation of students, adequacy of school buildings and educational equipment, length of school term, extent of curriculum— Negro students are invariably at a disadvantage."[96] The report was extensive and examined other areas, including housing, the military, health, law, foreign policy, and morality.[97] It concluded that the issue of civil rights was a national one, not regional.[98]

Truman would follow up on this report with his 1948 State of the Union speech. In his speech, he called for the minimum wage to be increased, public housing, national health insurance, extending rent control, and more aid to education.[99] Although these proposals would have helped all economic underdogs, they probably would have (in terms of their percentage of the overall population) disproportionately helped African Americans. His most controversial statement directly concerned equality. He remarked that "some of our citizens are still denied equal opportunity for education, for jobs and economic advancement, and for the expression of their views at the polls. Most serious of all, some are denied equal protection under laws.... The recent report of the President's Committee on Civil Rights points the way to corrective action by the Federal Government and by State and local governments. Because of the need for effective Federal action, I shall send a special message to the Congress on this important subject."[100]

His special message to Congress was sent on February 2, 1948, and called for Congress to enact wide-ranging civil rights laws. He wanted poll taxes to end, lynching to be made illegal under federal law, and an end to discrimination in interstate travel by airplane, bus, and rail. He also ordered the military to end discrimination and requested Congress to take action on the claims made by Japanese Americans concerning their World War II internment.[101] Most of Truman's proposals went nowhere, but one did become law fairly quickly: Executive Order 9981. It was issued on July 26, 1948, and ordered the desegregation of the armed forces.[102]

It was a controversial move. Only 13 percent of Americans supported what he wanted to do. General Omar Bradley believed it would ruin the army. Georgia Senator Richard Russell said that rates of crime would increase among the military and more men would become disabled because of contracting communicable diseases.[103] African Americans in the military at this time were obvious underdogs who were treated unequal and unfairly. In an essay, Republican Colin Powell refers to himself in the third person as he thanks *Democrat* Harry Truman for making his underdog career possible:

Many years later when he became chairman of the Joint Chiefs of Staff, he would be asked by inquisitive reporters who had forgotten their history, "Well, General Powell, when you were growing up in the South Bronx, did you ever think or dream that you would grow up to become chairman of the Joint Chiefs of Staff of the Armed Forces of the United States?" And I would smile patiently and say "No," because such a dream would have been impossible for that eleven-year-old kid. But that kid didn't know that President Truman had just signed an executive order that would permit such a dream to come true. And the dream did come true, not just because President Truman signed an executive order, but also because after he signed the order, he went about the task of knocking the ears off the Pentagon to make it happen.[104]

Even though his other proposals on equal protection had very little chance of becoming law, they still scared much of the south. His call for racial equality of opportunity splintered the party. Southern political leaders recognized that their region's way of life could be in danger. Alabama governor James Folsom announced that he would run for president in 1948. Folsom wanted other states to back him.[105] The civil rights message was a lynching of the Constitution, according to Tom Connolly of Texas. South Carolina Senator Olin Johnston boycotted the Jefferson-Jackson Day dinner because he feared sitting next to a black.[106]

Alabama's American Bar Association president made it crystal clear about how he saw the future for his state: "No Negro is good enough and no negro will ever be good enough to participate in making the law under which the white people in Alabama have to live."[107] Truman aide Clark Clifford recounts the southern reaction to Truman's proposals: "Immediately, letters began to pour in from all over the South charging that President Truman was breaking up the Democratic party. Most of the letters were bitter, and many of them contained ugly or obscene racial slurs directed at the President, his family, and some of his staff, including me. Arkansas governor Ben Laney branded the civil rights message 'distasteful, unthinkable, and ridiculous.' "[108]

Truman's proposals were further evidence that a new Democratic coalition was emerging, one that would eventually dislodge most southern whites from the party. As historian Gary A. Donaldson writes, "South Carolina governor Strom Thurmond and Mississippi senator James Eastland, saw the president's civil rights message as an indicator for the future. There did not seem to be enough room . . . for both the southern conservatives and the new liberal coalition of northern liberals, African Americans, and organized labor."[109]

Many conservative southern Democrats walked away from him in the 1948 election. One of the most prominent was Strom Thurmond, who ran for president as a candidate for the State's Rights (Dixiecrats) party. The Dixiecrats wanted to win enough states to deny any candidate an electoral vote majority. If that happened, the presidential election would have been decided by the House of Representatives, where the south could decide who was an acceptable candidate. The strategy did not work, Thurmond carried only four southern states and Truman won the election.[110] The Dixiecrat rebellion was mainly a Black Belt uprising that indicated more precisely (if that was necessary) that race was the primary motivation in the bloc.[111]

Truman later reflected on what he tried to do in 1948: "I said what I thought had to be said. You can't divide the country up into sections and have one rule for one section and one rule for another, and you can't encourage people's prejudices. You have to appeal to people's best instincts, not their worst ones."[112] To many, the best instincts in people involve trying to help the underdog.

In other ways, Truman can be linked to the underdog concept by the following:

- Israel: His 1948 recognition of Israel as a state eleven minutes after it came into existence[113] was an important step in legitimizing the Jewish state. To many, Israel at that time possessed the following underdog characteristics; it was not expected to survive,[114] and Jews were an object of sympathy from many around the world because of the Holocaust.
- Health care: In 1945, he proposed to a plan that would have offered health care for all Americans. He was the first president to do so.[115] On many occasions in his presidency, Truman kept pushing for national health insurance. It never happened. It was an underdog battle, as Brian Hamel reports: "powerful interest groups were aligned against this proposal. The AMA spent millions to defeat it. Enrollment in voluntary insurance was growing rapidly...[and] congressional committee politics managed to tie [it] up...so that it never came to a vote on the floor of either house."[116]
- The 1948 campaign: Harry Truman was widely expected to lose the general election to Republican Thomas Dewey. Much of the press thought the election was over in October. Author Zachary Karabell offers an example: "for its last issue before the election, *Life* featured a full-page photograph of Dewey and his wife in San Francisco, with the caption 'The Next President Travels by Ferry over the Broad Waters of San Francisco Bay.'"[117]

John F. Kennedy

Was John F. Kennedy an underdog? He certainly was thought of that way by many people because of his family; they were *seen* as underdogs. The Kennedy family was viewed as underdogs because they were Irish-Catholic in Massachusetts. The Irish had been historically discriminated against by the power elite in the state.[118]

The 1960 Presidential Election

It was the 1960 presidential race that created John Kennedy's image as an underdog in the minds of many. This was a deliberate strategy used by his campaign.[119] During the Democratic primaries, he fashioned himself the underdog because of his religion. The dynamics of the May 10 West Virginia primary illustrates why.

There were not many Catholics in West Virginia.[120] Before the primary, Kennedy held a lead in polling in the state. However, as the contest got closer, Kennedy found himself twenty points behind his principal rival, Hubert Humphrey. The reason for the change was that more West Virginians found out that he was Catholic.[121] One person said, "We've never had a Catholic president and I hope we never do."[122] He decided to tackle the religious issue straight out.[123]

He used rhetoric cleverly, for instance, when he publicly asked, "Is anyone going to tell me I lost the primary before I was born?"[124] He also tied religious prejudice to military service. In a speech in Morgantown, West Virginia, he declared: "Nobody asked me if I was a Catholic when I joined the United States Navy." In the same speech, he poignantly brought up his late brother: "nobody asked my brother if he was a Catholic or a Protestant before he climbed into an American bomber plane to fly his last mission."[125]

Associated Press West Virginia statehouse reporter Herbert C. Little recounted part of the media strategy of the Kennedy campaign:

> The Kennedy people seemed determined to make a bigger thing out of the religious issue than it really was. They tried to convey the idea that JFK was an underdog fighting against great odds. It was the rare case among political campaigns where a candidate's handlers would take offense if you wrote something suggesting that he might be the favorite.... JFK would... often solicit questions at the end of his speech. And after a while, nobody was bringing up the matter of his Catholicism. So, about midway through his campaign, he changed his tactic: he began bringing up the issue himself. The Kennedys played the underdog role to the hilt.[126]

In the end, the topic of religion was successfully framed by Kennedy as tolerance against intolerance and he won the primary. That night, Humphrey dropped his presidential bid.[127] It was brilliant political theater by Kennedy; tolerance was the heroic underdog, as writer Theodore H. White observes, "no voter could prove his tolerance by voting for Hubert Humphrey, but any voter could prove to his own conscience in this state of ninety percent white Protestants that he voted without prejudice by voting for Kennedy."[128]

There was another area in the battle for the Democratic nomination where Kennedy was clearly not an underdog; his finances. Kennedy was from a rich family and Humphrey was not. According to syndicated columnist Sandy Grady, "Kennedy…unleashed…gobs of money…JFK would hop to the airport in Charleston, W.Va., in his Convair turboprop (the Caroline) while Humphrey grinded around coal-mine hamlets in a rattletrap bus."[129] Journalist Sander Vanocur wrote that "how much money Kennedy had spent no one will ever know."[130]

The Kennedy campaign also used his underdog persona during the general-election campaign as well. The debates with Nixon were critical to his eventual victory. According to writer John Hellmann, the first debate was the significant one: "Kennedy went into it the underdog, an unproven leader facing the heir apparent of a highly popular administration; he emerged the favorite."[131] The collective memory of that event is also relevant to his perception as an underdog. As Kurt and Gladys Engel Long wrote in 1986, "Those old enough will remember how in that first meeting Kennedy…stood up to the more seasoned politician to prove that he was indeed presidential timber."[132]

Ideology

Liberals were suspicious of Kennedy in the 1950s. There were many reasons for this: the 1952 account in *The New Republic* that described Kennedy as being happy that Richard Nixon beat Helen Gahagan Douglas in the 1950 California U.S. Senate race, his refusal to confront Senator Joseph McCarthy and his father's business practices and politics.[133] As Michael O'Brien states, "The 'true' liberals, those influenced by Eleanor Roosevelt and Adlai Stevenson, thought Jack was too detached, too cool, too devoid of commitment."[134]

In preparation for a possible run for the presidency, Kennedy tried to cultivate an image as a "new" Democrat, one that was not a knee-jerk liberal. He did not join the Americans for Democratic Action (ADA) in his first year as a senator. After the 1956 election, he refused to become a member of the Democratic National Committee established Democratic Advisory Council (DAC). The DAC was to devise liberal policies for future platforms. Legislatively, Kennedy did not want to irritate Senate Majority Leader Johnson and House Speaker Sam Rayburn, who thought that their leadership was being hindered by the Democratic National Committee.[135]

Kennedy eventually associated himself with more liberal causes after 1958, though his stances on civil rights issues were shaded; after all, he wanted to maximize his potential to attract southern votes in 1960.[136]

JFK's domestic policy strategy after he became president was to first concentrate on achievable goals, the small victories that would eventually help him win on more contentious issues. This caution bothered many liberals, as they unfavorably compared him to FDR's first 100 days.[137]

Kennedy did help economic underdogs in his years in office. He was victorious in securing wins in several important policy areas: urban renewal, improved benefits for social security, and an increase in the minimum wage. The Peace Corps also was started.[138] Kennedy was never able to significantly help what is historically the biggest underdog group in American society: African Americans. He was beginning to move more clearly on civil rights, but was assassinated before he had the opportunity to act bolder.[139]

The assassination of JFK is the most obvious link to the underdog concept; his ideals and his promise became the objects of sympathy for millions of people. His tragic death produced sympathetic reactions from not only Americans, but from all over the world. These included statements from Queen Elizabeth, German Chancellor Erhard, Austrian President Scharf, and Swiss President Spuhler.[140] It would be the new president, Lyndon Johnson, who would harness the sympathy for JFK to help him win the most significant advances for African Americans in a hundred years.

Lyndon Johnson

Johnson grew up poor in Texas. His home did not have indoor plumbing or electricity.[141] Historian Henry F. Graff describes Johnson's early life: "there was never enough money, and Lyndon would often speak with disdain of the steady diet of grits, greens, and cornbread, and fatback of his early years."[142] The deficiencies in Johnson's early life were not confined to physical needs; as historian Robert Dallek explains, "Johnson was an emotional orphan. He was the offspring of 'absent' parents: his father was a self-absorbed character who was often away from the household, and his mother was usually too depressed to fill her children's emotional needs."[143]

Early in his career, Johnson worked for the underdog by teaching young children. He taught for a year in Cotulla, a small town in south Texas.[144] He personally witnessed the effects of poverty and discrimination of Mexican American children while there. He claimed that his backing for civil rights legislation was inspired (or justified) by his time there.[145]

When Johnson was a member of Congress, he was like many other southern politicians; he was for helping out white underdogs, but would not take much meaningful action to help out African Americans. From 1940 to 1960, he voted for segregation in the military (twice), against ending the poll tax (six times), against plans to end discrimination in federal programs (six times), and to preserve the District of Columbia's segregation (once).[146] When he became president in 1963, however, he would use JFK's legacy to build support to help out African Americans. In a speech before a Joint session of Congress five days after Kennedy's assassination, he said,

> No memorial oration or eulogy could more eloquently honor President Kennedy's memory than the earliest possible passage of the civil rights bill for which he fought so long. We have talked long enough in this country about equal rights. We have talked for one hundred years or more. It is time now to write the next chapter, and to write it in the books of law. I urge you ... to enact a civil rights law so that we can move forward to eliminate from this Nation every trace of discrimination and oppression that is based upon race or color.[147]

Johnson would harness the emotional sympathy that poured out after Kennedy's death as a means to help African Americans move toward equality.[148] On Thanksgiving Day in 1963, Johnson fused religion with American creedal values in a televised speech: "Let us today renew our dedication to the ideals that are American. Let us pray for His Divine wisdom in banishing from our land any injustice or intolerance or oppression to any of our fellow Americans, whatever their opinion, whatever the color of their skins."[149]

After months of legislative struggle, Congress passed the Civil Rights bill, and Johnson signed it in July 1964.[150] Johnson's lobbying for the bill stemmed from his ability to identify with people who had little power in their lives, as Robert Dallek writes: "Johnson—the prominent politician, the great Majority Leader, the Vice-President, the all-powerful President—was at the same time Johnson the underdog, the poor boy from Texas struggling to escape from the shadows and win universal approval."[151]

The Civil Rights bill did not make him popular in the south. Johnson suspected what would happen to his party once he signed the bill, as he told presidential aide Bill Moyers: "I think we just delivered the South to the Republican party for a long time to come."[152] He turned out to be right.

Although Johnson sympathized with African Americans, he nonetheless used the FBI to spy on civil rights advocates whom he thought could damage him politically. At the 1964 Democratic National Convention in Atlantic City, Johnson was afraid that a challenge to the credentials of the Mississippi delegation might cost him the election.[153] The members of the Mississippi Freedom Democratic Party (MFDP) were one target for Johnson. In July 1964, the MFDP had challenged the "regular" party over who should be the official Democratic Party of the state.[154]

The MFDP was composed primarily of blacks who were disenfranchised.[155] It was devoted to empowering underdogs, as author Kay Mills explains: "people living amid violence and discrimination needed a way to overcome their justifiable fears in order to take action. MFDP provided them with a vehicle through which they could learn about the political system and see how its decisions affected them, even if they lived in the poorest, most remote hamlets."[156] The atmosphere for racial equality in Mississippi was brutal in 1964. In June, three civil rights workers were killed. Their bodies were found near Philadelphia, Mississippi, in August. There was widespread harassment of civil rights workers, with arrests, beatings, and church burnings.[157]

The MFDP went before the party's credentials committee to plead their case. What happened next was dramatic. Fannie Lou Hamer "told her story about trying to vote in Mississippi.... Johnson quickly preempted Hamer's televised testimony with an impromptu press conference. But later that night, Hamer's story was broadcast on all the major networks. Support came pouring in for the MFDP from across the nation."[158]

After intense maneuvering, the dispute was solved: the "regular" Mississippi Democrats were to be seated and the MFDP received two at large seats.[159] In addition, delegations in the future were banned "from states where the Party process deprived citizens of the right to vote by reason of their race or color."[160] The MFDP did not accept the solution but it was imposed anyway.[161] The clash between the MFDP, the "regular" Mississippi Democrats and the Johnson White House was not put on display on the floor of the convention. Even though Hamer's testimony was televised, there was no fight on the floor of the convention or debate over which delegation deserved to be seated.[162]

This was a pivotal event for the Democratic Party and underdogs. Kay Mills writes that "the Mississippi challenge...was one more link in a chain of events that brought black Americans and then women, Latinos, and Asian Americans into fuller political participation."[163] At least as far as conventions, the national party in 1964 began to put itself on record of insisting on racial equality within the structures and rules of *all* state parties for the future. Equality, justice, and fairness, all core ideas of the underdog concept, would begin to grow in importance for the party. These ideas would be used in the future to justify arguments over issues (such as Vietnam) and procedures (the nominating process itself).

Lyndon Johnson sympathized and worked for the underdog in his war on poverty. Part of the reasons for Johnson's leadership on this agenda involved his childhood, as author Nick Kotz recounts: "his passion for helping the underdog stemmed from his own deep feeling of being an outsider, excluded and looked down upon in the dusty hill country town where he grew up—a victim, he felt, of his father's economic failure."[164] Populism made an impact on him from other sources, as he used to listen to the speeches of Louisiana Senator Huey Long when he was a Senate aide.[165]

On January 8, 1964, LBJ officially announced his war on poverty in his State of the Union address. It was a call for widespread action to help underdogs:

> We must enact youth employment legislation to put jobless, aimless, hopeless youngsters to work on useful projects. We must distribute more food to the needy through a broader food stamp program. We must create a National Service Corps to help the economically handicapped of our own country...We must, by including special school aid funds as part of our education program, improve the quality of teaching, training, and counseling in our hardest hit areas...We must provide hospital insurance for our older citizens financed by every worker and his employer under Social Security, contributing no more than $1 a month during the employee's working career to protect him in his old age in a dignified manner without cost to the Treasury, against the devastating hardship of prolonged or repeated illness. We must, as a part of a revised housing and urban renewal program, give more help to those displaced by slum clearance, provide more housing for our poor and our elderly, and seek as our ultimate goal in our free enterprise system a decent home for every American family.[166]

Programs that were either created or altered included the School Breakfast Program, the Special Milk Program, the Food Stamp Program, the College Work-Study Program, and Head Start.[167] Thus many groups could be considered underdogs as a result: school children, the poor and college students. They were unfairly discriminated against because they (or their families) were short of money.

Two of the most significant programs were Medicare and Medicaid. While Medicaid helped the poor, Medicare helped seniors *escape* poverty. Senior citizens were truly underdogs in 1964; more than 33 percent of people over 65 were living in poverty. This was more than twice the rate of younger people—an obviously unfair and unjust situation to many Americans.[168]

There were many other laws that were passed during Johnson's presidency that helped underdogs, including voting rights in 1965, rent supplements in 1966, age discrimination in 1967, and the Indian Bill of Rights and fair housing in 1968.[169] It would be the Vietnam War that would compel him to end his fight for underdogs and choose an early retirement.

Eugene McCarthy

Opposition to the war in Vietnam helped create many more Democratic underdogs. The most prominent underdog was Minnesota Senator Eugene McCarthy. In 1967, he published the book, *The Limits of Power: America's Role in the World*. In November 1967, he decided to challenge LBJ for his party's presidential nomination.[170]

He was instantly a romantic underdog, with many antiwar college students attracted to his campaign. They were known as the Children's Crusade and went door-to-door campaigning for him in New Hampshire.[171] He got a surprising 42 percent of the vote in the 1968 New Hampshire primary, enough to force Johnson to abandon his reelection hopes shortly afterward.[172]

Some of the speeches he made during the campaign illustrate his sympathies for the underdog. On March 23, 1968, McCarthy spoke in Milwaukee, Wisconsin, and lambasted President Johnson: "It is after all the poor and the sick and the distressed who are being called upon to pay the price of the war in Vietnam. Providing most of the manpower...the poor of this nation are bearing the principal cost of it in inflation and higher interest rates and are being asked to submit to an across-the-board surtax."[173]

The charge that the poor was being asked to pay the surtax was not accurate, in that Johnson's plan to help pay for the war exempted the lowest tax brackets.[174] It was correct in many broad ways, in that it was the poor and non-college educated who made up the majority of the soldiers sent to Vietnam and that inflation and macro economic worries were created by the "guns and butter" policy of Johnson.[175]

In a 1996 interview, McCarthy recalled his thoughts about his chances to win the nomination against LBJ: "Well, we didn't really know...we never thought we had a chance. Maybe for four or five hours after New Hampshire."[176]

He was the classic underdog, a person who was expected to lose. To understand more about underdogs, however, it is important to understand why he even attempted his improbable quest. He decided to run for the presidency because he, and other opponents, could not even engage in a debate on Vietnam in the Senate.[177] He was desperate. Perhaps underdogs become well-known when they are desperate enough. They do something out of the ordinary to attract attention to their powerlessness.

Bobby Kennedy

Bobby Kennedy was also unhappy with Johnson's Vietnam policy, but he did not want to challenge Johnson. Opposing him would divide the party and make Nixon president.[178] He eventually changed his mind, however, and entered the race on March 16, 1968.[179]

Before he made the decision to run for the presidency, Kennedy had felt pressure. When he spoke at Brooklyn College, he saw a sign that said, ROBERT KENNEDY—HAWK, DOVE, OR CHICKEN? This shocked him. Activist Alfred Lowenstein had been pressuring Kennedy to run for the presidency since September 1967. When he would not declare his candidacy in early 1968, Lowenstein told him, "You could've become president...but you don't have the balls."[180]

The pressures on Kennedy illustrate the relationship between underdogs and bravery. One has to be brave to fight for a side that will most likely lose. Is that willingness courage or stupidity?

The desire to help underdogs was not something new to Bobby Kennedy in 1968. It was woven into much of his adult life. At Milton, Arthur Schlesinger, Jr. writes, he "rushed to the side of the underdog and never worried about embarrassing his friends. Life had only enlarged his knowledge of underdogs—first the Rackets Committee, then the civil rights movement, then the poverty wars. His convictions about participation, his readiness to bypass established bureaucracies, his impulse to experiment with new institutional forms, above all, his instinct for sympathy: these were the key to his growing identification with the minorities of the republic."[181]

The assassination of his brother was a key factor into how Bobby Kennedy embraced the underdog. After JFK's death, Bobby publicly identified with the underdog.[182] As C. David Heyman wrote, "The humane 'liberalism' of RFK's last years came to fruition only after the death of his brother. While he would remain an astute politician, RFK could now gradually allow the compassionate side of his nature a more forceful expression then was possible when Jack was alive."[183]

Robert Kennedy's brief campaign for the presidency was full of references to helping the underdogs in American society. His speech at the University of Kansas on March 18, 1968, illustrates this:

> I have seen children in Mississippi starving, their bodies so crippled from hunger and their minds have been so destroyed for their whole life that they will have no future....I have seen Indians living on their bare and meager reservations, with no jobs, with an unemployment rate of 80 percent, and with so little hope for the future, so little hope for the future that for young people, for young men and women in their teens, the greatest cause of death amongst them is suicide....I have seen proud men in the hills of Appalachia, who wish only to work in dignity, but they cannot, for the mines are closed and their jobs are gone and no one—neither industry, nor labor, nor government—has cared enough to help....I have seen the people of the black ghetto, listening to ever greater promises of equality and of justice, as they sit in the same decaying schools and huddled in the same filthy rooms—without heat—warding off the cold and warding off the rats.[184]

Retrospectively, his candidacy was unusual for a contemporary Democrat running for president. It has come to be viewed as remarkable because it appealed to social class, rather than simply gender or racial identities. This was a major part of his strategy to win the 1968 California primary. It was a successful strategy, as he defeated Eugene McCarthy, 46.3 percent to 41.8 percent. He won because of his support from working-class whites, Latinos, and African Americans.[185]

Earlier in the year, Kennedy made a trip to Delano, California, to visit Cesar Chavez. Chavez was a Latino labor organizer who supported the rights of poor farm workers in California. His supporters asked Kennedy to visit him and ask him to end his hunger strike. Kennedy's trip was successful in that Chavez ended his hunger strike. Kennedy's presence was a visible stand for the underdog farm workers, who were generally unorganized and thus relatively powerless to substantially affect their working conditions, wage levels, and other elemental conditions.[186] His stand was used to gain support for his candidacy. Chavez was quoted in a bilingual campaign pamphlet:

> Senator Robert F. Kennedy is a man whose many selfless acts on behalf
> of struggling farm workers have been expressions of love through prac-
> tical deeds. Senator Kennedy came at a time when our cause was very
> hard pressed and we were surrounded by powerful enemies who did not
> hesitate to viciously attack anyone who was courageous enough to help
> us. He did not stop to ask whether it would be politically wise for him to
> come . . . nor did he stop to worry about the color of our skin . . . or what
> languages we speak. . . . We know from our experience that he cares, he
> understands, and he acts with compassion and courage.[187]

In his 1968 campaign, Kennedy did not emphasize separating out these
groups. Instead, he stressed what many had in common with each
other.

Neither Bobby Kennedy nor McCarthy became the Democratic presidential nominee in 1968, but their antiwar campaigns influenced the
future of the party. It deeply wounded Hubert Humphrey's attempt
to win the presidency later that year. It also helped change party rules
that allowed the antiwar George McGovern to become the party's
standard-bearer in 1972.

Hubert Humphrey

The strongest link between underdogs and Humphrey was civil rights.
Humphrey, who was the mayor of Minneapolis then, made a dramatic
speech to the Democratic National Convention in 1948 on the topic.
He spoke in favor of a minority report that the party establishment was
against. He wanted his party to act, not just talk:

> There will be no hedging, and there will be no watering down—if you
> please—of the instruments and the principals of the civil-rights program.
> My friends, to those who say that we are rushing this issue of civil rights,
> I say to them we are 172 years late. To those who say that this civil-rights
> program is an infringement on states' rights, I say this: The time has
> arrived in America for the Democratic party to get out of the shadow of
> states' rights and to walk forthrightly into the bright sunshine of human
> rights.[188]

In his autobiography, Humphrey described his decision to make the
speech: "for me personally and for the party, the time had come to suffer

whatever the consequences."[189] He waged a classic underdog battle, and this time the underdog won.[190] Some southern delegates walked out in response.[191] Illinois Senator Paul Douglass remarked, "No braver David ever faced a more powerful Goliath."[192] According to a biography of him from the U.S. Senate, "although no strong constituency existed for this issue in Minnesota, the position was in line with Humphrey's championing of others among his state's underdogs, including farmers, labor, and small business."[193]

Before he became vice president, Humphrey was a U.S. Senator from 1949 until 1964.[194] As a senator, he backed fair employment, social welfare, and civil rights.[195] In particular, he wanted a health insurance program, an expanded Labor Department, and increased school aid.[196] When he ran for president in 1960, it was clear how he wanted to be viewed ideologically, as *Time* wrote: "of all the leading candidates and contenders, he is the only one unashamedly setting himself out in the fine old-fashioned role of the poor boy who values above mother's milk the purest, hundred-proof liberalism, bottled 25 years ago in the bond of the New Deal."[197]

Humphrey's commitment to civil rights was genuine and deep. He played a major role in helping pass the 1964 Civil Rights Act, over the objections of many southerners.[198] When the Senate finally voted to end its filibuster, he was very content: "it was the culmination of the full year's fight for the Civil Rights Act, of fifteen years' battle for civil rights in the United States Senate, and of a lifetime in politics in which equal opportunity had been *the* objective above all others."[199]

Equal opportunity was very important to Hubert Humphrey. Why? One of the reasons was because of when and where he grew up. Humphrey was born in 1911 and grew up in Doland, South Dakota.[200] Humphrey was in scouts and evenhandedness was an important ideal to uphold. As his friend Julian Hartt said, "Fair play was an ideal of transcendent importance. It ordained sympathy and help to any deserving underdog."[201]

Unfortunately for him, all of his work toward helping underdogs was of secondary importance in 1968. To many, he was only Lyndon Johnson's loyal lieutenant on Vietnam. That was enough to make him the enemy of many of the insurgent Democrats who had supported Eugene McCarthy and Bobby Kennedy. He narrowly lost the general election to Richard Nixon.[202]

Even though he lost that election, he would be elected again to the U.S. Senate in 1970. He served until he died on January 13, 1978.[203]

Less than three months before he died, he said, "The moral test of government is how that government treats those who are in the dawn of life, the children; those who are in the twilight of life, the elderly; and those in the shadows of life—the sick, the needy, and the handicapped."[204] In other words, the underdogs.

CHAPTER 6

The 1970s and 1980s: McGovern, Carter, Hart, and Jackson

George McGovern

The 1972 Democratic presidential nominee, George McGovern, sympathized with the underdog from a very early age. An important influence was his father, who was a Methodist preacher. When McGovern was young, he read about the Social Gospel.[1] While attending Dakota Wesleyan University, he won the South Dakota oratorical contest. His winning entry was about personal responsibility to humankind: "My Brother's Keeper."[2]

McGovern's interest in underdogs also extended to his graduate work in academia. In 1953, he earned a PhD in history from Northwestern University. The subject of his dissertation was the Colorado coal strike of 1913–1914.[3] The strike was violent and produced many casualties. Even though the United Mine Workers did not prevail, the strike was viewed as a victory for the union, as it indirectly led to labor relations reform.[4]

His rhetoric supported moral causes. His political life's underlying concerns included making peace and feeding the hungry.[5] Early in his career, he was given a chance to act on these values when President John F. Kennedy appointed him director of the Food for Peace Program in 1961. Millions of tons of food were donated to developing nations under his direction.[6] As a U.S. Senator in the late 1960s and early 1970s, McGovern was a strong advocate for food stamps. He wanted to increase participation and add funds to the program.[7] He had a high profile on the issue, through his chairmanship of the Senate Select Committee on Nutrition and Human Needs. As *The Bulletin* (Bend, Oregon) of May 7, 1969, reported, "The presence of hunger in the country has been dramatized through the hearings of the Committee, whose Chairman, George McGovern...maintains that 10 million to 15 million Americans are malnourished or underfed. Witnesses before his Committee have talked of children with bone deficiencies and retarded growth due to improper diets. Welfare mothers have pleaded for programs that would enable them to buy more food for their children."[8]

These produced images of society's underdogs; children who needed food and mothers who could not afford to buy it for them. Over many years, he teamed up with Republican U.S. Senator Bob Dole of Kansas to increase the availability of food to poor Americans by funding the WIC (Women, Infants and Children) program, greatly increasing spending for the Food Stamp program, and financing reduced-price or free school lunches for children.[9] In later years, he continued his dedication to the cause of battling hunger. Many of the McGovern Center at Dakota Wesleyan University's annual conferences have addressed the issue: "Ending Hunger in Our Time" (2002), "The Hungry Child" (2003), and "Battling the Death Spiral: Hunger and HIV/AIDS" (2005).[10]

Reforming the Rules

One of the most significant ways that McGovern helped underdogs is through his work in reforming Democratic Party rules for selecting delegates to the national convention. After the bedlam of the 1968 convention, McGovern joined with others to try and come up with procedural changes that would make the nominating process fairer and less discriminatory. In January, 1970, McGovern wrote an essay in *Harper's Magazine* that spelled out the need for reform and some of the steps needed to improve the system. The need for reform was illustrated by the 1968 nomination of then Vice President Hubert Humphrey: "Though the Vice President chose to enter no primaries, partisans of his cause and of the war did seek to mobilize write-in support at the various primary way stations. In no election did the Vice President receive more than a tiny fraction of the votes. Yet he arrived at the Convention the clear favorite for the nomination, with perhaps 1,700 delegates out of a total of 2,500 pledged to him."[11]

Even though *how* Humphrey received the nomination was not historically extraordinary,[12] the result was seen as unfair by many. Why? Because it revealed disrespect for the majority will of the party, at least in how it was expressed through voting. As McGovern stated, "In the primaries, Democrats had spoken out unmistakably against the war, yet now the party machinery was treating them with contempt."[13]

McGovern listed many examples of procedures that were unfair, unequal, and discriminatory. For example, if one wanted to participate in selecting delegates (in some states), there were no codified party rules. In other states, the rules might not have existed. If there *were* any rules in some states, they were almost unattainable. In addition, women and young people were severely underrepresented. Also, in some states, there were high costs to try and become a delegate. That discriminated against poor Democrats.[14]

Eventually the McGovern-Fraser Committee was created. It democratized the process and gave average Democrats more control over who would be the presidential nominee. As political scientist Andrea Louise Campbell writes, "Delegates could no longer be selected by party committees, which were dominated by party leaders, but only by participatory convention or caucus or by primary election.... thus control over party nominations was handed from party elites to primary electorates, and the way to win the nomination altered from courting party leaders to campaigning directly to the public."[15]

On one level, the procedural reforms were transformative. The delegate selection changes gave the media a much bigger role in the process, indirectly reformed the way the Republican Party chose its candidates, and gave insurgents (in both parties) a structure they could use to gain power. George McGovern would use this system to win the 1972 nomination as would Jimmy Carter in 1976.[16] The politics of picking a presidential nominee were now open to more genuine public participation *and* increased media interpretative spin.

The genuine public participation, as reflected by increased primary and caucus voting and citizen volunteering, was a huge victory for underdogs. For example, more people of different economic, ethnic, and social backgrounds could now help shape the outcome of party nomination battles. Women could force men to listen to issues that were never much of a priority for many of them in the past. The causes of fairness and equality were advanced.

At another level, the root of the procedural reforms was Vietnam. If the Democratic Party elites and Vietnam dissenters would have somehow produced (at least the image of) a compromise, or middle ground, on the issue, perhaps a broad-based restructuring would not have occurred. But it did not happen. The Vietnam War was still going on when the 1972 campaign began.

His Stance on the Vietnam War

The specific themes of his 1972 campaign reflect this commitment. By far, his most significant issue was the American involvement in the war in Southeast Asia.[17] He was the antiwar candidate. McGovern toured college campuses in the late 1960s and spoke of his opposition to the Vietnam War.[18]

He officially announced his bid for the presidency in January 1971.[19] He called for America to be great again by directly confronting the issue of the Vietnam War: "First, we must have the courage to admit that however sincere our motives, we made a dreadful mistake in trying to settle the affairs of the Vietnamese people with American troops and bombers. I have opposed that intervention from the beginning, while our President and other presidential prospects were supporting it. There is now no way to end it or to free our prisoners except to announce a definite, early date for the withdrawal of every...American soldier. I make that pledge without reservation."[20]

By not shading his views, McGovern opened up himself to clear, negative reactions by the public. Many citizens did not want to be told that the nation had wasted countless billions of dollars with the U.S. military involvement in Southeast Asia. More significantly, many citizens did not want a future president to admit that the human casualties were caused by a mistake and thus could be considered in vain.

McGovern's view was not an underdog position, in that he was actually verbalizing the will of the majority. In 1971, a Gallup Poll found that 60 percent of Americans believed that it was a mistake to send troops to Vietnam.[21] I suspect, however, it was the *way* he conceptualized and spoke about this "mistake" that made him unpopular with many Americans; his criticism was just too direct and not nuanced enough. Throughout his career, his rhetoric was often harsh on Vietnam. In 1970, he spoke before the U.S. Senate in support of an amendment that would have set a timetable for withdrawal and a cut-off of funds: "Every senator here is partly responsible for that human wreckage at Walter Reed and Bethesda Naval [hospitals] and all across our land-young men without legs, or arms, or genitals, or faces, or hopes.... we are responsible for those young men and their lives and their hopes."[22]

Perception as a Radical

This type of rhetoric contributed to his underdog status by making it easier for his political opponents, and thus also the media, to characterize his Vietnam position as out-of-the-mainstream.

Examples of this image are numerous: there was an article in *Newsweek* in 1972 whose title was "How Radical Is George McGovern?"[23] Even though the title of a 1972 *Time* article was more objective ("How Voters

Assess George McGovern v. Richard Nixon"), part of the article dealt with the perception of McGovern as radical. *Time* surveyed 205 citizens and found that "panelists from both parties feel that he [McGovern] represents a broadly based constituency and not just a small radical minority.... Despite charges that he is 'the Goldwater of the left,' only one panelist in ten considers McGovern a radical."[24] Despite the results of the survey, he was constantly on the defensive over his suspected radicalism.

The image of McGovern as a radical was not an accident. Arguably, it was most significantly formed by Hubert Humphrey, in three debates held before the 1972 California primary. Humphrey, trailing McGovern in the polls, needed to raise doubts about McGovern to capture the nomination. A May 15 syndicated column by Rowland Evans and Robert Novak illustrates Humphrey's strategy: "A backstage decision by Senator Humphrey's campaign to finally take off the gloves against Sen. McGovern will become clear within the next week... 'We are going to show that McGovern is a radical, just like Goldwater was in 1964,' one highly placed Humphrey operative told us."[25]

McGovern's plans to reduce the size of the military were fodder for Humphrey's hawkish attack in the first debate: "I submit that the McGovern defense proposals cut into the very muscle of our defense...without any regard as to what kind of negotiations you can make with the Soviet Union."[26] McGovern's welfare plan "would be an unbelievable burden on the taxpayer."[27] Humphrey dominated McGovern, as the South Dakota Senator was put on the defensive.[28]

McGovern had been painted as a radical by Humphrey; Nixon now had ideological grenades for use in the general election campaign, courtesy of the leader of the establishment Democrats.[29]

Thus the word radical can be used pejoratively, to create fear of sudden political change. Because very few people (certainly not a majority) want sudden political change, radicals are expected to lose. Underdogs are expected to lose. In this way, McGovern shared a similar experience with William Jennings Bryan. Bryan was characterized as a radical by some of his opponents in the 1896 election.[30]

Moreover, "Radical?" is the title of Chapter six of *The Liberals' Moment*.[31] More interestingly, there is a particular section of that chapter labeled "Hard Truths."[32] Here we have it: Radicals, Hard Truths, Underdogs, and Losers. How do all of these concepts connect with each other?

Author Hunter S. Thompson connects the dots in his classic book, *Fear and Loathing: On the Campaign Trial '72*: "McGovern...lines out the painful truth, and his reward has been just about the same as that of any other politician who insists on telling the truth: He is mocked, vilified, ignored, and abandoned as a hopeless loser."[33]

Sympathy for Vietnamese Civilians

Some of McGovern's words also sympathize with underdogs that are *not* American, like the civilians of Vietnam:

> We have steel fleshettes that penetrate the skin and cannot be removed. We have napalm-jellied gasoline that sticks to the skin as it burns. We have white phosphorous that cannot be extinguished until it burns itself out.... Now, these are some of the weapons that produced that picture we saw in the press not too long ago of the little girl, Kim, running away from a school that had been hit by American napalm. She was naked, her clothing had been inflamed, and she was running directly into the lens of a cameraman nearby.... And I want to say to my fellow Americans that that picture ought to break the heart of the people of America.[34]

This is in stark contrast to Richard Nixon. According to 1972 tape recordings, he thought that Henry Kissinger was too concerned about civilian casualties in Vietnam. He also talked about dropping a nuclear bomb.[35]

It can be argued that it was the estimated four million Vietnamese civilians[36] who were the preeminent underdogs in the conflict. They were subject to massive amounts of injustices—either from the American military, their own political and military leaders, or both. Thus it seems that nationalism trumps support of foreign underdogs during a war. The following analysis supports this contention. Understanding the schema (defined as the conceptual or organizational framework in the mind) of individuals can illuminate psychological knowledge. In his article, "When the Underdog Scheme Dominates the We-Ness Schema: The Case of Radical Leftist Jewish-Israelis," clinical psychologist Aner Govrin links the concept of the underdog to a schema. He describes the underdog schema in the following way: "the universal tendency to feel empathy toward the underdog and condemn its oppressor. Its basic component is salient asymmetry between the underdog and the oppressor in terms of power, resources, and control. Another component is the oppressor's intention to harm the underdog or ignore its needs."[37]

What is the we-ness schema? It is "the universal tendency for human beings to differentiate themselves by group membership." Its elementary "component is that in-group members will behave more negatively towards out-group members of their own group."[38]

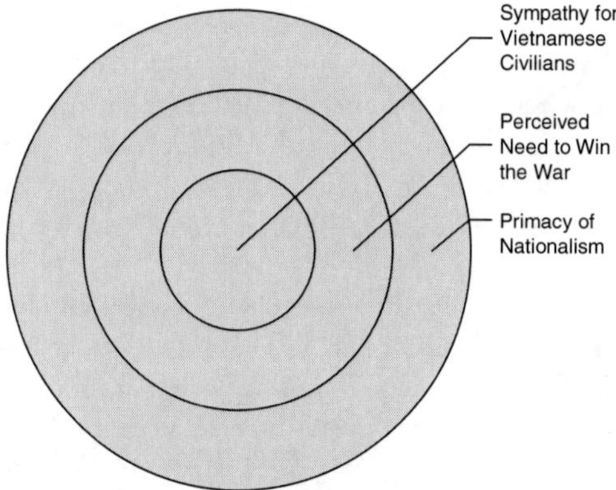

Figure 6.1   Sympathy, war, and nationalism

It is very human to feel empathy for the underdog. There are restrictions to this sympathy, however: the in-group cannot be threatened by the underdog. In addition, when the underdog becomes the enemy, the underdog schema usually is not very powerful.[39]

McGovern's sympathy for Vietnamese civilians did not move enough Americans to his side in 1972. The enemy was still North Vietnam and the Vietcong, and the United States was still at war. This is illustrated in figure 6.1.

The Eagleton Choice and Other Sympathies

The dynamics of McGovern's ill-fated choice of Thomas Eagleton as his first vice-presidential running mate can also be explained, at least in part, by his relationship with mental illness. One of McGovern's children, Terry, had mental illness and McGovern was familiar with its difficulties. He recounted an important moment in a conversation with Eagleton during the crisis. He first excused Eagleton's refusal to tell him of his illness earlier: "he had omitted the truth at the convention, but Eleanor and I understood how anxious he had been to close a painful series of events in his life that he believed belonged to the past." He then revealed that "for several years we had lived with a deep emotional disturbance involving one of our children. We saw the same tormented look on Tom's face as he told his story and, as Eleanor described it, 'We literally reached out our arms to him.' "[40]

Even though he eventually wanted Eagleton off the ticket because of his past mental illness, McGovern probably felt an *initial* impulse not to discriminate against him because of Terry's illness. According to McGovern's campaign manager, Frank Mankiewicz, if he had dropped Eagleton earlier, "he would in effect be saying to her, 'You're not fit.' "[41] McGovern wrote in 1994: "I could not in effect punish him for being a victim of depression."[42]

The mentally ill fall into the category of society's underdogs. Until somewhat recently, this class of people was not widely encouraged to triumph in life. To many in society, if they survived, or functioned, that was enough. The Eagleton episode raises critical issues: should McGovern have tried more to *initially* separate out his parental feelings of sympathy from his (potentially future) public responsibilities as president? Or would that have been impossible for him? Was taking Eagleton off the ticket punishing him for depression or potentially protecting the country's national security? *Are victims entitled to equal treatment in all ways?*

George McGovern also expressed sympathy for criminal suspects. His support for the criminally accused extended to controversial activist Angela Davis. Davis was an activist/professor who was fired for being a Communist Party member in 1969. She has fought for underdog causes throughout her life.[43] At the time of McGovern's campaign, she was accused of being involved in a judge's murder and kidnapping. He signed a petition calling for bail for her.[44]

George McGovern was also forthrightly for school busing to achieve desegregation.[45] If African Americans are considered the most prominent underdog in American society, then his advocacy of the issue represents his commitment to help the underdog. He was also for raising the corporate income tax, abolishing welfare, and creating a minimum income grant and guaranteed health care.[46]

McGovern lost the 1972 presidential election to Richard Nixon in a landslide. The 1976 Democratic presidential nominee was an unlikely choice for the party; a rural Georgia peanut farmer. Although not as traditionally liberal as McGovern, Jimmy Carter also championed the underdog cause.

Jimmy Carter

African Americans and Georgia Politics

Jimmy Carter's belief in human rights and equality helped shape many of his policies in his political career. His empathy for the disadvantaged came from his mother, who Carter admitted he was more like than his father.[47] While Carter was not a leader in the civil rights movement in the south, he was ill at ease with segregation. According to Rosalynn Carter, "Jimmy was never really critical [about segregation]...He just quietly let people know about what he thought. He never had any hot arguments or debates on it."[48]

While Carter served on the Sumter County (Georgia) school board in the 1960s, he was pressured to join the local White Citizens Council. The council wanted to fight integration. According to author Martin Schram, "several influential Plains men told him that he was the only white man in the area who had not joined." He was warned that his business would be negatively affected unless he joined. He did not become a member.[49]

While a Georgia state senator, he spoke out for political equality for blacks. As he recalls in his 1977 book, *A Government as Good as Its People*:

> The first speech I ever made in the Georgia Senate, representing the most conservative district in Georgia, was concerning the abolition of thirty questions that we had so proudly evolved as a subterfuge to keep black citizens from voting...questions...which were applied to every black citizen that came to the Sumter County Courthouse and said, "I want to vote." I spoke in that chamber, fearful of the news media reporting it back home, but overwhelmed with a commitment to the abolition of that artificial barrier to the rights of an American citizen.[50]

As governor of Georgia, Carter also realized the reality of blacks as economic underdogs. A good illustration of this is his remarks at Bethune-Cookman College in Daytona Beach, Florida, on October 29, 1975. He was asked what the most urgent problem was in black America. He responded by emphasizing social class: "I have been in every single prison in Georgia to visit while I was governor and there's one characteristic of the inmates there; they're poor. And quite often they are not well educated." He went on to list other inequities:

> Where are the streets paved last in your [*sic*] country? You know where they were paved last. Where are the poorest educational facilities in your county? You know. What farms are the last ones visited by the county agents in your county? Who are the people who have the last access to a doctor or registered nurse? You know. Where is the last place served effectively by the rapid transit system or the bus system in a community? You know. Among black people.... *You can name almost any sort of thing that affects poor people and it affects poor black people worse.*[51]

Some of his speeches as Georgia's governor further illustrate his emphasis on viewing inequalities in American life through the prism of economic and social status. In May 1971, Carter spoke to a Lions Club Convention about "a mandatory relationship between the powerful and the influential and the socially prominent and the wealthy on the one hand, and the weak, the insecure, and the poor on the other hand...In a free society we do see very clearly that one cannot accept great blessings bestowed on him by God without feeling an inner urge and drive to share those blessings with others of our neighbors who are not quite so fortunate as we."[52] Economic and social status cannot be very neatly, and completely, conceptually divorced from social justice. And striving for social justice is what motivates many people who fight for underdogs.

Although Carter understood blacks as societal underdogs, he was not above using racism as a way to win an election. For example, he appealed to segregationists to win the 1970 Democratic gubernatorial primary. His main opponent was Carl Sanders, a former governor. As Historian Burton I. Kaufman writes, "He spoke out against busing, visiting a segregated private academy, and said he would welcome a meeting with Alabama's openly racist governor, George Wallace."[53] Moreover, according to author Martin Schram, "Pro-Carter forces distributed in redneck areas an Atlanta newspaper photo showing Sanders getting doused with champagne by two black Atlanta Hawks basketball players in a victory celebration."[54]

African Americans and His Presidency

As president, Carter had a mixed record on issues affecting African Americans. He was very successful in appointing blacks to federal judgeships. He appointed twenty-eight to district courts and appointed nine to appeals courts. This record is significant, in that he tried to give an underdog group power that would last past one election. He also had faith in this group, as judge A. Leon Higginbotham wrote in 1992: "to the extent that the appointment of judges is a barometer of a President's feelings about placing historically excluded groups in positions of power, Jimmy Carter showed that he had complete confidence in African-Americans."[55]

However, on economic issues that disproportionately affected African Americans, Carter was less successful. The Congressional Black Caucus was critical of Carter in many areas, including his urban policy, ineffectiveness in creating enough new jobs, and housing and economic development policies.[56] These problems with blacks were over economic ideology and social class; concerns that most party liberals shared.

Relationship with Liberals

Liberals in the Democratic Party did not believe that Carter stood up for underdogs enough. He was not their first choice in the 1976 primaries and they never really trusted him. Liberal hostility started early in his term. Most of the unfavorable press coverage toward Carter during his first year came from Democrats, more often than not from party liberals.[57]

Liberals continued to display their distrust of his motives throughout his presidency. A good example that demonstrates this is Paul O'Dwyer. O'Dwyer was a former New York City Council president. In early 1979, he began a dump-Carter movement and met in secret with New York Democrats in the hopes of rebuffing Carter's renomination. He did not like Carter's move to the right during the last years of his presidency. A statement attributed to him in the *New York Times* illustrates his reasoning: "A true Democrat looks for the underdog, not for military budget increases at the expense of social programs."[58]

Other influential liberals came out against Carter because they thought that he was governing too conservatively. Speaking before the Americans for Democratic Action's (ADA) annual meeting in June 1979, Arthur Schlesinger, Jr. urged Democratic liberals to abandon Carter and seek a more traditional Democratic candidate. Ted Kennedy would be welcomed, if he chose to run.[59]

Some prominent Democratic politicians were also worried about the direction of the party. The most well-known was Massachusetts Senator Ted Kennedy. This culminated in the decision of Kennedy to seek the Democratic presidential nomination in 1979. More than a year before his official announcement, Kennedy made a dramatic speech to the 1978 Democratic Party's midterm conference in Memphis. In that speech, he criticized Carter's military spending and the neglect of social programs.[60] Carter's press secretary Jody Powell recalls both the substance and the theatrics of the divisions between Kennedy and Carter that were on display in Memphis:

> [Kennedy's] . . . principal theme at the convention was national health insurance. He insisted that the President endorse a comprehensive plan to be funded entirely from the federal treasury . . . the principal vote of the conference . . . was on two competing budget resolutions, one of which

had been drafted for the express purpose of embarrassing the President. His partisans worked hard for the anti-administration resolution and to prevent any compromise that would avoid a confrontation. We won the vote, anyway, and also a CBS survey of presidential preference, by large margins. Nevertheless, the political analysis on the networks and in print was that Carter might have "controlled" the organization, but Kennedy had won the "cheers" and "hearts" of the delegates.[61]

It was clear that Kennedy had the hearts of liberals who wanted to see equality and justice for underdogs. To many of them, Carter was an imposter; his tenure as defender of the liberal faith somehow false.

Carter's commitment to helping economic underdogs was constrained by economic conditions; he was governing in a decade (the 1970s) that was extremely difficult for the American economy. As author Daniel Horowitz states, "Rising house prices and decreasing rates of home ownership, declines in productivity and shortages of key goods made the lives of millions of Americans more economically difficult. Stagflation— the simultaneous combination of rising prices, high unemployment, and slow economic growth—seemed resistant to policy remedies."[62]

Arguably, the biggest problem was inflation. In 1978, it was at more than 10 percent for an annual rate. Carter wanted voluntary wage and price controls as a method to control it. That approach, however, was not very popular.[63]

Carter was in a dilemma. He needed to achieve an intricate political-economic balance. As political scientist Erwin C. Hargrove writes, "His fiscal conservatism and dislike of interest groups disposed him to resist inflationary demands. But his leadership of the Democratic coalition required him to balance his apprehensions about the new economic conditions against the claims of Democratic groups."[64]

Both labor unions and liberal interest groups could plausibly claim that they represented the interests of the underdog. So Carter compromised between solid economic management and the demands of key parts of his electoral coalition. However, that was not how it was perceived. According to economist W. Carl Biven, "the attempt to find a compromise between his own sense of a need for restraint, and the demands of some members of the party for a continuation of the spirit of the 1960s, gave the appearance of indecisiveness."[65]

The culmination to the challenge of Carter came at the Democratic National Convention in August 1980. Kennedy had challenged Carter in the primaries but had come up short. The fight would now be over the platform and the convention schedule.[66] There were disputes between his forces and Carter's over the economic plank. Jobs policy was a key issue. A proposal by Kennedy labeled it "our single highest domestic priority."[67] The battle between the two candidates was nothing less than a war over the party's core. As journalist Elizabeth Drew observed, "Kennedy, with his jobs proposal, is trying to show Carter, as he did in Memphis, who really owns the Democratic Party."[68]

Kennedy's speech to the convention mesmerized the crowd, as he captured much of the essence of the party's commitment to helping underdogs:

> My fellow Democrats and my fellow Americans, I have come here tonight not to argue as a candidate but to affirm a cause.... I am asking you to renew the commitment of the Democratic Party to economic justice.... Let us pledge that we will never misuse unemployment, high interest rates, and human misery as false weapons against inflation.... Let us pledge that employment will be the first priority of our economic policy.... Let us pledge that there will be security for all those who are now at work, and let us pledge that there will be jobs for all who are out of work; and we will not compromise on the issues of jobs.... These are not simplistic pledges. Simply put, they are the heart of our tradition, and they have been the soul of our Party across the generations. *It is the glory and the greatness of our tradition to speak for those who have no voice, to remember those who are forgotten, to respond to the frustrations and fulfill the aspirations of all Americans seeking a better life in a better land....* We dare not forsake that tradition.[69]

Although Kennedy has lost the nomination, he had won the affection of many traditional Democratic liberals. The disconnect between Carter and Democratic liberals was a major weakness that undermined him throughout his presidency. The challenge by Kennedy was the vital factor in his general election defeat, according to Carter aide Hamilton Jordan: "If we'd had the whole year to pull the party together and to try and work on the economy, I think Carter would, or at least could, have won."[70]

Human Rights and His Religious Beliefs

Carter's greatest commitment to the underdog was expressed through his human rights policies. His policies were very controversial, with them being viewed hypocritical by some,[71] and naïve[72] by others.

One of his first major speeches as president explained the significance of publicly supporting human rights. In May 1977, he spoke at

Notre Dame University: "In the life of the human spirit, words are action, much more so than many of us may realize who live in countries where freedom of expression is taken for granted. The leaders of totalitarian nations understand this very well. The proof is that words are precisely the action for which dissidents in those countries are being persecuted."

Within the same speech, he placed his policies squarely within the American political tradition: "In ancestry, religion, color, place of origin, and cultural background, we Americans are as diverse a nation as the world has even [*sic*] seen. No common mystique of blood or soil unites us. What draws us together, perhaps more than anything else, is a belief in human freedom."

He linked this tradition to the historical moment, and believed that America should elucidate this ideal: "Throughout the world today, in free nations and in totalitarian countries as well, there is a preoccupation with the subject of human freedom, human rights. And I believe it is incumbent on us in this country to keep that discussion, that debate, that contention alive. No other country is as well-qualified as we to set an example."[73]

In his memoir *Keeping Faith*, Carter recounts the expansiveness of his policies, how they applied to domestic as well as foreign policies: "Human rights was not merely a matter of reducing the incidence of summary executions or torture of political prisoners. It also included . . . the right to emigrate and reunite families, and protection against discrimination based on race, sex, religion, or ethnic origin . . . . but the right of people to a job, food, shelter, medical care, and education could not be ignored. At home I concentrated most of my energies on them."[74]

Supporting human rights was not just rhetoric for Carter. According to writer Tamar Jacoby, "the president . . . signed three international human rights accords—the hemispheric American Convention on Human Rights and two United Nations covenants, one on civil and political rights, the other on economic and cultural rights—that had been languishing for years without U.S. approval."[75] In addition, political backing and aid to countries were influenced by how well foreign governments treated their people. In particular, any government receiving foreign aid was subject to a State Department evaluation that would be made public.[76]

Emphasizing human rights did complicate his policies on many foreign policy issues: What if a major regional ally (Iran, Nicaragua) treats their citizens horribly: does the United States mute its criticism so the country remains a strong ally? Would the emphasis on human rights damage arms control talks with the Soviet Union? These were not just theoretical questions. They were dilemmas for his administration. The following newspaper stories on arms control negotiations and Soviet relations illustrate this:

- A headline in the *Eugene (Oregon) Register-Guard* (March 27, 1977) read "Tough negotiation expected." The story led with "As [Secretary of State Cyrus] Vance was warmly greeted by Foreign Minister Andrei A. Gromyko, Moscow television was broadcasting a strident commentary on Washington's rights criticisms, denouncing 'interference in the Soviet Union's internal affairs.' "[77]
- A headline in the *Kingman* (Arizona) *Daily Miner* (March 31, 1977) read "Carter reaffirms 'rights crusade.' " The Associated Press story led with "President Carter says he'll 'hang tough' when arms limitations negotiations with the Russians begin again in May and that he has no intention of dropping his human rights crusade."[78]

Carter believed that his emphasis on human rights was a triumph for many *individual* underdogs. As he recounts, "I was never criticized by the people who were imprisoned or tortured or otherwise deprived of basic rights. When they were able to make a public statement or to smuggle out a private message, they sent compliments and encouragement, pointing out repeatedly that the worst thing for them was to be ignored or forgotten."[79] Early in his administration, he showed his support for individual underdogs Andrei Sakharov and Vladimir Bukovsky in very public ways. Both were Soviet dissidents. He sent a letter to Sakharov and invited Bukovsky to the White House.[80] On a trip to Brazil, Rosalynn Carter met with two U.S. missionaries who had been arrested and detained for three days without being allowed contact with American diplomats. Her recollection of the incident illustrates the importance of individuals in Carter's human rights policy:

I called Jimmy to see if he thought I should meet with them. These were our people being mistreated...and I thought I should see them even though such a meeting might be unpopular with the Brazilian government. He agreed.... The meeting with the missionaries caught everyone by surprise, including the governor of the state, with whom I met later in the day to make clear our dissatisfaction with the way the Americans had been treated. The incident created a small flurry of excitement among the government officials in Brasila. However, it was not significant enough to be mentioned in the State Department cables back to Washington except to say that the governor expressed regrets and said he wanted everyone who visited his state to have proper treatment. Our point about human rights had been made.[81]

His concerns for individual underdogs were also exemplified with his efforts to free the American hostages that Iran held for 444 days. The Americans who were taken hostage by Iranian militants in November 1979, had many characteristics of underdogs; their captivity was unfair and unjust and they had gained the sympathy of most Americans. Bruce Laingen, the American charge d'affaire in Iran at the time, describes solitary confinement, a method of captivity that some of the hostages went through: "Living alone in a cell with no light except a dirty window at the top of the cell. One light, one bulb hanging from the ceiling. Denied the right to do anything except when I needed to go to the bathroom to bang on the door and be blindfolded and be taken down the hall to the bathroom."[82]

The psychological pressure that some of the American hostages were under was intense. This is revealed in the diary that one hostage kept (retired diplomat Robert C. Ode) during his captivity. For a while, Ode was kept with Jerry J. Meile, a communications officer at the embassy. In an August 25, 1980, entry, he describes Meile's mental condition:

> Talked quite a while with Jerry who is, in my opinion, letting his imagination run away with him, as he keeps thinking that the students are persecuting him-playing music from the "Godfather" (he is of Italian origin) and singing words long with it that sounds like the posts where he has served previously. I'm sure it's all part of his imagination and that he is worrying unnecessarily. He seems to think that they have singled him out, since he was a TCU (communicator) and that they are trying to drive him mad and that he will be tried and sentenced to prison and will never leave this place![83]

Getting all the hostages back alive was very personal for Carter, as he recounts in *Keeping Faith:* "The safety and well-being of the American hostages became a constant concern for me . . . I would walk in the White House gardens early in the morning and lie awake at night, trying to think of additional steps I could take to gain their freedom without sacrificing the honor and security of our nation."[84] The description of the hostage crisis on the Jimmy Carter Library and Museum's official Web site illustrates how he wants the incident to be remembered in history: "President Carter committed himself to the safe return of the hostages while protecting America's interests and prestige. He pursued a policy of restraint that put a higher value on the lives of the hostages than on American retaliatory power or protecting his own political future."[85]

Carter made a major mistake in how he dealt with the crisis, according to historian Douglas Brinkley: "Carter had made a fatal error to state at the outset that his primary concern was bringing the hostages home alive. The Iranians used this to blackmail the Carter Administration."[86] It is plausible that the revolutionary interests in Iran that wanted to hurt the U.S. government (by dragging the hostage situation out as long as possible) *used* Carter's empathy toward the hostages to solidify their power. If Carter would have publicly hinted that protecting American honor and security might result in the hostages becoming casualties, *perhaps* they would not have been held as long.

Undoubtedly, some of the Iranian militants conceptualized themselves as underdogs; expected to lose in any political struggle with the biggest superpower on the planet. Well, they had finally triumphed. As one of the Iranian guards watching the American hostages said after Carter had lost his reelection bid: "we have changed your president."[87] The hostage crisis in Iran mythology remains a significant cultural event as author Mark Bowden observes:

> For many Iranians... the hostage crisis was an unalloyed triumph. From the earliest moments of the takeover, artists, poets, journalists, politicians, mullahs, and historians began wrapping it in the cloak of legend, shading the actual incident with historical and mystical significance. It remains for the true believers a keystone of the national mythology, the epic tale of a small group of devout young gerogan-girha who, armed only with prayer and purity of heart, stormed the fortress gates of the most evil, potent empire on the planet, faced down the infidels' rifles and tear gas, and secured it without shedding a drop of blood, reclaiming the heart of Iran from the clutches of the devil himself.[88]

This would not be the last time the Iranians would exploit an American president's empathy for hostages. Just a few years later, Lebanese groups affiliated with Iran took American hostages. The Reagan Administration eventually responded by allowing arms to be sold to Iran in an effort to get the hostages released. This was part of the Iran-Contra scandal of the 1980s. According to Professors Athan G. Theoharis and Richard H. Immerman, Reagan felt sympathy for American hostages in Lebanon.[89] It would be difficult to suggest that sympathy was *not* involved in Reagan's decision to allow arms to be sold to Iran.

Jimmy Carter's commitment to life's underdogs seems almost too expansive. This impression changes when you factor in his religious beliefs. Carter is a born-again Christian. He is generally considered as the first president who was open about his spiritual new-birth.[90] His human rights policies can be understood by comprehending how he tried to apply his religious beliefs to policy.

Carter's understanding of theologian Reinhold Niebuhr's view of justice and morality greatly influenced him.[91] Niebuhr was an influential professor and author who linked modern politics to Christianity in the twentieth century.[92] During his 1976 presidential campaign, Carter read *Courage to Change: An Introduction to the Life and Thought of Reinhold Niebuhr*.[93] He wrote to Niebuhr's widow on August 1, 1976, and told her that his acceptance speech included an idea of the professor's.[94] His convention speech included the following lines: "I have spoken a lot of times this year about love. But love must be aggressively translated into simple justice."[95]

In June 1978, Carter was still thinking of Niebhur. According to journalist Carl Cannon, he mentioned one of his books, *Moral Man in Immoral Society*, and "pointed out the difference between a society and people. The expectations and demands on a person are a much higher standard. A person should have as our [*sic*] goal...complete agape love....The most we can expect from a society is to institute simple justice."[96] Thus, according to Carter, fighting for human rights is trying to establish justice. Justice is a central part of the underdog concept.

This reading of Niebuhr was flawed, according to historian Eyal J. Naveh, "Carter missed Niebuhr's essential argument, his insistence that love has a dialectical relationship with justice and that religious concepts can never be translated directly into politics. Therefore, the quest for justice in politics...would always fall short of the realization of the love ethic [agape]."[97]

Perhaps Carter intellectually accepted the truth that there would *always* be some injustice in the world, no matter how much public policy was based on love. However, admitting this truth did not necessarily translate into trying to do less. He could act upon his religious commitment to help underdogs while still privately acknowledging that he would always, in some way, fail.

Carter's farewell speech as president on January 14, 1981, illustrated the importance of human rights with three short sentences: "America did not invent human rights. In a very real sense, it is the other way round. Human rights invented America."[98] Carter would later go on to help underdogs all over the world through his work with the Carter Center.

Gary Hart

Gary Hart fit the classic definition of a Democratic underdog when he announced his presidential candidacy on February 17, 1983. He was not expected to win the nomination. He had only been a U.S. Senator since 1975 and thus did not have the Washington relationships that many people believed were necessary for winning the presidency.

Relationship with Liberalism and Walter Mondale

His policy views were not identical with the traditional approaches that liberals took to help economic underdogs. Although it was standard for many national Democrats to equate the interests of economic underdogs with the policy positions of labor unions, Hart took a more independent approach. He wanted to create the image that he did not necessarily agree with them all the time. For example, he publicly challenged Mondale in an Iowa debate to name "one major domestic issue in the last three or four years" in which he did not agree with the AFL-CIO.[99] More generally, he characterized the front-runner, Walter Mondale, as an " 'old-fashioned' New Deal Democrat who symbolized 'failed policies' of the past."[100]

His economic ideas were not orthodox for most Democrats. For example, in his June 1982, policy paper titled "Restoring Economic Growth," he claimed that "our economic reforms must recognize that people are motivated by more than money," and that "our economic reforms must be tested in practice, and abandoned if they do not work."[101]

The paper states that "the policy ideas...are designed to stimulate a Democratic Party debate about our economic agenda for the 1980s...[and] they are only the first step in what should be a lively process of discussion, analysis and testing to identify the policies and initiatives which will allow us to meet our greatest economic challenge: the restoration of growth in an era of economic change."[102]

These ideas, however, *indirectly* criticize many of the assumptions that underlay some of the key government programs that Democrats champion. For example, if a policy assumes that there is more than money in motivating people, then it is not too difficult to rationalize policies that cut spending on them. If money is not the determining factor in getting people gainful employment, marketable job skills, or healthy habits, then it is rational to cut spending for these programs, such as welfare. These ideas could also diminish the power of labor unions in negotiations with owners. Owners can claim that raises for workers are not *as* important, as say, having them appreciate their place in international markets.

To abandon economic reforms that have failed would be to challenge the power of powerful and vested interest groups that support and sustain the programs that are the result of the "reform." That envisions a possible reduction of the size of some governmental bureaucracies. These were not traditional economic ideas for orthodox Democrats in the early 1980s.

His willingness to explore this ideational territory was noticed by the media. In May 1982, Norman C. Miller wrote in the *Wall Street Journal* that "Sen. Hart's approach…is grounded in a belief that the public won't buy the Democrats' traditional big-government programs and will also become disenchanted with the Reagan ideology of cutting taxes and domestic spending while vastly increasing defense outlays."[103]

The disenchancement with Reagan's economic polices was a given for most Democrats. However, it was Hart's willingness to break with reflexive support for government solutions to social and economic problems that helped create his perception as an early neoliberal. Neoliberalism was a nonideological approach to politics that emphasizes technology and effectiveness.[104]

The front-runner for the Democratic presidential nomination, Walter Mondale, did not think neoliberalism and Democratic Party ideology matched. In March 1984, he told Dan Balz of the *Washington Post*, "I think there's always been this neo-liberal approach that disdains what I view to be a fundamental and sacred objective of the Democratic Party, which is to pursue fairness and stand up against interests that are powerful and that only a President can resist effectively."[105] These remarks imply that Hart was not sufficiently for the interests of economic underdogs and thus was not a "real" Democrat.[106]

Hart's voting record in the U.S. Senate, however, was liberal in many regards—for example, on civil rights and women's issues.[107] He earned a rating of eighty on the Americans for Democratic Action (ADA) list. Mondale had a ninety-two rating.[108]

Gary Hart was considered the presidential candidate of the Yuppies (Young, Urban Professionals or "young, upwardly mobile professional") in 1984.[109] Yuppies were socially liberal, yet fiscally conservative and Hart appealed to them.[110] The economically conservative and upwardly mobile part of the Yuppie equation created a gap between Hart and the traditional economic underdogs of the Democratic coalition. Many upwardly mobile people were not as supportive of the traditional government programs that old-fashioned liberals supported.

The Mondale-Hart divide is central to understanding the gap between Hart and economic underdogs. Upwardly mobile young professionals could be perceived as more selfish and individualistic than their parents. These characteristics suggest that Yuppies trust more in market economics, and thus might support Republican economic ideology. Evidence of this is suggested by remarks of Reagan political strategist Richard Wirthlin on yuppies in the 1984 presidential campaign: "We did look at the Yuppies very carefully. We found that from our perspective, which was that of the general electorate, the Hart people were picking up the Democratic yuppies, but the yuppies, as a group, we felt we had a very good chance of getting."[111]

The ideological gap between Hart and Mondale, however, should not be exaggerated. Some view the primary differences between the two owing more to generational differences and dissimilarities over questions of leadership style.[112] If these are the critical differences, then the following questions become salient: Should Democrats wear their ideological sympathies "on their sleeve," or should they appear more managerial and technical? Do you lead by emphasizing solidarity or effectiveness?

Campaign Strategy as an Insurgent

Where Hart has the strongest conceptual link to underdogs is in his nomination challenge to Mondale. Hart had very little money and institutional support compared to Mondale. He was not expected to become the Democratic presidential nominee. Nevertheless, he almost won.

Gary Hart probably thought of himself as an underdog when he first ran for president. Susan Berry Casey was codirector of his 1984 New Hampshire campaign. Hart's own words on the first page of her 1985 book, *Hart and Soul*, support this conception of himself as an underdog: "I thought about it a lot. It's a long-shot, dark-horse, uphill battle; the odds are long. But all signals seemed to be go. Not that if you run, you're going to win, but it's worth a try."[113]

Hart captured the mantle of the alternative to Mondale when he finished second in the Iowa caucuses. Although he won only 16.5 percent of the vote to Mondale's 49 percent, he unexpectedly beat more experienced politicians, like Ohio Senator John Glenn.[114] Hart was in the position of the party insurgent, the underdog poised to take the Democratic Party into the future and away from its failed past (at least as represented by the rout of 1980). If he won next week in New Hampshire, then he would have the momentum to win the nomination. As Jules Witcover writes, "Hart, the old McGovern campaign manager who was in New Hampshire that night, knew how to make the most of it. He talked by phone to the press room in Des Moines, where his Iowa campaign manager relayed questions from reporters and he answered them. Hart...had worked the Iowa rural vote and got just enough of it to make himself suddenly Mondale's chief challenger."[115]

The headlines in many New Hampshire newspapers after the Iowa results were perfect for Hart's positioning. The *Concord Monitor* read: "HART SAYS IOWA MEANS IT'S A TWO MAN RACE." The *Keene Sentinel* read "IOWA GETS MONDALE OFF TO A FAST START, MAKES HART THE ALTERNATIVE."[116]

Hart won the New Hampshire primary, beating Mondale 39 to 27 percent.[117] Although not the front-runner, if he could keep the momentum he earned with these early results, Mondale may not have been able to come back. There were caricatures of Hart and Mondale on the cover of *Time* on March 12, 1984. The caption was "Now It's a Race."[118]

It was at this point, however, that the underdog persona stopped working for him. Instead of the press silently routing for the unexpected (which makes a more interesting story than the expected outcome), now Hart was in a position to actually win the nomination. The underdog is expected to lose. This was not quite as certain as it was before Iowa and New Hampshire.

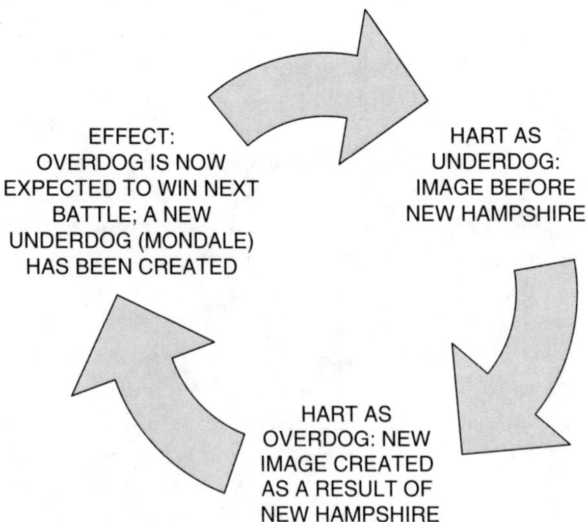

Figure 6.2 The transformation of an underdog to an overdog and the creation of a new underdog

The next big battles were the contests on "Super Tuesday" two weeks later on March 13. Although Hart won seven of the nine states, he lost the media "spin." Because Mondale won Georgia, the dominant media narrative became Hart's lost opportunity. If only Hart could have put Mondale away then.

The reality, as Jack Germond and Jules Witcover write, was quite different from the image: "two weeks earlier, Gary Hart had been naked in the South; now he had won the largest prize in Florida and come very close to taking Georgia from Mondale. But the television networks viewed the results very differently."[119] Peter Hart of the Mondale team stated that "TV basically declared us a winner after winning two of five primaries, and it changed the whole psychology of the campaign."[120]

The label of "Fighting Fritz" was now in vogue, as the media now began to focus on Mondale's comeback.[121] Bob Beckel, Mondale's campaign manager, made a well-timed appearance on NBC's *Today Show* the morning after "Super Tuesday." The dominant media interpretation of the previous night was solidified, as the following exchange reveals: " 'Congratulations,' the host, Bryant Gumbel, told him. 'Yup.' Beckel said. 'It's the comeback of the year.' "[122]

Of course, you have to be behind to come back, so Mondale was now the underdog. Key ingredients to the underdog image are perception and timing. Mondale had turned the perception around, at least temporarily. The timing of the perceptual shift was central to his success.

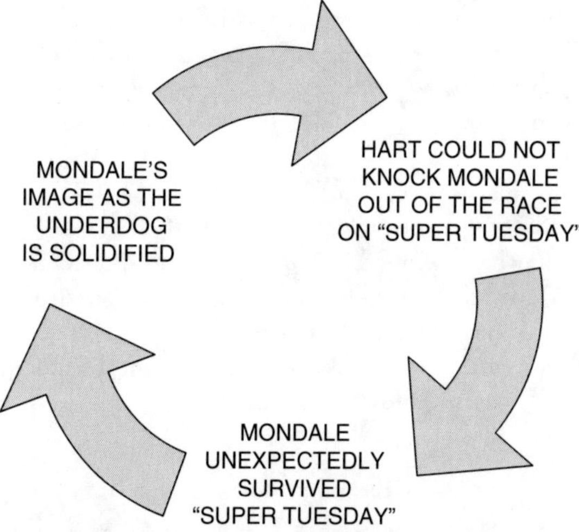

Figure 6.3   The media and the underdog image

In the end, the favorite of the Democratic establishment, Walter Mondale, won the 1984 nomination. He was trounced by Republican Ronald Reagan in the fall; Mondale won only 40.56 percent of the popular vote and 13 electoral votes.[123]

When Mondale lost the general election to Reagan, Hart was in position to become the favorite to win the 1988 Democratic presidential nomination. He ran a close second in 1984 and had name recognition. Hart could no longer be considered the underdog. He officially entered the race on April 13, 1988. However, in early May, he was accused of an extramarital affair with a young model. There was expansive and intensive media coverage of the controversy. He quit the race on May 8.[124]

The Romantic Hero

Hart reentered the 1988 presidential race in December 1987.[125] He had again become the underdog, a position he perhaps felt most comfortable with. His words announcing his reentry is evidence of the challenges any underdog faces: "I don't have a national headquarters or staff. I don't have any money. I don't have pollsters or consultants or media advisers or political endorsements. But I have something even better. I have the power of ideas."[126] The image of the romantic underdog warrior was the aura that Hart was trying to tap into. As writer Walter Shapiro argues, the Democratic Party is open to such an impression: "There is a strong romantic streak in Democratic politics… For the party that nominated William Jennings Bryan three times, choosing a candidate is not a cold calculation of self-interest but a leap of faith, an idealistic commitment. *Hart creatively and perhaps cynically used this imagery in recasting himself as the ultimate guerrilla insurgent, scorned by his party and tormented by the press.*"[127]

Hart received only 4 percent of the vote in the New Hampshire primary and pulled out again from the race.[128]

There was another Democrat who ran for the presidency in 1984 and 1988 who appealed to the more traditional constituents of the Democratic coalition. His rhetoric would often raise the hopes of underdogs while at the same time scare much of the Democratic Party establishment. His name is Jesse Jackson.

Jesse Jackson

The 1984 and 1988 presidential campaigns of Jesse Jackson were self-consciously structured on coalitions of, and appeals to, underdogs. In these campaigns, he attempted to lift the spirits of the seemingly forgotten traditional constituencies of the Democratic Party during the Reagan era. He seemed to be the only national political leader during the 1980s who was at least attempting to speak to the progressive issues that the 1960s brought up. As Jackson's former press secretary and journalist Elizabeth O. Colton writes, "For those of us who had come of age in the sixties, all we had worked for appeared to have been forgotten in this new Reagan era. The only politician in the mid-eighties who seemed courageous enough to address the important issues was Jesse Jackson."[129]

Similar to Ted Kennedy, Jackson can be characterized as a liberal lion, as journalist Marshall Frady did in 1996: "he has become one of the few remaining voices of any force in the land still unabashedly campaigning, like the Last Believer, for the old, liberal conscience in American politics."[130]

1984 Presidential Campaign

Jackson's first presidential campaign officially began on November 3, 1983.[131] It was a guerilla campaign; with few resources and money. To rationalize their lack of organization and money, one staffer labeled it a movement, not a campaign.[132]

One of Jackson's speeches during the winter of 1983–1984 explicitly compared his cause with the biblical story of David and Goliath. Journalists Jack Germond and Jules Witcover recount his speech: Jackson was "David and Ronald Reagan was Goliath. The stones for David to use as weapons were unregistered black voters. 'I think about David picking up his rocks, using what he's got,' he told the rapt congregation. 'Illinois—Reagan won by 376,000; 700,000 unregistered blacks, 500,000 unregistered Hispanics. Rocks—just layin' around. New York—Reagan won by 165,000; 900,000 unregistered blacks, 600,000 unregistered Hispanics. Rocks—just layin' around....Little David! Throw your chest out! Don't feel inadequate anymore!...Use what you got! Use your slingshot!'"[133]

The first major event that put Jackson in the limelight during his first campaign was his mission to Syria. Jackson wanted to free Navy pilot Robert Goodman, who was shot down over Lebanon in December, 1983. Goodman, who was black, was in a military prison in Damascus. Jackson wanted to fly to Syria and get Goodman released.

It was truly an underdog mission; Jackson had many huge obstacles in his way that would make success improbable. The Reagan

Administration did not want him to go and complicate matters, and it was illegal for a private American to officially negotiate for the U.S. Government.[134] According to Jackson, "In effect, Reagan's policy was just to leave Goodman there to rot. He wouldn't even return my calls before I left."[135] Jackson succeeded in securing Goodman's release in early January 1984. The Navy pilot was welcomed home with a ceremony at the White House.[136]

Relationship with Jews

Jackson's relationship with Jews was controversial. Within a month after his return from Syria, he was talking about the Jewish constituency and New York City. The New York primary was scheduled for April. He used the words Hymie and Hymietown in a conversation with reporters. An uproar over these remarks ensued, created in part because of his 1979 embrace of Yassar Arafat.[137]

He also had a relationship with Louis Farrakhan. Farrakhan sometimes introduced Jackson at rallies and provided body guards for him. Farrakhan was controversial for many Jewish (and non-Jewish) voters. Farrakhan labeled Judaism a "gutter religion" and admired the leadership traits of Hitler.[138] In addition, the formation of Israel was called an "outlaw act."[139]

The relationship between African Americans and Jews is central to understanding the role of the underdog in the Democratic Party. In both of his campaigns and afterward, Jackson was at the center of this nexus. As Marshall Frady writes, "It was almost as if to Jackson there was some running competition between blacks and Jews for primacy among the historically abused . . . he regularly elected to employ the long ordeal of blacks from slavery through segregation as 'our one trump card.' "[140]

Several essential questions are: what group is the greatest underdog? Which group has been discriminated against more? Which people have been hurt the most and lost the most important struggles? To put it crassly, which group is the biggest loser?

These are not insignificant questions. They go to the heart of many assumptions on which public policies are based on, such as affirmative action, economic assistance to urban areas, and foreign policy. On many occasions, the competition for public dollars and political priorities makes the conflict between these two groups a zero-sum game. Should the United States support the creation of a Palestinian state? If so, what are its borders? Should United States' aid to Israel be reduced and have the balance given to expanding economic opportunity for residents of the inner cities (many which are African American)?

People without a home are underdogs. Homeless people have gotten that way usually as a result of some sort of injustice. They are also more likely to lose any struggle with an enemy, or opponent, who has a geographical home. Jackson realized that Jews needed a home: "been homeless two thousand years, suffered, been persecuted—they ought to have a *home*. 'Cause that's *right*." However, the homelessness argument applied to the Palestinians as well: "it's just as true now for the Palestinians, they got to have a homeland, too."[141]

African American Pride

Even though a great deal of the black political establishment favored Mondale,[142] many African American voters took great pride in seeing Jackson being accepted as a respected candidate for the Democratic nomination. He helped boost black participation in many 1984 primaries.[143] He won 75 percent of the black vote in Pennsylvania, 74 percent in Illinois, and 89 percent in New York.[144] Although many blacks were motivated to vote against the economic policies of Reagan, Jackson also exemplified the positive; how far blacks had come in American politics. Not surprisingly, Jackson pointed this out to his audiences. Right before the Illinois primary, he affirmed that: "We're moving on up. At the '72 convention...Rueben Askew was the keynoter...I was just fighting for a seat in the hall...and I beat 'em in New Hampshire....Fritz Hollings...When he was governor of South Carolina, I couldn't use the bathroom in the state capitol. I beat Fritz Hollings!...John Glenn was up there orbiting the earth when I was scuffling for dimes down here. Now he's gone and I'm still in the race. We're moving on up!"[145]

The 1984 campaign ended with Jackson coming in a respectable third behind Mondale and Hart. He had done very well in various states, winning 3.5 million votes, 41 congressional districts, and 7 major cities. Even though he won 21 percent of the votes, he ended up with only approximately 11 percent of the convention delegates. The reason for this disparity was the common requirement of a 20 percent minimum vote (with thinly spread graduations upward) in order for a candidate to receive any delegates. He complained that this was unfair.[146]

It was unfair, as former Carter Administration official Bert Lance admitted: "the rules *had* been fixed so that the nominee in '84 had to be either Ted Kennedy or Fritz Mondale. They sat down and figured out how to make the results consistent with what they wanted."[147]

Changing the Rules to Help Underdogs and the 1988 Presidential Campaign

In a meeting with southern party chairmen in which these rules were discussed, Jackson compared the Democratic committee to the Pharisees of the Bible.[148] Jackson also did not like run-off votes and the power of superdelegates. According to Lucius J. Barker, a Jackson delegate to the 1984 convention, "the entire character of Jackson's campaign demanded that he raise such issues, attack rules and structures that, on close examination, would disadvantage blacks and minorities from full and effective participation in the political game."[149] Blacks and minorities are the traditional underdogs in American society. Jackson was seeking to politically empower them.

Jackson's 1988 presidential run was even more successful than his 1984 campaign. He started out with strong showings when he came in second in Minnesota and Maine and won outright in Vermont.[150] The biggest day of the campaign was Super Tuesday, March 8. More than 50 percent of the delegates needed to win the nomination were up for grabs. Before these contests, Jackson went down south to campaign. This was logical since, of the twenty-one contests, fourteen were in southern and border states.[151] He did very well that day, as Marshall Frady wrote: "Jackson ran first or second in sixteen of them. In the South, he finished first in five states and second in nine others, winning 27 percent of the popular vote, more than anyone else, and claiming almost a third of the region's delegates."[152]

Jackson benefited from a number of factors on Super Tuesday. The threshold for receiving convention delegates was now 15 percent, not the 20 percent it had been in 1984.[153] In addition, he did well in southern states that had a substantial amount of blacks; he won Virginia, Mississippi, Louisiana, Alabama, and Georgia.[154]

Coalition of Underdogs

Jackson's appeal to southern voters was based on portraying the south as underdogs; the region always seemed to get the short stick of everything. His campaign crafted a "New South Agenda" that included the following positions: "We must stop drugs from flowing into our country and protect families. 85% of the drugs flowing into this country comes through the South and only 10% was stopped. . . . We must provide decent housing. The South has more substandard housing than any other region, yet we cut housing spending from $32 billion to less than

$10 billion under Reagan.... We must protect our environment—three Southern states account for more than half the hazardous—waste dump capacity in the country."[155]

It would be difficult to argue that homosexuals, as a group, are not underdogs. Their historical persecution is well-established. In his 1988 campaign, he openly accepted them as part of his rainbow coalition. As Elizabeth Colton writes, "He was the only presidential candidate who dared joined in the National Gay Rights March on Washington in October 1987. His Rainbow Coalition had a special section for them, called the Lavender Stripe."[156] Jackson also supported banning discrimination based on sexual orientation in the military and the federal government.[157]

In the 1980s, people with AIDS were expected to die. Moreover, fear was prevalent because the disease was associated with homosexuals and no one was sure how the disease was spread. In Minnesota, Jackson made a speech that directly addressed some of the issues and concerns associated with AIDS. Speaking before the Lavender Stripe Conference, he urged the nation to "develop a compassionate response to AIDS." There were three parts to this response: "Effective, preventative education which targets high-risk behaviors rather than stigmatizing certain societal groups.... Massive federal funding to research AIDS prevention, treatment and cure.... [and] a national health care system which would include programs of voluntary and confidential testing and counseling."[158]

Jackson tried to create a coalition of underdogs in his 1988 campaign: workers, gays, racial minorities, and the poor. His campaign had its biggest victory on March 26th in Michigan, when he won 55 percent of the caucus vote. He won 20 percent of the white vote in the state.[159] He appealed to autoworkers who were fearful of losing their job and talked of a workers bill of "rights."[160]

The next big contest was Wisconsin. Although Dukakis eventually defeated him in the primary, Jackson was riding high, with his coalition of underdogs at its zenith. Writer E.J. Dionne, Jr. describes a scene in LaCrosse: "Jackson landed at the local airport sometime after ten in the evening, and about four hundred people had jammed an airport hangar. Virtually all of them were white. Many had voted for Ronald Reagan in 1984. Yet they cheered Jackson's defense of the common people, his proclamations that what unified blacks and average whites was far more important than what divided them, his calls for a coalition of 'working people' against the 'merger maniacs' at the investment banking houses."[161]

Dionne then goes on to describe how Jackson views race within his coalition: "whites of modest means were no less the victims of racism than blacks. Racism…was not a sin of the white masses, but a technique used by white elites to divide the natural coalition of the downtrodden. In effect, Jackson was separating himself from white liberals who looked down upon average whites. The white liberals might blame white working people for racism, but…its real cause lay elsewhere."[162]

According to Jackson, race was used to divide underdogs from each other, so basic power relations would remain unchanged. This is not new, as writer Ron Daniels states, "historically, racism has been used…as a mechanism and a strategy to divide and exploit people of color and poor and working people, particularly to divide between white working class people and poor people and whites in general and people of color."[163]

Jackson made a dramatic speech at the Democratic National Convention in Atlanta. He mentioned many underdog groups that Democrats traditionally defended, including the poor. He stood up for their dignity and asked for equality and justice:

> Most poor people are not lazy. They are not black. They are not brown. They are mostly White and female and young. But whether White, Black or Brown, a hungry baby's belly turned inside out is the same color— color it pain; color it hurt; color it agony. Most poor people are not on welfare. Some of them are illiterate and can't read the want-ad sections. And when they can, they can't find a job that matches the address. They work hard everyday. I know. I live amongst them. I'm one of them. I know they work. I'm a witness. They catch the early bus. They work every day. They raise other people's children. They work everyday. They clean the streets. They work everyday. They drive dangerous cabs. They work everyday. They change the beds you slept in in these hotels last night and can't get a union contract. They work everyday. No, no, they are not lazy! Someone must defend them because it's right, and they cannot speak for themselves. They work in hospitals. I know they do. They wipe the bodies of those who are sick with fever and pain. They empty their bedpans. They clean out their commodes. No job is beneath them, and yet when they get sick they cannot lie in the bed they made up every day. America, that is not right. We are a better Nation than that.[164]

However, he also talked about underdogs in other nations. He supported the African National Congress' quest for majority rule in South Africa.[165] He also went to Cuba in 1988 and secured the release of 48 Cuban American prisoners in jail.[166] That act linked him with two underdogs: Fidel Castro and the prisoners held in his jails.

Perhaps Jackson's most famous line from his presidential campaigns was "Keep hope alive." If you are expected to lose, and have been discriminated against and oppressed, hope is critical to survival. It helps underdogs survive. Four years later, a man from Hope, Arkansas, would also champion the cause of underdogs: Bill Clinton.

The 1990s to 2004: Bill Clinton, Al Gore, and Howard Dean

Bill Clinton

Bill Clinton grew up in very difficult circumstances in Arkansas. His father died before he was born. In 1950, his mother Virginia married a man who was an alcoholic and eventually assaulted her. They divorced, but she allowed him to live in the same house afterward because she felt sad for him (they remarried a few months later). Bill Clinton played a key role in defending his mother from his stepfather, contacting her attorney on several occasions when there was physical violence (or the threat of it), and reassuring her during these difficulties.[1]

Part of Clinton's personality can be explained as a child living with an alcoholic parent. There are many ways for a child to cope with the uncertainty that such a household creates. One is to be a "family hero." This role has two main roles: redeemer to the external world or as family protector. Author David Maraniss believes Clinton played both roles during his high school years.[2]

Maraniss explains this redeemer role: "the Family Hero is often excused from the family's inner burdens and dispatched into the world to excel and to return with praise and rewards that will make the entire unit feel worthy.... the Family Hero becomes a vessel of ambition and the repository of hope."[3] It is this role that is most relevant to the underdog. Clinton's family is in an underdog position, with his mother a victim of domestic abuse but unable to make a clear break with the man responsible for it. Why did his mother stay in the relationship? Either she was not financially well-off enough, did not think it was best for the children or she thought the conflicts were partially her fault.[4]

If Clinton could shine and make a name for himself, then everything in the family would be okay. This is the point where the hero and the underdog meet; the dysfunctional family will be saved by the sheer persistence and diligence of the child. Bill Clinton, the hero-underdog.

On policy positions, Clinton supported underdogs. Clinton was a supporter of civil rights for African Americans early in his life.[5] He liked both Lyndon Johnson and Hubert Humphrey in the 1960 Democratic primaries, partially because of their action and advocacy of civil rights. One reason he wanted John Kennedy to win in 1960 was his public support of Dr. Martin Luther King, Jr. when he was put in jail before the election.[6]

When he was sixteen years old, Clinton participated in Boys Nation, a civic engagement group. He went to Washington, DC, and debated political issues with other boys from across the nation.[7] Clinton was a proponent of government action on civil rights during the rhetorical clash between the boys. His side believed that discrimination must be eradicated, although action was not enough. His group said, "Legislation alone cannot change the hearts and minds of men. Education is the primary tool which we must employ...it must begin in the home, in the church and in the schools."[8]

Even though he supported action on civil rights, Clinton was not an activist himself. As Maraniss states, "He had not publicly protested the patterns of racism he grew up with in Hot Springs, where the schools, swimming pools, clubs, and motels had been segregated, where 'Dixie' was the high school fight song until his junior year, and where the local Lions Club recruited members of the high school choir to appear in blackface for the annual minstrel show."[9]

Arkansas Political Career

1976–1980

Clinton's first success at public office was in 1976, when he was elected attorney general of Arkansas. He fought for consumers in that post, by trying to stop utility rate hikes. Paying utility bills was more difficult for poor people than rich and thus Clinton's stand can be considered helping economic underdogs.

Prisoners are at the bottom of society. Successful, long-term rehabilitation of prisoners is more the exception than the rule. Because of that, prisoners can be viewed as underdogs, a class of people who will most likely fail in their attempt at reintroduction into society. Clinton wanted prisoners to be better equipped for life on the outside, so he expanded the work-release program that also relieved overcrowding.[10]

In 1978, Clinton was elected governor of Arkansas. He pledged to address several issues that affected underdogs in his first inaugural speech, including tax relief for the elderly, helping emotionally disturbed children, and altering the system for rural health care. He wanted to help the perennial underdogs of society: the needy, weak, and old.[11]

Clinton had many setbacks in his first term as governor. His proposal to raise vehicle license fees (for road improvements) caused him trouble. The proposal was altered so that the final legislation negatively affected owners of older, and heavier, cars. These owners were inclined to be poor and ended up paying more than owners of lighter, smaller, and newer cars.[12] This issue penalized economic underdogs—people who could not afford new cars.

1980 was a bad year to be a Democrat in Arkansas. State revenues were down because of the poor economy. The Ku Klux Klan was active and truck drivers were on strike.[13] It was the situation with the Cuban refugees of the Mariel boatlift, however, which may have sealed Clinton's electoral fate that year.

Fidel Castro let 125,000 of his people leave Cuba in 1980 in what is known as the Mariel boatlift. Many of these people were mentally ill or criminals. 20 percent of them ended up in Fort Chafee, Arkansas. For the most part, they were not welcomed by the local community. In the spring of 1980, there was a riot and approximately 300 of them escaped. There were injuries to the military guards and the refugees before they were recaptured.[14]

This incident reveals the tension when underdogs are pitted against another. It can be argued that the state of Arkansas was an underdog in 1980. Bill Clinton did not want the refugees there, but the Carter Administration did. Underdogs are expected to lose a fight. Clinton lost that fight. In August, he found out that all the Cuban refugees in resettlement camps in Florida, Pennsylvania, and Wisconsin would be transferred to Fort Chafee. Clinton shouted at a White House official after learning of this decision: "How could you do this to me? I busted my ass for Carter. You guys are going to get me beat. I've done everything I could for you guys. This is ridiculous!"[15]

The underdogs that were pitted against the state of Arkansas were the Cuban refugees within Fort Chafee. Some refugees were subject to violence within the fort. There were local people marching through streets with rifles. They could not leave the fort until they found sponsors.[16] The refugees were human pawns played by Castro in his long-standing grudge match with the U.S. government. They were forced to leave their country—they became underdogs to the power of the Castro government.

Before the refugees came to Fort Chafee, Clinton suggested an alternative course of action to the Carter Administration; separate out the criminals and mentally ill from the others before they were relocated to the U.S. mainland and send them back to Cuba.[17]

Clinton's proposal, if accepted, could have helped the Cuban refugees who were eventually let into the country. Those healthy and noncriminal underdogs would gain political freedom. But what would have happened to the mentally ill and criminals who were dumped back into Cuba? It is difficult to believe that their conditions would have improved had they been forced back to Cuba.

Undoubtedly, some of the ones classified as mentally ill were homosexual.[18] Would the conditions of the Cuban gays who were deported have improved if they were forced back into a country whose government had rounded them up and kicked them out of the country? One of the reasons people were allowed to leave was because they were perceived as harmful to Cuban society. The primacy of nationalism trumped the need to help the underdogs who needed the most help—the ones who had some of the longest odds for acceptance, success, or security.

Years after the Mariel boatlift, nationalism still seems to be the trump card when it comes to the diplomatic relationship between Cuba and the United States. As journalist Mirta Ojito wrote in 2005, "twenty-five years after the events that altered so many lives, Mariel lives on as a much-abused point of reference in political rhetoric on both sides of the Florida straits, U.S. lawmakers talk about never allowing another Mariel—which... [is] a code word for uncontrollable immigration—while their Cuban counterparts play the Mariel card: the implied threat that Cuba has millions of people who are desperate to leave and a government ready to let them loose whenever it is politically convenient."[19]

The lessons seem all too clear: in the United States, if the perceived national interest is threatened, the humanitarian needs of foreign underdogs are not a priority. In Cuba, the interests of the government take precedence over the needs of domestic underdogs (dissidents, gays, the mentally ill, criminals). As president, Clinton would learn from Mariel. In 1994, he ordered Cubans on boats to be sent to the U.S. military base in Guantanamo. If Cubans reached land, they would generally be allowed to stay in the United States. Cuban underdogs were welcome in the United States, but in a limited and controlled fashion.[20]

Even though he lost his reelection bid in 1980, Clinton had accomplished a lot. The *Arkansas Gazette* noted that the then 34 year old had "provided the single largest increase in teacher's salaries ever, extended health insurance to school employees, provided the first incentives for school programs for gifted children, established the first accountability program through standardized testing of students and new teachers, expanded special education and kindergartens and achieved some equity in the distribution of school funds."[21]

1982–1992

Clinton ran again for governor in 1982. He was involved in a three-way primary against Joe Purcell and Jim Guy Tucker. Both Tucker and Clinton clashed with each other, both trying to outdo each other as to who was more conservative and strong.[22] As journalist David Maraniss writes, "Tucker attacked Clinton for commuting or cutting the sentences of thirty-eight convicted murderers during the final weeks of his first term. Clinton . . . portrayed Tucker as a tool of labor and the special interests and as a bleeding heart on welfare issues."[23] Neither candidate was supporting traditional societal underdogs.

Clinton won the June 8, 1982, primary with 54 percent. With the help of his campaign team, he deliberately chose a populist message to bring to the voters. He wanted to turn the Public Service Commission into an elected body. The commission was responsible for utility rates. He also spoke extensively in black churches and sent out operatives to secure the black vote.[24] Clinton had pivoted, back to supporting the underdog interests of consumers and appealing for the support of one of the oldest underdog groups: African Americans.

Clinton's gubernatorial comeback was complete when he won the November general election, defeating Republican Frank White. He enlisted the help of Dick Morris, a political consultant, as he crafted an image of helping the underdogs, while White protected the powerful. The consumers were the underdogs, and the utility companies were the powerful.[25] Clinton recalls how Morris helped created an image of White being against underdog interests, particularly the elderly poor: "Dick Morris did a devastating ad taking White to task for letting utilities have big rate increases while cutting back from four to three the number of monthly prescriptions the elderly could get from Medicaid. The tagline was: 'Frank White—soft on utilities. Tough on the elderly.'"[26] He was now the "Comeback Kid." One can only come back if you are an underdog.

Education reform was a key issue for Clinton once he got back into office. To pay for it, Clinton proposed raising taxes. His 1983 proposal included many ways to get money, including increasing the severance tax on natural gas, taxing membership in country clubs, and raising the state sales tax to 4 percent from 3 percent. The sales tax increase was opposed by an alliance of community, labor, and consumer organizations because there were no exemptions for utility and food bills. After the state legislature considered his proposals, the sales tax increase was the only thing left. Arkansas law made it easy to increase it, because only a one-third vote was needed. Other taxes required three-fourths, or two-thirds vote.[27] Authors Charles F. Allen and Jonathan Portis describe the atmosphere: "So, the lowly sales tax became the whipping boy—the easiest way to raise revenue. Food and groceries were not exempt from the sales tax in Arkansas. Critics called it a 'regressive tax,' because it had its greatest effect on lower-income people, the people who could least afford it."[28]

Clinton believed education reform was the fundamental issue. His proposed standards were sweeping; they included increasing the school year, making twenty the maximum class size for a part of elementary school, uniform testing of selected grades and required kindergarten.[29]

Even though a regressive tax hurts economic underdogs more than the middle-class or the wealthy, improved education provided hope and potential economic mobility. As authors Allen and Portis observe, he knew what forces he did not want to anger in pursuit of his goals: "for all his talk of risking his career for the program, Bill Clinton was not ready to risk it in a major fight with the business community....Bill Clinton's 'idealism' had vanished, to be replaced with an expedient program."[30] Corporate interests would *not* pay for education reform.[31]

Ultimately, the hope was that education would decrease the number of underdogs in Arkansas. How? Improving education would attract more companies. More companies means more jobs, jobs lead to opportunity, opportunity leads to more economic security, and economic security decreases the chances that one would be always behind and prone to becoming a victim.

Clinton *did* improve education in Arkansas. For example, in 1983–1984, 68 percent of the state's high schools offered chemistry courses and 46 percent offered physics courses. In 1990–1991, all high schools offered these courses. In 1983–1984, 38 percent of high school graduates went to college. In 1990–1991, 48 percent did.[32]

The truth is that the improvement in education was minimal. It was the attention he devoted to it, however, that was more significant. As authors Allen and Portis report, "he initiated an incremental change that, if perpetuated, promises to pay off in years to come. He instilled in Arkansans an awareness of the importance of education. That may prove to be his most valuable accomplishment."[33]

Clinton tried to improve health care for the poor in Arkansas. While he was governor, the state started new programs for health care for poor children and prenatal care.[34] Some of his initiatives, however, had only limited success. For example, the state's infant mortality rate only improved from 33rd to 34th from 1982 to 1992.[35]

Most people realized that Clinton's ambitions were higher than Little Rock. Ever since 1980, he had been searching for ways for Democrats to regain a majority for change.[36] This pursuit had actually started much earlier, as author David Maraniss relates: "Clinton had long since turned away from what he viewed as the politics of nostalgia. Going back...to...1970, he had been searching for new formulas for Democratic success. By the time his party gathered in August in San Francisco for the 1984 Democratic National Convention, he believed that the great divide that needed to be narrowed was not so much between liberals and conservatives as romantics and realists."[37]

Bill Clinton would run for, and eventually win, the White House in 1992 by distancing himself from nostalgia and romanticism. He would be a "New Democrat," fully aware of the need to look ahead for the party's best days. But would that also mean he would turn away from the party's historic link to helping society's underdogs?

Rhetorically, he had almost the perfect line that would appeal to underdogs: "I feel your pain." Underdogs are full of pain, with unrealized ambitions, physical suffering, societal discrimination, lack of understanding, psychological and emotional suffering, or simple economic poverty. Even though the "I feel your pain" line eventually became an unflattering caricature of him, Clinton did have more genuine empathy than most other politicians. As author John F. Harris states, "Clinton's gift was not simply a put-on: he did have an authentic superior sense of human dynamics."[38]

1992 Presidential Campaign

On October 3, 1991, Bill Clinton officially announced his bid for the White House. One of the biggest underdogs that Clinton hoped to stand up for was the middle class. He believed that it has been neglected during the Reagan and GHW Bush Administrations: "Middle class people are spending more hours on the job, spending less time with their children, bringing home a smaller paycheck to pay more for health care and housing and education."[39]

A few weeks later, he made a major speech at Georgetown University titled "The New Covenant: Responsibility and Rebuilding the American Community." Within the speech, he continued his defense of the middle class: "For 12 years, the forgotten middle class watched their economic interests ignored and their values run into the ground. In the 1980s, nothing illustrates this more clearly than the fact that charitable giving by middle-class families went up as their income went down, while charitable giving by the wealthiest Americans went down as their incomes went up. Responsibility went unrewarded and so did hard work."[40]

Later, he rhetorically affirmed the suspicions of government that many middle-class people have: "Out there, you can hear the quiet, troubled voice of the forgotten middle class, lamenting that government no longer looks out for their interests or honors their values—like individual responsibility, hard work, family, community. They think their government takes more from them than it gives back, and looks the other way when special interests only take from this country and give nothing back. And they're right."[41]

The middle class *were* underdogs in the 1980s. Economic inequality greatly increased during this decade. Scholarly research confirmed this while many general-interest books popularized this trend.[42]

Bill Clinton's strategy for the middle class was contained in his campaign pamphlet, "Putting People First": "during the 1980s...while the rich got richer, the forgotten middle class—the people who work hard and play by the rules—took it on the chin. They paid higher taxes to a government that gave them little in return."[43]

Two basic components to his plan included increasing the amount of taxes that the wealthy pay and increasing government spending that helps the middle class. Middle-class taxes would go down. The revenue lost because of the decrease in taxes paid by the middle class would be replaced by the increased taxes on the wealthy and reforming tax policy for corporations.

Government spending would encompass many areas and programs. For example, health care costs would be controlled and accessibility increased, new transportation projects funded, information technology expanded to more citizens, family and medical leave legislation would become law, and worker retraining would be mandatory.[44]

Clinton campaigned on these ideas, as well as many others, during his 1992 presidential race. He successfully portrayed himself as a posttraditional liberal Democrat, one who would not always be seeking more government programs as the exclusive method to redress inequities in American society. He mixed in other, more conservative, themes so that he could not be easily labeled as just another tax and spend Democrat. He was for welfare reform, placing 100,000 new police officers on America's streets, international trade liberalization, cutting profligate government spending, and reducing the budget deficit.[45]

Clinton was almost knocked out of the race before the February New Hampshire primary when two scandals hit. One involved Gennifer Flowers. She claimed that she had had a twelve-year affair with Clinton and played tapes to prove her accusation. The other involved Clinton's lack of military service in Vietnam. There was an assertion that Clinton had signed up for the ROTC to deliberately evade the draft. A letter from Clinton was released that laid bare Clinton's thinking at the time and crassly displayed his future political calculations. His poll numbers declined dramatically in New Hampshire. Former Massachusetts Senator Paul Tsongas was now tied with him.[46]

He was able to come back, however, and do well in the primary by his campaign's management of media expectations. According to Jules Witcover, "the Clinton campaign now cast its candidate as the beleaguered underdog against Tsongas.... All Clinton campaign operatives of importance were moved from Little Rock to New Hampshire, led by campaign chairman Mickey Kantor, working with a sense that unless Clinton made a respectable showing there, his candidacy could be finished before it really began.... On election day... Clinton was second with 25 percent... Accentuating the positive, Clinton proclaimed himself 'The Comeback Kid' in a primary that he had been expected to win."[47]

Clinton campaign aide James Carville wrote about how the campaign helped create this media narrative: "we set about writing a speech for the governor. Bill Clinton had been given up for dead, in the space of a month he'd taken every hit a politician could take. Now he'd made up ground... and finished strong. Paul [Begala] came up with the line about the 'Comeback Kid.' It was perfect."[48] This is the same tactic that was successfully used by the Mondale campaign against Gary Hart in the 1984 nomination battle.

Clinton's campaign began to take off after New Hampshire. He did very well in the Super Tuesday primaries and had become the front-runner by early spring.[49]

On the key issue of race, Clinton made a bold move that won him praise from moderates. He publicly criticized an African American cultural figure when she made outrageous racial comments about whites in the aftermath of the 1992 L.A. riots. Sister Souljah remarked to the *Washington Post* that "if black people kill black people every day, why not have a week and kill white people?...So if you're a gang member and you would normally be killing somebody, why not kill a white person?"[50] Clinton said, in part, "If you took the words 'white' and 'black' and reversed them, you might think David Duke was giving that speech....We have an obligation, all of us, to call attention to prejudice whenever we see it." What made Clinton's statements even more powerful was that he spoke them before Jesse Jackson's Rainbow Coalition.[51]

Clinton was seen as courageous because he stood up to an important base of his party. His "Sister Soulijah" moment signaled that a likely Democratic presidential nominee could forcefully, clearly (and safely) criticize a prominent African American over remarks that were considered reverse racism.

Political courage, or at least the perception of it, is also newsworthy. When Clinton made his remarks, Clinton was behind in the polls. The perception of the news media was that his Sister Soulijah remarks were an attempt to get media coverage.[52] Putting an underdog in their place was not something that many expected from a prominent Democrat.

He had more standing than many other Democrats to criticize an African American because he had talked previously of racial divisions.[53] He was the presumptive Democratic presidential nominee partially because of African American support. As the late political scientist Wilson Carey McWilliams explained, "Clinton's nomination...turned on Jesse Jackson's decision to stay out of the race and on the fact that Governor Douglas Wilder did not prove to be a viable candidate. Everywhere, Clinton had a decisive advantage among black voters, and that edge was critical to his victories."[54]

Clinton condemned the underdog. He was unafraid of the potential backlash that could be just beneath the surface: the sociological explanation (or rationalization) that, because of their oppressed history, extreme rhetoric by prominent blacks should be tolerated.

Or perhaps it was a calculated move, designed to stand up to the "demands" of blacks. Historian Roger Wilkins thought so. In an interview with columnist Anthony Lewis, he does not defend her comments, but says,

Clinton didn't know what had gone on at that Rainbow meeting. And he didn't ask Jesse Jackson, didn't give him any warning of what he was going to do. At the panel the night before, Jackson stood up to Sister Soulijah, insisting that you can and must work within the system. And she finally agreed with him....In that context Clinton's speech was arrogant, and it was cheap.[55]

Whatever his intentions, Clinton was seen as distancing himself from some blacks. Was he taking them for granted and using them to try and win the general election?

Presidency

Haiti

Clinton started his first term with high expectations from underdogs. He had promised many things in his campaign, including treating the Haitian refugees who were trying to flee their country differently than the GHW Bush Administration did. The refugee crisis was triggered by a 1991 military coup and the economic sanctions placed on the country in response to it.[56] The Bush Administration had issued an executive order in May 1992 that ordered the refugees stopped at sea and accompanied back to their country.[57]

Clinton differentiated himself from Bush by saying, "I wouldn't be shipping those poor people back." He charged Bush of playing "racial politics."[58] Many Haitians were full of hope if Clinton was elected president. Perhaps things would begin to change for the poorest country in the Western Hemisphere. As writer Howard W. French put it in the *New York Times* in November 1992: "in conversations with dozens of people along the Caribbean coastline, Haitians spoke with giddy conviction that Mr. Clinton's Administration would either quickly restore democracy and set things right in their poor and broken country, or welcome them with open arms when they set out in small boats to reach American shores."[59]

As the CIA found out with satellite photos, there were tens of thousands of people in Haiti making boats from trees and even wood from their own homes. They were planning to come to America. They were to be disappointed. Even before he was inaugurated, Clinton shifted his policy. He would not give all the fleeing refugees temporary asylum.[60] Clinton had abandoned these underdogs. Perhaps he deliberately wanted to separate himself from two controversial stands that George McGovern and Jimmy Carter had made in the past. McGovern's rhetorical support of Vietnamese civilians and Carter's acceptance of the Cuban refugees in the Mariel boatlift were not big vote getters for them. Moreover, the 1980 Mariel boatlift was a contributing factor to Clinton's gubernatorial defeat.

Clinton defended his policy because of the fear that many of the Haitians would drown in their boats trying to make it to the United States. He also claimed that the deposed president, Jean-Bertrand Aristide, supported his position.[61] The new policy would save lives at sea. The military government, at least for now, would stand.

So the lives of some underdogs would be saved, but their political freedom would not be restored. At least not yet. Thus Clinton's decision left much of the Haitian people still political and economic underdogs.

The United Nations and the Clinton Administration tried to get the military government to step down for the next year and a half, but they would not. In September 1994, things were becoming horrible for the Haitian people; specifics atrocities included killing priests and executing orphans.[62]

The United States threatened to invade and restore Aristide to power unless the military government stepped aside. Eventually, a mixture of diplomacy and military threats compelled the military leaders to agree to step down and allow Aristide back into power. Aristide returned in October 1994.[63]

Thus Clinton did eventually help the underdogs in Haiti. It is notable because Clinton threatened military intervention even though most of Congress and public opinion was against using force.[64] Even though some of the realities of the way Clinton handled the crisis were less than flattering to him, author John F. Harris has praise for him: "This was an act of statesmanship. There were no U.S. military casualties, and Aristide was returned to power. As an exercise in nation building, the Haiti intervention was a modest and incomplete project; the island nation's future, like its past, continued to be marked by violence and poverty. *But Clinton had at least given the Haitians a chance to govern themselves.*"[65]

Gay Rights

One of Bill Clinton's 1992 campaign promises was to lift the ban on gays in the military. He considered issuing an executive order to do that early in his presidency, but his plan was met with hostility and suspicion from much of Congress and senior military officials. In response to this pressure, the "don't ask, don't tell" policy was created.[66] It was a compromise that did not fully satisfy either side of the controversy.

Although this issue was not the most important concern for the gay community,[67] it could have helped lessen discrimination, and increase acceptance, of gays in American society.

His political opposition was skillful in helping create a perception that he was more interested in helping gays, than in fixing the economy. As Clinton recollects, "[Republican] Senator Dole won big. By raising the issue early, and repeatedly, he guaranteed it so much publicity that it appeared I was working on little else, which caused a lot of Americans who had elected me to fix the economy to wonder what on earth I was doing and whether they'd made a mistake."[68]

Although Clinton was committed to the ideal of equal opportunity and non discrimination, he also had priorities. His economic plan was more important than the lifting of the ban on gays in the military. If enacted, it would have affected many more underdogs.

Did Bill Clinton sell out gays with this compromise? Some gay rights groups were critical of the outcome, but Clinton thought he did as much as he could, considering congressional opposition and a closely divided public opinion.[69]

In 1996, Clinton retreated further from supporting gay rights. He signed the Defense of Marriage Act. It allowed states not to recognize gay marriages from other states and declared that same-sex marriages would not be recognized by the federal government.[70] Even though he had criticized it earlier, he still signed the bill.[71] Congress was controlled by Republicans then and it was a presidential election year.

Fiscal Policy

Clinton's economic and budget proposals during his first year in office reveal the difficulties that he had in both standing up for underdogs, and the challenges in communicating exactly *how* his policies did that. The big battles involved cutting the deficit, expanding government to help underdogs and tax policy. Clinton is perceived by many as siding early with the deficit hawks and not helping traditional underdogs very much in his first year.

The White House aide who was most disturbed by this was probably Paul Begala. Along with James Carville, Begala played a critical role in the 1992 Clinton campaign. Begala did not like the emphasis on deficit reduction. He thought Clinton's economic advisors had swayed Clinton too much: "They came to the President and said, 'We're talking to the business community, and they say you're being punitive and judgmental and participating in class warfare. Every American wants to be rich, and you're suggesting there's something wrong and dirty about that, and you're going to hurt yourself with the business community.' So our rhetoric became focused on deficit reduction."[72]

Begala talked directly to Clinton on this, as author Bob Woodward mentions in his book, *The Agenda*: "'Mr. President.' Begala said, 'why are listening to these people? They did not support you. It's not what you're about.' 'We need them,' Clinton said, his temper rising. 'We can't do anything for people unless we reduce the deficit.' The Republicans certainly created the legacy, but they didn't make up the numbers. They were real and Clinton had to deal with the problem he had inherited."[73]

To support his viewpoint, Begala even drafted a memo. The theme was "It's not the deficit, stupid."[74] Clinton had won in 1992 partially because of his laser-like ability to concentrate on one issue: the economy. However, the deficit was not the essence of his economic plan, according to some of his political advisers. Yet lowering the deficit was supposed to help the middle class—a key underdog group that Clinton wanted to help.[75]

Clinton's speech to Congress on February 17, 1993, laid out many of the details of his economic plan. He called for incentives so that more people would attend college, increased money for public education, and a plan for national service. He also wanted to raise taxes on the wealthy and increase the corporate income tax. In addition, he called for empowerment zones and community development banks. These would theoretically bring money to poor areas.

These were classic liberal approaches—tax and spend to help the disadvantaged, or underdogs. This approach also used financial institutions and structures to create economic opportunities for people and areas that needed them. The image of his speech, however, was tilted toward emphasizing his fiscal responsibility and sensible economic policy, not his spending initiatives: Hillary Clinton sat with Federal Reserve Chairman Alan Greenspan in the gallery of the House.[76] Eventually, the middle-class tax cut was discarded and a new energy tax was proposed.[77]

Did Clinton abandon the middle-class underdogs by rejecting their tax cut? In one sense, he did not: the premise of lowering the deficit was that the middle class would benefit from that result.[78] From a policy perspective, the middle class would have to realize that the totality of Clinton's plan would eventually help them. The partisan spin put on his plan, however, was made up of images and code words that were designed to hurt him politically. Even though the Clinton economic team thought that public investment and spending were conceptually dissimilar, they could easily be perceived as a unified notion: simply "more government spending" as the proposals worked their way through the system and became interpreted by the public.[79] Instead of helping middle-class underdogs, he was simply raising taxes and spending more money—just like all liberal Democrats do.

Lani Guinier

In 1993, Clinton nominated Lani Guinier to be the assistant attorney general for civil rights. She was a law school professor who had published some innovative ideas on minority rights and majority rule. She sought minority empowerment through changing voting procedures and laws. They would be altered in a way that supported a results-oriented test.[80] She was attacked as a "quota queen" and portrayed as a radical, leftist academic by some conservatives in the press.[81]

Guinier's writings were misrepresented in the press. Much of the coverage of her was based on fear that her writings might, at least in part, "represent an agenda for reorganizing democratic institutions."[82] However, she did not believe in quotas or "race-conscious districting."[83] She was actually for expanding the number of people who might participate in democracy. This would have to include the underdogs of society—the ones who have been discriminated against or seem to always lose in struggles. As law professor Randall Kennedy writes, "Far from abandoning democracy, Guinier maintains that, in all too many circumstances, too few people have too little say about the rules and rulers that govern them. An adherent to a consensus (as opposed to a simple majoritarian) model of democracy, a self-described 'democratic idealist' who unashamedly invokes the 1960s rhetoric of 'participatory democracy,' a synthesizer of John Stuart Mill, Arend Lijphart, and Fannie Lou Hamer, Guinier favors rules of self-governance that she believes will encourage more participation by a wider array of people."[84]

Guinier proved to be an unnecessary liability to Clinton and he withdrew her nomination.[85] Why? According to some, he needed to be perceived to be moving to the center, and jettisoning her nomination would be evidence of just such a shift.[86] The tragedy of the Guinier episode is the lost opportunity to educate the American public on the links between political structures and democracy. According to Kennedy, "Senate hearings on Guinier's nomination might have facilitated a widely watched, widely debated, public seminar about contending conceptions of democracy, the strengths and weaknesses of various electoral and legislative schemes in the United States and around the world, the means and ends of the Voting Rights Act, and other important issues."[87]

An open debate on the means and ends of the Voting Rights Act could have been particularly useful in bringing to light critical issues that relate to underdogs. Related issues such as affirmative action and federalism could have been debated. Americans could have been educated (not lectured) about the progress (and lack of it) that the nation has made in realizing political equality.

But did Americans really want to be reminded of these underdog struggles? It depends on which Americans are affected by these struggles and also the degree to which they *see* themselves as affected by them.

The first six months of Clinton's first term were hardly a victory for underdogs, as writer Barbara Ehrenreich summed up:

> Clinton came to office with support from underdogs of all descriptions—gays, women, minorities, union members and those of the poor who manage to vote. They were hoping he might arrest the upward flow of wealth and generally take a stand with the oppressed and the harassed against the bigots and the bullies. But this never, even in a rhetorical sense, became a consistent Clinton theme. He dropped the gays like a flaming potato...he abandoned the Haitians on their leaky rafts...[and] he snubbed the unions by sticking to NAFTA.[88]

Health Care

In February 1993, Clinton helped parents, caregivers, and the seriously ill when he signed the Family and Medical Leave Act.[89] With some exceptions, this law allowed new parents to take unpaid time off to take care of their child, care givers to take unpaid time off to care for their spouse, child, or parent who is seriously ill. It also allowed seriously sick employees to take unpaid time if they cannot do their job. While they are away, they cannot be dropped from the employer's health plan.[90] Clinton, however, had bigger plans for health care. He wanted universal coverage.

His health care proposal was a bold, sweeping attempt to help underdogs. According to writer Elizabeth Drew, "it pledged universal coverage by January 1, 1998, and security from the inability to obtain coverage because of 'preexisting conditions,' or being charged more for having an illness, or having a policy revoked because one became ill or changes jobs."[91]

There were many underdogs when it came to health care. The biggest ones were the 37 million people without insurance at all.[92] The people with "pre-existing conditions" who could not get insurance were also underdogs, victims of economic discrimination by the health care system. Paying higher premiums because of illness naturally elicits sympathy, a characteristic of underdogs. In addition, losing your policy *because* one got sick or chose different employment creates sympathy. It also puts one at an economic disadvantage compared with people who are healthy or stay in their jobs.

The contested conceptual points that link health care to underdogs revolve around responsibility and control. Who, or what institution, has responsibility for making sure that Americans receive the health care they need? How much control does one individual *really* have in maintaining one's health?

More specific questions are also important: Are individuals responsible for their preexisting conditions? What if these conditions were genetic? Even if the individual is responsible for their preexisting conditions, denying adequate health care to treat their conditions would hardly help the person get better. If the person does not get better, they might have a more difficult time contributing to society (e.g., through steady employment). They could eventually become a drain on society, soaking up the tax dollars or insurance premiums of the healthy.

How does responsibility and control correlate with Americans who work but cannot afford the health insurance that is offered to them by their employer? From one perspective, they control their ability to have health care coverage: they chose that job. But what if that job had other benefits that were critically important to the worker? For example, they have built up seniority, the job is close to home, it is near their children's school or child care, or has good wages. That situation puts the person in a quandary: they can go without health care coverage or leave that job and lose those other advantages associated with it. But they cannot leave both.

In addition, because of the cost of health care, many people were one major illness away from becoming bankrupt. Bankruptcy also creates economic underdogs.

Many of the people who were concerned over the cost and availability of health care were middle class. The health care issue could be the magic bullet that brought the middle class back to the Democrats, as author E.J. Dionne, Jr. states, "having the federal government ensure that all Americans would have health care coverage seemed a perfect step toward reconnecting middle-class voters with Washington. After all, many in the middle-class... feared that they were in danger of losing some or all of their health benefits."[93]

William Kristol, an influential Republican strategist, realized this. According to him, Clinton's plan must never be tried because if it did, it just might be successful: "it will relegitimize middle-class dependence for 'security' on government spending and regulation." This would help Democrats by reviving "the reputation of the party that spends and regulates... as the generous protector of middle-class interests." Most frighteningly "it will at the same time strike a punishing blow against Republican claims to defend the middle-class by restraining government."[94]

The Clinton health care plan never got enacted. The middle class was never reconnected through the issue of health care as much as Clinton and other Democrats hoped. One reason was that it was subjected to the same framing as his first economic plan was. It was criticized by opponents as a massive increase in government spending and control. The media campaign framed middle-class people and families as potential victims of an unresponsive federal bureaucracy. The operation is depicted in a *Wall Street Journal* article of April 29, 1994:

> The baby's scream is anguished, the mother's voice desperate. "Please," she pleads into the phone as she seeks help for her sick child. "We're sorry; the government health center is closed now," says the recording on the other end of the line. "However, if this is an emergency, you may call 1-800-GOVERNMENT." She tries it, only to be greeted by another recording: "We're sorry, all health-care representatives are busy now. Please stay on the line and our first available..." "Why did they let the government take over?" she asks plaintively. "I need my family doctor back."[95]

The mother in the above scenario is a victim of government; she has been turned into a sympathetic underdog by the successful framing of the issue by the opponents of Clinton's health care plan.

Another reason why Clinton's health care plan failed related to his romanticism. In his nationally televised speech in September 1993, he stated that he would veto any bill that did not have universal coverage. He was boldly standing up for underdogs. He would finally defeat the American Medical Association and the other groups who had fought against government guaranteed health care over the last forty-five years.

No more would any American have to worry about whether they could afford to get sick. It would be a right. However desirable this goal was, its insistence affected his judgment as to how to move progressive legislation forward. Hillary Clinton also agreed with this insistence, since she was in charge of the plan. Author John F. Harris analyzed how this romantic fight for the underdog helped defeat the plan: "The problem...was that his judgment was invariable clouded...more focused on expansive ends than on realistic means for attaining them. When the person he relied on most to provide realism and prudent judgment [Hillary Clinton] was herself in a vainglorious mood, it was a volatile combination."[96]

Even though Clinton might have envisioned himself as Franklin Roosevelt when he began his quest for universal health care coverage, he ended up like Don Quixote.

Rwanda and Kosovo

On two other foreign policy issues, Clinton took differing approaches to helping underdogs. His administration essentially did nothing to prevent the massacre that started in Rwanda in April 1994. The tribal conflict took more than 800,000 lives, most of them Tutsi.[97] John F. Harris captures the inaction of the Clinton Administration during this episode: "Historians have searched in vain for a fateful moment of decision...There was none...the State Department labored to avoid declaring the mass killings a 'genocide.' Invoking that term, lawyers warned, imposed an obligation to intervene....Meanwhile, the Pentagon rejected even modest measures, such as bombing the radio facilities that were spewing hateful propaganda and instructing Hutus to kill their Tutsi neighbors."[98]

The Clinton Administration did not act forcefully because the Somalia debacle was not that old, Bosnia was absorbing their time, and there was congressional opposition.[99] The reluctance to act in Rwanda was similar to Clinton's decision to help, or not to help, other foreign underdogs caught up in violent conflicts, such as the Somalis and Bosnian Muslims. As author E.J. Dionne, Jr. explains, these struggles "placed a distant second in importance, behind dealing with economic dislocation and criminal disorder at home. If the United States could not keep its own streets safe, many asked, how could it dare attempt to impose order on nations thousands miles away?"[100]

Clinton *did*, however, act decisively in Kosovo in 1999. Kosovo was a province of Serbia, with a population that was predominantly Albanian. In 1989, their autonomy was taken away by Yugoslav leader Slobodan

Milosevic. Over the next ten years, Kosovo voted to break away from Serbia and Yugoslavia. A separatist movement was created. Parallel structures in taxation, medical care, and education were developed. There was tension between the KLA (Kosovo Liberation Army) and Serbs. Ethnic Albanians suffered during the period when Slobodan Milosevic was in control of Yugoslavia. Carla del Ponte, a prosecutor for the International Criminal Tribunal for the former Yugoslavia, stated in 1999 that her prosecutors have reported to her more than 11,000 deaths.[101]

In March 1999, the Yugoslavs refused a settlement that would have given Kosovo temporary autonomy. Later that month, there were NATO airstrikes on Serbia. In June 1999, a negotiated settlement was reached: NATO stopped their bombing and Serb troops withdrew from Kosovo.[102] Clinton explains some of his rationale for the bombing campaign in a speech on March 24, 1999: "Milosevic has stripped the Kosovars of their autonomy, denying them their constitutionally guaranteed rights to speak their own language, run their own schools, and govern themselves. I described the Serb atrocities: killing civilians, burning villages, and driving people from their homes. . . . I put the current events in the context of the wars Milosevic had already waged against Bosnia and Croatia."[103]

Clearly, Clinton had portrayed the Kosovars as underdogs—people who were being discriminated against and thus deserved our sympathy. Moreover, like all underdogs, they were expected to lose. Clinton used NATO to defend them and change the power relationship between the Kosovar Albanians and the Serbs. He wanted these underdogs to win.

NAFTA

The movement toward trade liberalization also created a discourse in which underdogs were prominently featured. In 1993, Clinton fought for Congress to approve NAFTA, the North American Free Trade Agreement. NAFTA was an agreement that liberalized trade between Canada, the United States, and Mexico. It was controversial because many thought the agreement would create a "race to the bottom," in terms of wages and environmental protection. Labor unions, in particular, were against it. As writer Elizabeth Drew put it, "labor feared not only a loss of jobs but that NAFTA would accelerate the existing trend of forcing down entry wages or holding down wage increases, or benefits."[104]

One of the fiercest Democratic critics of NAFTA was Michigan Representative David Bonior. He spoke in Congress on July 28, 1993, on how it would negatively affect Americans: "NAFTA has the potential to impact us all in intangible ways in our daily lives, and unfortunately for most of us, that impact I believe is negative. The people who work in the factories, of course, and those whose paychecks depend upon those factories, stand to lose the most. But when the factories shut down, we all suffer. It hits the neighborhood gas station, the local restaurant, the clothing store, the hardware store, the school system."[104]

Clinton directly confronted a fundamental tenet of the Democratic ideology when he supported NAFTA. That tenet was that the party would protect the interests of workers, or the working class. However, by 1993, the working class was not much of a self-conscious social class anymore in the United States, if it ever was one to begin with. There was not much class solidarity, and unions had dramatically declined in their numbers and influence over the last forty years.

Clinton believed in free trade.[105] He described the ideological coalition that was opposing NAFTA in his autobiography: "NAFTA faced intense opposition from an unusual coalition of liberal Democrats and conservative Republicans, who shared a fear that a more open relationship with Mexico would cost America good jobs *without helping ordinary Mexicans*, who they believed would continue to be underpaid and overworked no matter how much money their employers made out of trading with the United States."[106]

He shared some of the concerns of the critics: "*I knew they might be right about the second part*, but I believed NAFTA was essential, not just to our relationships with Mexico and Latin America but also to our commitment to building a more integrated, cooperative world."[107]

One of the assumptions that some of the opposition had was that NAFTA would be acceptable if it was guaranteed that ordinary Mexicans would be treated better (higher wages, better working conditions) under NAFTA. Many ordinary Mexicans are poor and could be considered economic underdogs. If NAFTA would really help them, then these foreign underdogs would be favored over the American factory workers who might lose their jobs due to this agreement. The affected Americans would then become economic underdogs.

From a macro perspective, however, American underdogs are not as economically disadvantaged as their Mexican counterparts. Moreover, there was help from the federal government for retraining when American jobs are lost to production shifts and foreign competition.[108]

The NAFTA vote revealed the split between, and among, the Democratic and Republican parties over markets and globalization.

The divide was more penetrating for Democrats, as author E.J. Dionne, Jr. notes:

> Republicans were torn to some degree by trade issues, but they were broadly committed to the same *system*, the largely unregulated free market, which logically entailed free trade. Democrats were committed to a *goal*, an expanding living standard for low-and middle-income workers. But there were wide differences within the party over how that goal could be reached, where and how much the government should intervene, and whether the whole globalization process was primarily benign or menacing. Trade issues brought all these arguments to the surface.[109]

This split laid clear the deep differences regarding the effect of economic markets on individuals: Do markets help underdogs? Should Democrats trust markets? The same, broad differences were played out later in his presidency over the issue of whether China should become a member of the World Trade Organization (WTO).

Enemies

With the Republicans in control of Congress from 1995 onward, Clinton was reacting more to Congressional initiatives than leading the policy discourse in Washington. Many progressives were asking: Where was Clinton's leadership? Some liberals felt Clinton needed to make more enemies. FDR had rhetorically demonized many interests in his successful quest to help underdogs in the 1930s. Why didn't Clinton use his rhetorical skill to do the same?

On April 12, 1995, Clinton went to Warm Springs, Georgia, to try and reenergize his presidency. It was the fiftieth anniversary of FDR's death. Prominent liberals Arthur Schlesinger, Jr. and John Kenneth Galbraith were in the audience that day.[110] The *Washington Post* reported the event and quoted their criticism of Clinton:

> *Galbraith:* FDR enjoyed his enemies. I'd like to see Bill Clinton enjoy them more.
>
> *Schlesinger:* I think Clinton very much sees himself in the FDR tradition, all things equal. Yet FDR loved a good fight; Clinton seems by temperament an accommodator. Accommodation has its uses but it can too easily become appeasement.[111]

In order to defend underdogs, do you need clearly recognizable enemies? If so, then which enemies?

There have been numerous books and articles that have detailed the efforts of some of Clinton's enemies to bring down his presidency. They include *The Hunting of the President: The Ten-Year Campaign to Destroy Bill and Hillary Clinton* and *Blinded by the Right: The Conscience of an Ex-Conservative*.[112] These efforts were sophisticated and organized attempts to politically weaken the Clintons. Both Bill and Hillary Clinton could be interpreted as underdogs to these right-wing efforts to politically destroy them. They gained the sympathy of many Americans as they were perceived as victims of a political witch-hunt.

The best example is the Monica Lewinsky scandal. Although Clinton was personally at fault and attempted a White House cover up, there were many who thought Special Prosecutor Ken Starr went too far. Former Arkansas Senator Dale Bumpers gave the closing argument for the defense in Clinton's Senate Impeachment trial. He described the context of the moment, thus helping to solidify Clinton's image as an underdog: "How did we come to be here? We're here because of a five-year, relentless, unending investigation of the President. Fifty billion dollars, hundreds of FBI agents fanning across the nation examining in detail the microscopic lives of people. Maybe the most intense investigation not only of a President but of anybody—ever." Bumpers then implied that Clinton was persecuted because of sexual immorality: "after all of those years and 50 million dollars of Whitewater, Travelgate, Filegate, you name it, nothing, nothing, the President was found guilty of nothing, official or personal. We're here today because the President suffered a terrible moral lapse, a marital infidelity; not a breach of the public trust, not a crime against society... It was a breach of his family trust. It is a sex scandal."[113]

Clinton was a victim of the Puritans, just like Hester Prynne was in Nathanial Hawthorne's *The Scarlet Letter*. He became an underdog to the power of Puritan morality over American politics.[114] Even though Clinton was impeached over the Lewinsky scandal, he managed to stay in office.

One can make the case, however, that he had the wrong *kind* of enemies while he was president; instead of Ken Starr and the Christian right, he needed to be seen (and most important, *felt*) as an enemy to more business interests. His relationship with the Democratic Leadership Council (DLC) helps explain why this did not happen. Formed in 1985, the purpose of the DLC was to offer a new, more business-friendly image of the Democratic Party to the public.[115] As expressed in the 1990 conference, their beliefs included that "the Democratic Party's fundamental mission is to expand opportunity, not government... [and] the free market, regulated in the public interest, is the best engine of general prosperity."[116] In 1991, the organization opposed organized labor's position on free trade. They also issued a statement that read, in part, "in the minds of too many Americans, the Democratic Party has stood for government programs that don't work... [and] special interests before the interests of ordinary people."[117] Clinton was its chairman from 1990 to 1991.[118]

The DLC and the Clinton Administration shared many similar approaches to governing. The DLC was effective; public policy was influenced and new laws were helped created by their ideas.[119] One of the biggest DLC-supported new laws was welfare reform.[120] In June 2009, Clinton attributed the organization with the achievements of his presidency.[121] To many others, however, the DLC is no friend of the underdog. As former U.S. Representative Major R. Owens acidly observed in January 2008, "contempt for inspiration and idealism. This is the mindset of the DLC....What matters most is money....For them causes are merely cute puzzles...Arrogance and insensitivity are trademarks of the DLC."[122]

Clinton tried to handover the office to his loyal vice president in 2000. How the underdog concept is linked to Al Gore is where this analysis goes next.

Al Gore

It is difficult to conceive of Al Gore as an underdog. He was born into prestige and power, the son of a U.S. Senator from Tennessee. He was vice president under Bill Clinton for two terms. A 2000 biography of him is called *The Prince of Tennessee*.[123]

2000 Presidential Campaign Themes

Al Gore took on characteristics of an underdog during the 2000 presidential election. His campaign had many different themes, including one that, at least rhetorically, emphasized a message of economic populism. He started this phase of his campaign in late June, 2000 as he linked the Republican Congress to many powerful interests: health maintenance organizations (HMOs) and large drug, insurance, and oil companies. The absence of cheaper drugs and an inadequate minimum wage[124] could be interpreted as examples of policies that kept too many elderly and poor as underdogs.

He delivered this message clearly at the Democratic National Convention in July. He emphasized his desire to fight against interests that were powerful and stand up for the "little guy":

> Big tobacco, big oil, the big polluters, the pharmaceutical companies, the HMOs, sometimes you have to be willing to stand up and say no, so families can have a better life. . . . I know one thing about the job of the president: It is the only job in the Constitution that is charged with the responsibility of fighting for all the people, not just the people of one state or one district, not just the wealthy or the powerful, all the people; especially those who need a voice, those who need a champion, those who need to be lifted up, so they are never left behind.[125]

Gore took the advice of Stanley Greenberg; a Democratic consultant who believed in a more direct approach to traditional Democratic constituents.[126] This strategy was controversial, as some of the more economically conservative Democrats thought his appeal was too class-oriented. The DLC thought this approach cost him the election.[127]

Some of his top advisors rejected that notion, however, explaining why they thought his defense of underdog interests, in conjunction with an appeal to more wealthy voters, was the right strategy. As Gore strategist Carter Eskew recalls, "Gore/Lieberman outpolled Clinton/Gore in the general election among African-Americans and among members of organized labor, but also did better than Clinton among Americans who make over $100,000 a year, the so-called 'new economy voters.' We matched Clinton's performance among suburban voters. The bottom line is that Gore received more votes than any other Democratic candidate in history, and he did it even while a third party candidate was running on the left, not the right."[128]

Gore lost a significant amount of the white working-class voters in the 2000 election. It was this group that was a critical factor in his loss in several states. However, it was not his defense of underdog economic interests, but rather a combination of various policy stands and his ties to Clinton that sealed his fate. As authors John B. Judis and Ruy Teixeira state (about Greenburg's findings): "In some states, such as West Virginia and Kentucky, Gore lost votes because of his specific stands on the environment, tobacco and coal. Many rural and small-town voters objected to Gore's support for gun control. And in most of the states, the single most important reason for voting against Gore was distrust of him stemming in large part from the Clinton Administration scandals."[129]

Nader's Challenge

Gore was forced to more explicitly champion underdog interests because of the challenge of third party presidential candidate Ralph Nader. As political scientists James W. Ceaser and Andrew E. Busch write, "Gore sought to limit defections and keep potential Nader voters in the fold. Nader's appeal figured importantly in Gore's thinking…and it had something to do with his adopting a populist stance."[130]

Nader, displaying his characteristic sarcasm, wanted to refresh the American political system with his candidacy by injecting "fresh political movements that will displace the control of the Democratic and Republican Parties, two apparently distinct political entities that feed at the same corporate trough."[131] With the Democratic Party's ties to corporate financing, Al Gore was not the best person to believably defend the interests of the underdogs in American society.

According to Nader, Democrats a long time ago had moved away from fighting for the interests of underdogs because of *where* they received their campaign money. "During the eighties, it became ever more clear that the Democrats were losing their will to fight. Business money pouring into party coffers melded into the retreat from progressive roots and then into an electoral tactic that argued for defeating Republicans by taking away their issues and becoming more like them."[132]

Former Texas Agricultural Commissioner Jim Hightower expressed his disenchantment with his party in explaining his support for Nader: "As a Democrat, I've been terribly disappointed. We've had these promises from Al Gore and Bill Clinton before, and they didn't deliver. They took progressives for granted and went along with Wall Street. I'm tired of being taken for granted."[133]

There were former associates of Nader, however, who did not believe that the two major parties were essentially indistinguishable on economic issues. During an August 2000 fundraiser, former associate Gary Sellers stood up to Nader on this claim: "You cannot claim there's no difference between the parties…Why is it that 95 percent of the time, we used to work with Democrats? We used to celebrate if a Republican signed on to one of your crusades."[134]

In a way, Nader could have perceived himself as the biggest underdog in the 2000 election. He was the underdog to the power of the Democratic Party. Democrats presumed that any Nader vote would take away a potential Gore vote. The tension between Nader and Democrats was widespread, but the pressure did not bother him. According to author Justin Martin, "Cursed in the halls of Congress, pilloried in numerous op-eds, urged by countless petitions to drop out, Nader responded instead—among other things—by actively campaigning in Florida, that most closely contested of states. The pressure should have been unbearable, but Nader seemed unfazed, which drove the Democrats to turn up the heat even more. Still he did not flinch."[135]

It can be argued that Nader acted to defend more of the underdog position of his *candidacy*, and less the underdog interests of the many causes and groups that he was championing. No credible analyst gave Nader a chance to win the election. The only positive effect for society's underdogs would be to help out the future interests of the Green Party and/or influence Gore to taking more liberal stands on issues.

Nader continued to campaign in some close states, ignoring the pleas of sympathetic ideogical allies. In an open letter to Gore, Gary Sellers and others tired to reason with Nader: "It is now clear that you might well give the White House to Bush. As a result, you would set back significantly the social progress to which you have devoted your entire, astonishing career."[136] Nader's response illustrates the central role emotion played in his actions: "All these good people who have

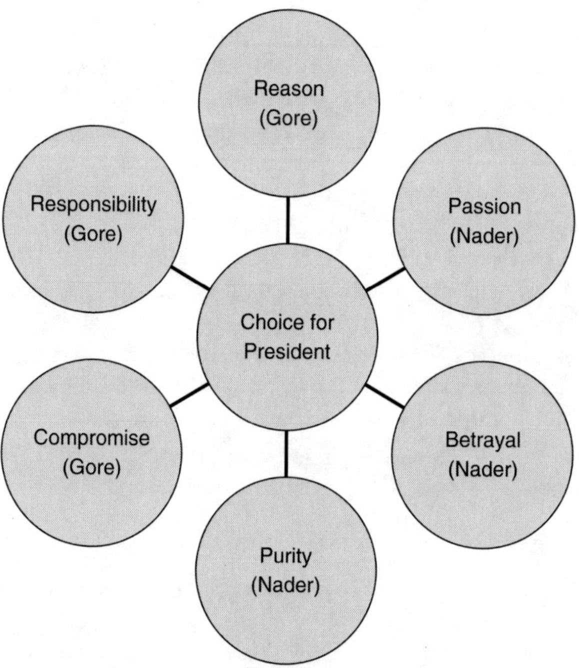

Figure 7.1   The 2000 presidential vote and underdogs

succumbed to the lesser-of-two-evils syndrome are setting themselves up for another cycle of political betrayal."[137] Many underdogs became that way because they were betrayed. Nader did not want to be betrayed by Democrats, once again.

The key questions for supporters of underdogs in the fall of 2000 were these: What was the best way to fight for their interests: Compromise and reason or purity and emotion? What was the responsible vote?

To some, standing up for the people who are discriminated against, or are most likely to lose, can best be accomplished by holding one's nose and voting for Gore. He should be supported even though, to many on the economic left, Gore was not on the side of underdogs when he fought hard for trade liberalization (NAFTA and the WTO). Even though the Clinton/Gore Administration failed to achieve comprehensive health care reform, their attempt to provide universal coverage should not be forgotten. Wrong on trade, impotent on health care, but still their administration's heart was in the right place.

To others, Democrats have taken underdogs for granted for too long. If eight years of a Democratic administration cannot achieve universal health care, why were they in power to begin with? If they sold out the interests of labor by pushing hard for economic globalization (with no effective safeguards for workers), why should the party be rewarded with votes from the people who struggle?

The debate between reason and compromise and emotion and purity was mainly focused on underdog economic interests. Nader's support of underdog social and cultural interests was questioned by some as election day approached. In particular, his support of women and gay rights was seen as not very solid.[138]

After Gore finally conceded the election in December, many Democrats were livid at Nader. They thought his candidacy cost Gore Florida, and thus the White House. According to Delaware Senator (and future vice president) Joseph Biden, Nader was to be shunned: "Ralph Nader is not going to be welcome anywhere near the corridors...He cost us the election...God spare me the purists."[139]

Election Night and the Recount

Gore and Bush ran close to each other during the fall. On election night, one state ended up deciding the contest: Florida. The state was first called for Gore at 7:49 p.m. (ET) by the Associated Press and the television networks. However the state was taken from the Gore column and moved to undecided at 10:13 p.m. At 2:13 on the morning after the election, FOX News finally declared Florida for Bush. The other networks quickly echoed FOX's decision.[140] Gore called Bush to concede.[141]

For approximately two hours, the networks characterized Bush as president-elect.[142] However, the raw vote difference between Gore and Bush began to shrink. Gore later retracted his concession to Bush. The networks were forced to withdraw their call for Bush. Regardless of the retraction, James W. Ceaser and Andrew E. Busch state that "it did create a clear disadvantage for Vice President Gore. No one could erase the 'fact' that George W. Bush had been declared president-elect, complete with new graphics, music, and two hours of pundits lauding his campaign strategy. *It was thereafter Vice President Gore who was in a position of reversing the presumption*"[143]

From that point on, Gore was on the defensive. Like all underdogs, he was expected to *ultimately* lose. How could he change the ultimate outcome when his opponent had more votes? People watching television that night (and early morning) went to bed with the image of Bush being ahead. He was the likely victor. This perception was an important component in helping Bush ultimately win the election. As historian Tracy Campbell points out,

> A central rule about recounts is that a candidate needs to immediately claim frontrunner status. Frontrunners can stake a claim to the office, while those who trail and contest the results can quickly be burdened with the mantle of "sore loser" and therefore the obligation of having to prove why the perceived frontrunner should be denied the office. In terms of public relations, frontrunners have all the political and legal advantages. Throughout the 2000 recount in Florida, the Bush camp quickly seized the role of frontrunner, while Gore accepted the role of the one behind in the count.[144]

His only strategy was to challenge the procedure. Unfortunately for Gore, procedure is complicated while numbers are simple. From that point on, Gore would never again have more official votes than Bush in Florida. Moreover, much of the procedural challenges could not be overcome by Gore. The main hurdle was time. Gore was an underdog to time. Ultimately, as long as the vote total did not officially change enough to put Gore ahead, all the Bush campaign had to do was run out the clock. And they did, with the help of a combination of public opinion, much of Florida's state government, local governments, and the federal courts.

The statewide machine recount (every county but one completed it) dropped Bush's lead to 327 votes. It was done by November 10. However, there were now deadlines, maybe not ironclad, but deadlines nonetheless. The November 15th deadline for the Florida Secretary of State to certify the election was one. The Electoral College vote in mid-December in Tallahassee was another. The certification of the Electoral College votes from all fifty states would have to be done by Congress in early January 2001.[145]

The meaning and importance of some of these deadlines were contested. Essentially, it boiled down to one core argument: accuracy versus speed. Does Florida need to "get it right," even if takes longer than a few weeks? Or is the alternative preferable: do the best to ensure the people's will (as expressed through their votes), but still adhere to the deadlines? But these questions assume that all that needs to be done is accurately tabulate the people's will and the genuine result will be revealed. That assumption was problematic, as the recount process unfolded.

The complete list of "mistakes" and partisan maneuvering associated with the Florida vote is beyond the scope of this study. But some can be identified: there were honest, yet tragic mistakes, like the butterfly ballot in Palm Beach County. There was deliberate stalling by the Bush campaign. There were attempts to "cherry pick" geographic areas to recount by the Gore campaign to find enough votes to move him past Bush. There were different ways to interpret voter intent. Voter rolls of suspected felons were purged that disproportionately disenfranchised African Americans. There was the disenfranchisement of thousands of voters in the central time zone of Florida due to the networks early initial call of the state. Overseas absentee ballots were counted (or not counted) by different standards.[146] There were blatantly partisan state and federal court decisions that affected how the recount proceeded and, ultimately, the end result of the election.

There was one particular group that a lot of people had sympathy for and felt were being discriminated against. This group is typically not thought of as underdogs: the U.S. military. There were many overseas ballots that had been ruled illegal, and thus they were not counted. These included votes from military personnel. The Republicans sought to get the votes of the discarded ballots from military personnel without postmarks *counted* while attempting to have the ballots of Democratic overseas ballots without postmarks *discarded* for the same reason. The key, as Tracy Campbell notes, was that "the difference was that since any questions concerning the overseas absentee ballots would be met with charges of disenfranchising military personnel, Republicans had political cover."[147]

Gore's running mate, Connecticut Senator Joe Lieberman took the Republican position and urged the election officials in Florida to reconsider these discarded military votes and give them "the benefit of the doubt."[148] War had been declared on American military personnel overseas, according to Montana Governor Marc Racicot. Who had declared the war? The Democrats and Al Gore.[149]

Benefit of the doubt? War being declared? How can these statements be reconciled with a group, or individual, that is as strong as the U.S. military? They seem to describe more accurately the characteristics of underdogs; groups or individuals who elicit sympathy and need help. So, in this way, the U.S. military were portrayed as victims, and underdogs. But what were they victims of? Underdogs to whom?

Was Gore an underdog during this recount? Absolutely. However, unlike many other underdogs, there was no lone, clearly identifiable and believable, villain to explain how the underdog's status was created. There was no evil scoundrel completely responsible for what happened to him. The one figure that came closest to this depiction was Florida Secretary of State Katherine Harris. There were other people responsible for Gore's fate as well, including various Florida Democrats and civil servants.[150]

It was clear to many people that if the U.S. Supreme Court got involved, Gore's status as the underdog would be solidified. If the contest needed an untouchable referee, Gore was bound to lose: the ideological and partisan composition of the court would guarantee that. The Supreme Court stopped what was to become the final official recount. The critical decision that effectively stopped Gore was written by five justices appointed by Republicans. Gore lost. Underdogs usually do.

In the 2004 presidential race, most Washington political analysts believed that the Democratic nominee would be either John Kerry or Richard Gephardt. Even though Kerry eventually won the nomination, he had to beat a challenger who most thought was not even in the first tier of candidates. He was Howard Dean.

Howard Dean

When Howard Dean decided to run for president in the 2004 campaign, most people believed he would not win. He was a governor from Vermont who was not well known in national politics. Initially, his central issues were the war, health care, fiscal responsibility, and early childhood education. He had a lot of obstacles in the way of winning the White House, as he described the beginning of his campaign: "I had no name recognition, to put it mildly, and no support from my party, to put it nicely. I had no campaign infrastructure, no press team, no handlers, no consultants, no 'oppo research.' "[151]

Dean declared his intention to win the White House on May 31, 2002.[152] His campaign did not attract a lot of attention and support initially, as Charles Lewis writes:

> As late as January 2003, the medical doctor, self-proclaimed outsider, and underdog remained virtually unknown to voters outside of his home state. A *Newsweek* poll of registered Democrats and independents taken that month, after most candidates were already in the race, showed 4 percent of respondents backed Dean, behind other long-shot candidates, Al Sharpton, Carol Mosley Braun, and Dennis Kucinich. Even the people who knew him best seemed doubtful...A March 2002 poll of Vermont registered voters found that only 23 percent would back him for the White House.[153]

Dean began to get more national notice with his March 15, 2003, speech to the California Democratic State Convention. It was a blistering speech that condemned what he saw as his party's capitulation to President George W. Bush. One issue he was upset over was health care: "What I want to know is why the Congress is fighting over the Patient's Bill of Rights? The Patient's Bill of Rights is a good bill, but not one more person gets health insurance and it's not 5 cents cheaper.... What I want to know is why the Democrats in Congress aren't standing up for us, joining every other industrialized country on the face of the Earth in providing health insurance for every man, woman and child in America."[154]

Dean was standing up for the millions of Americans who either did not have health insurance or had a difficult time affording it. Dean had fought hard to help more Vermonters get health insurance when he was governor. He was successful, as he pointed out in his 2003 book, *Winning Back America*: "While the number of uninsured Americans has been climbing, over the last ten years the rate of people who have no health insurance in Vermont has actually dropped from 17 percent to just under 8.5 percent."[155]

It was not his references to health care, though, which got him notice. It was his direct challenge to his party's support of the Iraq War so close to the actual invasion: "What I want to know is what in the world so many Democrats are doing supporting the President's unilateral intervention in Iraq?"[156]

Dean had spoken earlier about conditionally supporting the Iraq War. For example, in February 2003 he spoke in front of the Democratic National Committee (DNC). In that speech, he said he would only support an action if the United Nations authorized it and the organization would send its own troops.[157] The United States invaded Iraq without these conditions.

Dean was not alone in his opposition. On February 15, 2003, there were antiwar rallies all across the globe. These included big turnouts in the United States, including 300,000 in New York City, 30,000 in Los Angeles, and 20,000 in Seattle. On February 16, between 65,000 and 200,000 people protested in San Francisco.[158]

Was Dean's position on Iraq an underdog position? Was it a stance that would contribute to his defeat? Was it a minority view? It depended on who is surveyed. A *New York Times/CBS News* poll conducted between March 7–9, 2003, asked respondents whether they would approve or disapprove of removing Saddam Hussein militarily without U.N. approval. Of all respondents, 55 percent approved while 41 percent disapproved. Dean's position was out-of-step with the majority of Americans.[159] This is not surprising given the Bush Administration's inflammatory rhetoric leading up to the invasion.

The very same poll found that, among Democrats, the numbers were almost completely *reversed*: 55 percent disapproved while 42 percent approved. Similar polls found comparable results. For example, an *ABC News/Washington Post* poll conducted between February 26–March 2, 2003, found 59 percent approved of removing Saddam Hussein even without U.N. support. Among Democrats, only 37 percent approved.[160]

Dean was representing the underdog position in the country; a view that was suspicious of the stated urgency of the war *and* unwilling to act unilaterally at the time. Although many Americans may have doubted the urgency of the invasion, most were willing to "rally around the flag" and support the president.

Despite the rhetoric coming from many top Democratic leaders, presidential hopefuls and their aides, their views did not match the views of the majority of their party. Dean was criticized for his pro-U.N. view. For example, in February 2003, John Kerry's campaign manager stated that "Governor Dean, in effect, seems to be giving the U.N. veto power over national security decisions of the United States. That's an extraordinary proposition, one never endorsed by any U.S. president or serious candidate for the presidency."[161]

An insurgent campaign against key parts of the establishment of the Democratic Party was developing. Dean's criticism of fellow Democrats angered the DLC. The DLC is an ideologically moderate to conservative organization formed after 1984. Its purpose back then was to help Democrats nominate candidates who were not perceived as liberal to win back political power.

The DLC did not like Dean's position on Iraq, his rhetoric, tone, and his national security feebleness. They tried to weaken his appeal by creating a negative image of him.[162] As writers Jerome Armstrong and Markos Moulitsas Zuniga report, "the DLC attack plan focused on hitting Dean and defining him early enough in the primary as an unelectable northeasterner who was trotting out the tired, old, failed liberalism of McGovern and Mondale."[163]

Dean also stood up for another underdog group: the working-class, southern white male. In his speech to the California Democratic State Convention, he uttered an unusual line for a Northern Democrat: "I don't want to win without the South. I'm going to go to the South, and I'm going to say to white guys who drive pick-up trucks with Confederate flag decals on the back of their car, 'We want your vote too, 'cause your kids don't have health insurance either.' "[164] Campaigning in Iowa in the fall of 2003, Dean again mentioned the Confederate flag and talked about wanting to appeal to southern working-class whites.[165]

Democratic presidential opponents pounced on Dean. North Carolina Senator John Edwards said, "The last thing we need in the South is someone like you coming down and telling us what to do." Reverend Al Sharpton told him, "Most poor Southern whites don't wear a Confederate flag, and you ought not to try to stereotype that." Gephardt essentially accused Dean of pandering to racists by trying to get the support of voters "who disagree with us on bedrock Democratic values like civil rights."[166]

After Dean apologized for how his remarks had caused hurt, Massachusetts Senator John Kerry still went after him: "Howard Dean has finally admitted that his words have caused pain, but I am puzzled as to why he does not seem to regret the words that caused the pain."[167] Dean did not take the criticism lightly: "I think there are a lot of poor people who fly that flag because the Republicans have been dividing us by race since 1968 with their Southern race strategy."[168]

Obviously, Dean hit a nerve. The truth is that working-class whites are in many respects classic underdogs; economically discriminated against and, at least historically, always being bested by Northerners and Southern elites. In a column titled *Pickup Drivers for Dean*, writer Sam

Smith clearly states the veracity of Dean's intent: "what he was doing was simply reaching out to a constituency that Democratic liberals have too long dissed, the less successful white male.... By any traditional Democratic standards, this constituency should be a natural.... what more dramatically illustrates the failures of two decades of corporatist economics than how far these white males have been left behind?"[169]

The key to the Republican success in helping to elect presidents from 1968 to 2004 has been the working-class southern whites. In many respects, it is not so much that the Republicans appeal to this group than it is that the national Democratic Party has been successfully framed as their cultural enemy. Even though a lot of southern working-class whites are actually economic underdogs, many *identify* more as cultural underdogs: to the educated elite, the northern urbanites, and the mainstream media (to name just a few).

Dean's campaign picked up support throughout 2003. He went on a "Sleepless Summer Tour" in which, over a period of four days, he campaigned in eight states. He drew large crowds at many stops. Underdogs were attracted to Dean and his message of hope and revival of the Democratic Party. As he recounts in his book, *You Have the Power*, certain pictures stuck with him: "A woman in a wheelchair in Iowa who handed me a bag of fifty dollars in quarters that she'd saved from her monthly disability check."[170] People found empowerment: "Howard Vicini...whose life had ground to a halt after decades of chronic pain and the total failure of our health-care system to care for him, wrote of finding himself 'reacquainted...with hope and with the world-at-large...reawakened to a sense of community.'"[171]

Technology helped fuel Dean's rise throughout 2003. His campaign creatively used the Internet in a way that made it easier for average individuals to participate in the political process. Underdogs need to find a way to get their message out without spending huge amounts of money for advertising.[172] The campaign, under the direction of Joe Trippi, used meetup.com to grow, and also decentralize, the campaign. Meetup.com facilitates in-person meetings between people interested in a common topic, hobby, or subject. How does it work? According to Wikipedia, "users enter their ZIP Code (or their city outside the United States) and the topic they want to meet about, and the website helps them arrange a place and time to meet."[173] It was extremely successful. Trippi describes how it helped the campaign: "After we put Meetup on the web site, I checked back and suddenly there were 2,700 people who wanted to meet up for Dean. The number had taken one of those exponential leaps-what would turn out to be the first of many. The second-highest candidate, Kerry, had only gone up to 330 names. This was more than just a statistical quirk. Something was going on out there."[174]

Meetups provided a way for people who are not rich, middle class, or well-connected to help create the infrastructure of a national campaign. These people can be considered underdogs, in that they would be at a disadvantage in traditional campaigns. In traditional campaigns, they would have to plug into a structure already created by the campaign instead of helping to create one.

The nexus between underdogs and the Dean campaign can also be found in how they received their money. They attracted a tremendous amount of small donors. For example, in the third quarter of 2003, more than 200,000 contributions came into his campaign. The average contribution was $77.[175] In the past, major candidates for the Democratic presidential nomination had increasingly relied on big contributors for much of their money. With all of these small donors, the Dean campaign provided an outlet for people with modest financial means to build a national campaign.

As Dean became more popular and visible, the opposition to him from some establishment Democrats intensified. In November 2003, the group Americans for Jobs and HealthCare took direct aim at the former Vermont governor. This group was run by Democrats associated with House Minority Leader Richard Gephardt and Massachusetts Senator John Kerry (both contenders for the 2004 presidential nomination). Labor unions were also involved. The organization received $50,000 from the unused campaign funds of former New Jersey Democratic Senator Robert Toricelli.[176]

Americans for Jobs and HealthCare paid for television advertisements in Iowa that questioned Dean's progressivism. His commander in chief credentials were also questioned. A particularly strong advertisement used a picture of Osama bin Laden in a way that weakened him on national security. The advertisement, in part, said, "Americans want a president who can face the dangers ahead. But Howard Dean has no foreign policy or military experience. And Howard Dean just cannot compete with George Bush on foreign policy. It's time for Democrats to think about that…and think about it now."[177]

Dean could not be considered an underdog in the sense that he was gaining the support of the *majority* of Democrats, at least as surveyed in various polls.[178] He was becoming the favorite to win the nomination. Underdogs are not favorites. He could be considered an underdog in that he was trying to wrestle power away from a part of the Democratic establishment that did not want to lose it. Gephardt and Kerry were the safe alternatives to Bush; both voted for the Iraq War and thus could not be as easily painted as doves as Dean could.

Even though there were powerful Democratic Party forces working to try and cripple Dean, it could be argued that his campaign was doomed from the very beginning. That it could never win the nomination. Deep down, Howard Dean expected to lose. Like all underdogs. If this was the case, *how* was it doomed?

A big part of his campaign's predestination concerned Dean himself. Did he really want to win? According to his campaign manager, Joe Trippi, he did not. The campaign got really tough for Dean in December 2003. At that time, according to journalist Evan Thomas, "Trippi told his aides, Dean had come to him and tearfully confessed that he had run only to shake up the Democratic Party and push for health care reform, that he never cared about being president and never thought he could win." Dean denied saying that.[179]

Dean's pollster Paul Maslin lends credence to the spirit (if not the precise words) of the "confession." In December 2003, the media was pressing Dean to make public his gubernatorial records. Dean was reluctant to release them. Maslin described a meeting in which the issue came up:

> On Wednesday, December 3, in the campaign's ratty Burlington conference room, Dean met with about fifteen of his senior campaign staffers and top consultants. I felt that failing to release the records would be more damaging than anything the records might contain. It would fly in the face of the campaign's whole message of openness and change, and would reveal Dean as just another politician. But others, who had known him longer, were more circumspect. They were particularly concerned about the weekly memos Dean was given as governor, on which he would write comments. Nobody could remember a precise example, but all, including Dean himself, thought that he had probably insulted many major political players in Vermont in those comments, including Democrats and Democratically-leaning interest groups. Dean was increasingly uncomfortable with the discussion…in the end, he lowered his head and said to us all, but mostly to himself, *"I'd rather end the campaign than have the world see everything."* Seldom have I heard a candidate so open about his feelings…more seldom still have I seen someone on the brink of political success be so conflicted about it.[180]

Howard Dean did not become his party's presidential nominee in 2004. He finished third in the Iowa caucuses and dropped out of the race in February.[181]

Dean had a powerful effect on the Democratic Party. He was elected the chairman of the DNC in early 2005. As DNC Chair, Dean adopted a 50-state strategy; the party would put resources into states that were traditionally Republican to build a more national party.[182]

By doing this, he was empowering Democratic underdogs in traditionally Republican states. For example, before Dean's tenure, if you were a Democrat in Kansas, Alaska, or Idaho, you could not expect much (if any) help from the national Democratic Party. Dean gave resources, hope, and money to Democrats everywhere in the nation, not just in traditionally Democratic and "swing" states.

Democrats won back both houses of Congress in 2006. Dean's 50-state strategy was an integral component of the victory. As Joe Conasan wrote in Salon.com, "What Dean and his organizers created... was an environment that allowed insurgents and outliers as well as the party's chosen challengers to ride the national wave of revulsion against conservative rule. That enterprise, in turn, surprised and overwhelmed the Republican capacity to respond. Faced with many more viable challenges than anticipated, the Republicans made mistakes in allocating resources—and were forced to defend candidates in districts that are usually safe."[183]

Dean has also reached out to religious voters as party chair. This was a new experience for many in the modern Democratic Party. Dean realized that the party and Christians had some shared concerns. As author Amy Sullivan states, "By the fall of 2007, the party organization had developed a database to identify voters by religious affiliation, among other characteristics. And Dean's schedule was filled with appearances at black churches *and* religious colleges populated by those 'white Christians' he had once associated only with the GOP."[184]

Many Christians felt that the national Democratic Party discriminated against them because many of their positions on social policy were at odds with their faith. Other Christians believed that the party did not even try to relate to some of their concerns. Dean's purposeful outreach was a move to try and make Christians feel that they are not *always* ignored, discriminated against, or at a structural disadvantage in the party. In short, that they are not always an underdog component of the national Democratic Party coalition.

Dean's experience showed how underdog energy can have a lasting, positive effect on a political party. Under Dean's leadership (and helped to a considerable effect by Barack Obama), the November 2008 elections strengthened the Democratic control of Congress. A new era of Democratic dominance was about to begin. The person who would lead this epoch was Barack Obama. In the final chapter, we turn to his story and the future of the party.

CHAPTER 8

Barack Obama and the Future of the Democratic Party

Biography

By now, most of us are familiar with Obama's roots. Barack Hussein Obama was born in Hawaii in 1961. He was named after his father. His mother was from Kansas and his father from Kenya. His mother was white while his father was black.[1] The fact that he was a product of a racially mixed marriage gave him an underdog predisposition; he would be subject to at least *some* form of inequality and discrimination just because of his skin color. In his autobiography, *Dreams from My Father,* Obama recounts a few instances of how some of his family dealt with racial discrimination. For example, he describes an incident that took place in Honolulu involving his father and maternal grandfather. At the time, his father was a student at the University of Hawaii:

After long hours of study, my father had joined my grandfather and several other friends at a local Waikiki bar....a white man abruptly announced to the bartender, loudly enough for everyone to hear, that he shouldn't have to drink good liquor "next to a nigger." The room fell quiet and people turned to my father, expecting a fight. Instead, my father stood up, walked over to the man, smiled, and proceeded to lecture him about the folly of bigotry, the promise of the American dream, and the universal rights of man.

What happened next was unexpected: " 'This fella felt so bad when Barack was finished,' Gramps would say, 'that he reached into his pocket and gave Barack a hundred dollars on the spot.' "[2]

This incident illustrates that one way Obama's father dealt with discrimination was with intellectualism; instead of taking the insult personally, he put it in the context of a larger frame and disarmed the racial venom. Moreover, the hatred was neutralized by embracing hope.[3] To Obama's father, racial equality was obviously the future of the world.

Obama also recounts instances where his mother and maternal grandparents were exposed to racial discrimination while living in Texas. In his job as a furniture salesman, his grandfather was advised to cater to potential Mexican and black customers after the store's regular hours. These potential customers would also have to "arrange for their own delivery."[4] His grandmother was also disparaged at her workplace for calling a black man "mister." His mother, only 11 or 12, violated a defacto racial taboo by playing with a black child.[5]

Obama was also influenced by his mother. His mother's political orientation was clearly left of center; she has been referred to as "an Adlai Stevenson liberal" (by Obama's maternal grandmother), as well as a "secular humanist and an avowed New Deal, Peace Corps-loving liberal" (by Obama). Part of Obama's moral direction was from his mother's guidance.[6]

Writer Amanda Ripley has referred to Obama's mother, who was known as Ann, as a "romantic pragmatist" and a "dreamer." She had a great deal of cultural empathy and lived her life demonstrating it. For example, while in Indonesia doing research for her doctorate in the late 1980s and early 1990s, she wanted to help poor women. Her research helped establish Indonesia's microfinance program. Economist Richard Patten claimed that her anthropological investigations helped inform the policies of the Bank Rakyat Indonesia. These policies have had a lot of success; as of 2008, Indonesia's microfinance program has the most savers of any country in the world.[7]

Obama's mother was concerned with fairness. In particular, she was interested in calculating degrees of fairness. For instance, when she was living in Indonesia she sympathized with the many beggars present in that country. At one time, she gave money to every beggar who came to her door. However, as Obama states in *Dreams from My Father*, she later revised her actions: "when it became clear that the tide of pain was endless, she gave more selectively, learning to calibrate the levels of misery."[8]

Obama's mother may have been thinking the following: It is simply impossible to help *every* underdog I meet. Calibrating the difference in their misery levels is a pragmatic way to help the ones that need assistance the most.

Even though that process is very logical, many people do not let their sympathy control their actions. Obama got that message from his mother's second husband, an Indonesian named Lolo Soetoro. Soetoro tended to be harder about people who were less fortunate. He couched his differences with his wife in traditional gender stereotypes: "Your mother has a soft heart...That's a good thing in a woman. But you will be a man someday, and a man needs to have more sense."[9]

While in Indonesia, Obama did, at times, follow how his mother dealt with beggars, but he also listened to Soetero's advice. Synthesizing these two competing philosophies produced a general sympathy for underdogs that is protected by a hard shell of reality. This reality was described by Soetoro as "taking life on its own terms."[10] In many ways, Obama's relationship to underdogs fits that fusion.

As a child, Obama grew up in both Hawaii and Indonesia. When he was nine years old, Obama lived in Indonesia with his mother. He recounts a story in which he was looking at magazines in the library of the U.S. Embassy, where he was waiting for his mother, who worked there. He found a *Life* magazine that had a picture of a black man who had undergone a chemical treatment to make his skin lighter. At first he did not realize why the man looked so strange: "He must be terribly sick...A radiation victim, maybe, or an albino." When he realized that the man had done this to himself, he became upset: "I felt my face and neck get hot. My stomach knotted...I had a desperate urge to jump out of my seat, to show them what I had learned, to demand some explanation or assurance."[11]

His words revealed a visceral reaction to what is clearly an incredulous reality, at least to a nine year old. To him at the time, he might have thought that there was some incredible unfairness in the world that would convince this man to try and change his skin color. Underdogs fight unfairness. It was not just a theoretical concern to him, however. Since his skin was black, would he someday feel the need to try and change his skin color? Was he an underdog?

The shock of that photograph helped open Obama's mind to the destructive power of racism. It was a power that was often concealed, and thus impossible to be shielded from.[12]

When he was growing up in Hawaii, Obama did not experience as much racism as many blacks did on the mainland, though there were some incidents. One was a time when a tennis coach made a joke about Obama's blackness rubbing off. Obama quit the tennis team.[13] On another occasion, a student asked if his Kenyan father ate people.[14]

Although the image of Hawaii is that of a harmonious and racially tolerant society, the reality was not quite so ideal. A black schoolmate of Obama at Punahou School recalled the atmosphere: "A big joke amongst the brothers was you could be anything else but a brother and have free rein of the world in Hawaii."[15]

A major lesson that Obama learned from growing up in Hawaii was to embrace tolerance and diversity. In a 1999 essay for his alumni bulletin, Obama recalls how Hawaii shaped his values: "Hawaii's spirit of tolerance might not have been perfect or complete, but it was—and is—real. The opportunity that Hawaii offered—to experience a variety of cultures in a climate of mutual respect—became an integral part of my world view, and a basis for the values that I hold most dear."[16]

This was pragmatic, as Obama family friend Georgia McCauley explained: "If you grow up here, where we have no majority and there's a complete ethnic mix, people have learned how to get along with others who look different and are from different places."[17] Getting along with others who are different than you is very difficult unless you recognize that there is an egalitarian core value that trumps all other values. There is no room for racial discrimination.

Obama also recalled how his life concern for underdogs was shaped by these school years: "By the time I moved back to Hawaii...I had come to recognize that Hawaii was not immune to issues of race and class, issues that manifested themselves in...the glaring differences between the facilities we at Punahou enjoyed and the crumbling public schools that so many of our peers were forced to endure."[18]

Obama's link to underdogs is also illustrated by the fact that he chose to be a community organizer. In 1983, he decided on that career path because he wanted change. He thought mobilizing people at the grassroots was how change occurred.[19] While still in New York City, but after he had graduated from Columbia University, he decided to try his hand at helping the poor. He worked in Brooklyn and Harlem on a part-time basis.[20] Later, he moved to Chicago where he became a full-time community organizer on the city's south side. From 1985 until 1988, he was employed at the Developing Communities Project as their director. He created a tenants rights organization at a public housing complex, helped create a tutoring program for college preparation as well as an agenda for job training.[21]

The communities in Chicago that Obama tried to help organize were becoming *underdog communities*—ones that were expected to lose and clearly unequal (politically, socially, and economically) with nearby ones. These underdog communities were mostly made up of blacks.[22]

One neighborhood was Roseland. Author David Mendell described Roseland at the time Obama worked there: "about one in six Roseland residents lived below the poverty line. The ubiquitous presence of the poor created an emotional paradox for middle-class blacks. Residents of moderate wealth were mindful that their neighbors lived in deprivation, a situation that instills a sense of compassion for those less fortunate." Sympathy for these underdogs, however, was tempered by how they were being affected by the presence of the poor: "middle-class blacks...harbored some resentment toward their poor neighbors because they dragged down the community's overall standard of living."[23]

Obama's work in Chicago helped him understand the complexity of what nonblacks may label "the African-American experience." In particular, that within black communities, there were many traditional underdogs (people expected to lose, subject to discrimination and victims of injustice) *as well as* blacks who were middle class and stable. Obama identified this duality as "individual achievement *and* collective decline."[24]

What does this reveal about the links between Obama and underdogs? It foreshadowed a future time when Obama would successfully articulate this duality to bigger audiences. It would forever change the practice of traditional black politics. The national politics of Jesse Jackson, that had emphasized historical wrongs and sociological solutions, would give way to more a nuanced, and updated, narrative of African Americans. It would be a tale where two stories would share a single narrative: Although great progress had been made, the power of government was still needed to be used to address the historical legacy of slavery, Jim Crow and other forms of racism that still deeply affected millions of Americans.

Obama also realized that many African Americans were *psychological underdogs*. Deep within many blacks, there was a subterranean element of hate that was associated with whites. This hate coexisted with stories of sacrifice, courage, and success. Together, they "formed a counternarrative buried deep within each person and at the center of which stood white people—some cruel, some ignorant, sometimes a single face, sometimes just a faceless image of a system claiming power over their lives." Would "hating blue eyes" be necessary to reestablish community?[25]

If that was true, how could blacks be anything but permanent underdogs? Underdogs are expected to lose. If racial identity is the core element in political discourse and power, then racial minorities would always be at a disadvantage, destined to fall short in any struggle with the majority.

The forces of assimilation and the power of stereotypes also contribute to the links between African Americans and underdogs. Moreover, this is usually true for all minorities, as Obama wrote in *The Audacity of Hope*: "In general, members of every minority group continue to be measured largely by the degree of our assimilation—how closely speech patterns, dress, or demeanor conform to the dominant white culture—and the more that a minority strays form these external markers, the more he or she is subject to negative assumptions."[26] A negative assumption about a person, or group, is obviously disadvantageous, and thus can be the first step toward persecution and discrimination.

Obama recognized that the specific dynamics of the underdog status of minorities have probably changed over the last thirty years because of decency and antidiscrimination norms becoming internalized. He also believed that this "prevents most whites from consciously acting on such stereotypes in their daily interactions with persons of other races." Even so, discrimination is still a reality: "it's unrealistic to believe that these stereotypes don't have some cumulative impact on the often snap decisions of who's hired and who's promoted, on who's arrested and who's prosecuted, on how you feel about the customer who just walked into your store or about the demographics of your children's school."[27] Psychologically, the effect on minorities can be tremendous: "spending one's days refuting stereotypes can be a weary business. It's the added weight that many minorities, especially African Americans, so often describe in their daily round—the feeling that as a group we have no store of goodwill in America's accounts, that as individuals we must prove ourselves anew each day, that we will rarely get the benefit of the doubt and will have little margin of error."[28]

Obama eventually left Chicago to go to Harvard Law School. After graduating, he moved back to Chicago. In 1992, he worked for Project Vote, a voter registration organization, as its director. The organization wanted to register 150,000 unregistered African Americans in Illinois. That goal was met.[29] How did he meet that goal? He started a media campaign, helped educate deputy registrars, and made contact with black politicians, churches, and community groups. Sam Burrell, a local politician in Chicago's 29th ward, described what Obama helped create: "We were registering hundreds a day, and we weren't having to search them out. They came looking for us. African Americans were just so eager to have a say again, to feel they counted."[30]

Many underdogs *feel* that they do not have a say in how power is distributed. Project Vote helped many African Americans feel that they were counted, and thus were not disadvantaged, at least on election day. The numbers bear this out: As journalist Gretchen Reynolds wrote, "for the first time in Chicago's history...voter registrations in the 19 predominantly black wards outnumbered those in the city's 19 predominantly white ethnic wards, 676,000 to 526,000."[31] This was quite an achievement for African Americans, the historical underdogs in Chicago politics.

Obama became a full-time lawyer with the firm of Davis, Miner, Barnhill & Galland in 1993.[32] This organization was a natural match for someone who wanted to help underdogs; it was described as "a real do-good firm." Although Obama represented many different clients, many had common underdog characteristics. For example, he fought for blacks who thought that some Chicago voting districts were discriminatory. He helped ACORN (the Association of Community Organizers for Reform Now) force Illinois to implement a federal law making it easier to register to vote. In addition, he helped with a whistleblower that had been fired for exposing government corruption and waste.[33]

The Dynamics of His Political Career in Illinois

The next step for Obama was to enter elective politics. In 1996, he ran for a seat in the Illinois State Senate. He won the election and started his state legislative career in 1997.[34] He fought for underdog causes in his first three years in the legislature. For example, he cosponsored or introduced bills on ethics and campaign finance reform, causes that cynics and skeptics might consider destined to ultimately fail. He also fought for government action that would reduce health risks that disproportionately affected African Americans. Examples include more money for lead abatement and the founding of a prostrate cancer screening program.[35]

Obama would continue to fight for underdogs later on in his state legislative career. His visibility increased dramatically as a result of the 2002 elections when the Democrats took control of the Illinois State Senate. He stood up for the working poor by sponsoring legislation that expanded the Earned Income Tax Credit.[36] Before crowds of blacks, he would also emphasize his actions that targeted the unequal treatment that they received from government; such as getting health insurance to more poor children and attempting to stop racial profiling.[37]

While still in the state senate, Obama decided to run for Congress. He wanted the seat of Bobby Rush, an incumbent congressman. Rush was thought to be vulnerable because he had had recently lost his own challenge to an incumbent: Mayor Richard M. Daley.[38] Obama started off as an underdog in the race; most congressional incumbents do not lose their reelection campaigns.

Obama never seemed to connect with the majority of potential constituents in the primary campaign. Instead, he was viewed by many as too intellectual and out-of-touch. He was called "an educated fool" by Rush.[39] Writer David Mendell described the dynamics of the race: "By most accounts...Obama was too fond of reciting his impressive resume, too often mentioned that he had forsaken a high-priced law firm for public office and too often spoke in the high-minded prose of a constitutional law lecturer, all of which could make him appear condescending to his audience."[40] Rush won the primary easily, defeating Obama 61 to 30 percent.[41]

Rush could be considered a bigger underdog than Obama, as writer Edward McClelland observed: "You might say Rush has been running as an underdog his whole life. He dropped out of high school to join the army but now holds two master's degrees.... Once hunted by the Chicago police after fellow Black Panther Party leaders Fred Hampton and Mark Clark were gunned down, Rush went on to serve ten years as an alderman. He's fought off a stammer to become a fluid, if not dynamic, public speaker."[42]

Rush's underdog credentials were solidified by the tragic death of his son. Huey Rush was killed on a street on the South Side of Chicago five months before the primary campaign. Instead of the brash politician who lost to Mayor Daley, he now had the image of the brokenhearted parent.[43]

The next step for Obama was the U.S. Senate in 2004. His two principal challengers to the Democratic nomination were Blair Hull and Dan Hynes. Hull had made money in securities trading and was very wealthy. Hynes was the Illinois state comptroller. Obama was an underdog to both of these candidates. He was a financial underdog to Hull, who self-financed his campaign with $29 million. Obama did not have nearly as much name recognition as Hynes, whose father was well-known in Chicago Democratic politics. Moreover, Hynes had already been elected state-wide.[44] Dan Hynes's campaign never gained much strength; he finished a distant second to Obama in the primary.[45]

How Obama beat Hull is the more relevant portion of the underdog story in the primary. Hull was leading the race until the records from his divorce were unsealed. These records, made public by pressure from the political opponents and the media, showed some embarrassing revelations. He got into a physical fight with his (then) wife and was arrested for battery. She also claimed that he threatened to kill her. He ended up with 10 percent in the primary.[46] Obama took advantage of Hull's downfall and never looked back.

Obama was not the underdog anymore in the primary campaign. As author David Mendell states, "Momentum had swung his way and it seemed unstoppable. He was soaring in the polls. This was the very beginning of the Obama phenomenon that would sweep through Illinois and then spread nationwide."[47] Hull's own spokesmen remarked that "Obama is on fire!"[48]

Illinois Republicans nominated millionaire Jack Ryan as their candidate for the U.S. Senate. Just like Hull's did, Ryan's campaign stumbled when his divorce files were unsealed. They contained unsavory details that embarrassed him and doomed his campaign. In particular, his ex-wife (actress Jeri Ryan) alleged that he pressured her to have sex in public with him. On July 29, 2004, Ryan withdrew from the race.[49]

After his primary victory, it would be difficult to characterize Obama as an underdog in this race. A poll taken in May 2004 (before the salacious specifics of Ryan's divorce records were released), showed Obama leading Ryan by 52 to 30 percent.[50] One of the core characteristics of an underdog, that they will probably lose, no longer fit Obama's campaign. On the contrary, he was almost sure to win and was becoming nationally known through positive media exposure. He was a rising star in the Democratic Party. The pinnacle event of the year for Obama was his keynote speech to the Democratic National Convention in Boston.

As Obama was becoming more famous, he was also being scrutinized more. Some of this scrutiny would throw into question his commitment to underdogs. For example, Obama was a guest on *Meet the Press* on the Sunday before the Boston convention opened. One topic was the comments made in 1996 about accessibility and the Democratic National Convention in Chicago: "Chicagoans have grown especially jaded watching the Democrats raise cash for this month's national convention in Chicago. The convention's for sale, right? You got these ten-thousand-dollar-a-plate dinners, Golden Circle Clubs. I think when the average voter looks at that, they rightly feel they've been locked out of the process. They can't attend a ten-thousand-dollar breakfast. They know that those who can are going to get the kind of access they can't imagine."[51]

Host Tim Russert wanted to know how he felt about the big contributors at the 2004 Boston convention and the political symbolism it conveyed: "A hundred and fifty donors gave forty million dollars to this convention. It's worse than Chicago, using your standards. Are you offended by that, and what message does that send the average voter?"[52]

Where *in* the convention hall was the equality that underdogs fought for? Had he forgotten about the average Democrat in Boston who could not afford to get into the convention? Where was his sympathy for them?

Obama deflected Russert's question by noting the bipartisan problem of political money, minimizing the importance of the convention, and generalizing about the party's historic appeal to underdogs.[53] In *The Audacity of Hope*, Obama admits to privately liking his 1996 remarks better than what he said in 2004.[54]

The key word is privately. The future president was moving from being an outsider to an insider. He would have to compromise on his public commitment to standing up for *all* underdogs as a means to gaining more publicity, national exposure, and ultimately greater power. He would not be a political purist; a little hypocrisy would be an acceptable tradeoff to reach bigger goals. Underdogs would not be abandoned. Instead, he would try to fight for national legislation that would benefit them through public policies. To do that, he needed to have more power.

Obama became known nationally with his speech to the 2004 Democratic National Convention. It was a powerful speech that electrified the convention. He was interrupted thirty-three times by applause.[55] Obama skillfully coupled his personal story to the American dream. He also linked the plight of underdogs to a powerful emblem of the United States, E pluribus unum:

> If there's a child on the south side of Chicago who can't read, that matters to me, even if it's not my child. If there's a senior citizen somewhere who can't pay for her prescription and has to choose between medicine and the rent, that makes my life poorer, even if it's not my grandmother. If there's an Arab American family being rounded up without benefit of an attorney or due process, that threatens my civil liberties. It's that fundamental belief—I am my brother's keeper, I am my sister's keeper—that makes this country work. It's what allows us to pursue our individual dreams, yet still come together as a single American family.[56]

Helping our underdogs was the method to achieve national unity. Embracing the struggle for fairness and equality by the illiterate, the poor, and the ethnic minority was the way to transcend division.

But precisely how could this be done? What are the dynamics that connect society's underdogs to national unity? According to Rowland and Jones, the most important rhetorical move that Obama made was to emphasize what Americans have in common. In the speech, Obama mentioned both what Americans value and what they dislike. For example, that God is worshipped in Democratic states and that people in Republican states do not like their libraries being infiltrated by federal agents.[57]

However, it is in how Obama's *approach* differed from other progressives that gave him a greater potential to actually help underdogs. As Rowland and Jones note, "While many Democrats and other liberals emphasize the differences between rich and poor, white and minority communities, and men and women, Obama argued that the most fundamental definition of identity was found in simply being an American."[58] This was different, at least for many national Democrats.

Although emphasizing the economic and political gaps *between* people is the standard Democratic approach to gaining political power, it has not been very successful over the last thirty years for the party. If Democrats tried to point these gaps out, then the charges of class warfare would be brought up by many Republicans. This has been used successfully in the past to stifle candid debate on economic issues. According to Massachusetts Rep. Barney Frank, "One of the most successful right-wing ploys was to demonize any concern about the distribution of income in America as, quote, class warfare."[59]

Stressing the gaps to essentially shame Americans into passing legislation to help economic underdogs was not working as well. Many Americans had compassion fatigue. Ideological aversion to redistributive economic policies was also a roadblock to helping underdogs. Instead, according to Rowland and Jones, "it was more important [for Obama] to emphasize the similarities, *since once those similarities were recognized it was much easier to make a case for helping fellow Americans.*"[60]

Upon some introspection, American underdogs are really not that different from Americans who have "made it" in life. Many people realize how close they are to turning into underdogs themselves when a catastrophe occurs; perhaps a major medical emergency threatens to bankrupt them or a looming layoff will trigger an economic or psychological crisis. If one can look at the less fortunate and see themselves *in* them (at least partially or potentially), they might view government policies to help underdogs with less reluctance as many do now.

Obama also connected political hope to underdogs. For example, he dared his audience to hope through the use of historical and personal examples of underdogs: "It's the hope of slaves sitting around a fire singing freedom songs; the hope of immigrants setting out for distant shores...[and] the hope of a skinny kid with a funny name who believes that America has a place for him, too."[61]

Rowland and Jones observed that Obama's use of hope in his address skillfully blended personal values with communitarian actions. For instance, it was the personal strength of individual slaves that allowed African Americans to persevere and ultimately gain freedom. But it also took communal action (like the Civil War and the civil rights movement) for African Americans to both gain that freedom *everywhere* in the nation and experience it deeper. Fundamentally, hope is linked to equal opportunity: "Hope can only be achieved in an America where opportunity is available to all because shared identity means more than embracing strong personal values; it also means reaching out to help those in need."[62]

The link between helping underdogs and providing equal opportunity is complicated. At what point do underdogs feel entitled to help by the very nature of that status? What effect does government assistance to underdogs have on the strength of personal values (in general) and personal responsibility (in particular)? What effect does the persistence of underdogs have on the communal values of a nation?

Those are difficult questions, ones that the mainstream media rarely even ask. Instead, it is an image that has a commanding hold on the fortunes of politicians. On this level, Obama had become a hero. The media loved the speech. Pundit Mark Shields claimed, "A star is born." Television personality Chris Matthews said, "I have seen the first black president." The *Chicago Tribune* editorialized that Obama was " 'The Phenom.'"[63]

Although John Kerry lost the presidential race in November 2004, Obama handily won his U.S. Senate race. He won with 70 percent of the vote over Alan Keyes.[64] Keyes had become the Republican nominee in the summer when the GOP was left with no candidate after Jack Ryan dropped out. Keyes was a controversial choice for many reasons, including the fact that he became a resident of Illinois only days before his candidacy.[65] A *Chicago Tribune* poll found Obama ahead of Keyes by a huge margin: 68 to 17 percent. Obama was so far ahead that he campaigned for other Democratic candidates outside of Illinois. He even contributed $225,000 of his own campaign money to the Democratic Senatorial Campaign Committee and various state parties.[66] Obama officially became a U.S. Senator in January 2005. He would now have a bigger stage in which to fight for underdogs.

Career as a U.S. Senator

Obama was a U.S. senator from early January 2005 until mid-November 2008, resigning approximately two weeks after his election as

U.S. president.[67] Did he fight for underdogs as a U.S. senator? By many accounts, he was one of the most reliable defenders of their interests. For example, he supported the interests of the Children's Defense Fund more often than not. Obama backed the group's interests 100 percent of the time in both 2005 and 2006. Even though his support dropped off in 2007, he still backed them 60 percent of the time.[68] Did Obama suddenly fight a little less strenuously to defend children in 2007? Most likely not: his ratings could have been affected due to his being absent for many votes because of his presidential campaign.[69]

He compiled a high rating from many other liberal interest groups as well. Much of what these groups fight for are underdog interests. For example, the National Education Association gave him an A for 2005, 2006, and 2007.[70] Examples of key votes that were used in compiling the grades included supporting union rights, increasing the minimum wage, and spending more for education.[71]

Americans for Democratic Action gave him consistently high rankings: 100 percent for 2005, 95 percent for 2006, and 75 percent in 2007.[72] Examples of key votes that were used in compiling these rankings include one dealing with the tactics used in the war on terrorism (he voted for a provision that would have given detainees rights to use U.S. courts to contest their detention), one on economic policy (he voted against a capital gains tax cut), and another one on employment and immigration policy (he voted for a provision that would have made grossly or willfully negligent violations of the Occupational Safety and Health Act a felony and also would have given back pay to undocumented workers who were denied their employment rights).[73]

There were times that Obama did not seem to stand up for underdogs. For example, he sided against trial lawyers when he voted for a bill that would have limited class-action lawsuits. Although it is hard to see lawyers as underdogs, consumers who get cheated by unethical business practices are classic underdogs; they have not been treated fairly and they elicit sympathy. His vote was against the interests of labor, civil rights, and consumer groups.[74] He defended his vote by pointing out that justice and truth were not being served by the present system: "When multimillion-dollar settlements are handed down and all the victims get are coupons for a free product, justice is not being served," he said in a statement. "And when cases are tried in counties only because it's known that those judges will award big payoffs, you get quick settlements without ever finding out who's right and who's wrong."[75]

However broken the system was, many liberal groups did not think the bill he voted for was in the best interests of underdogs. The truth was, according to writer David Sirota, that "everyone in Washington knew the bill's real objective was to protect corporate abusers."[76]

Sirota described a conversation that Joan Claybrook, a longtime consumer activist, had with Obama after this vote. Obama was meeting with public interest groups. He defended his vote by saying, "Sometimes you have to trim your sails." Claybrook asked herself, "Trim your sails for what? You just got elected by a wide margin—what are you trimming your sails for?"[77] For a potential future presidential run. Perhaps Obama knew that he might someday get a chance to be able to help underdogs from an even bigger stage than the U.S. Senate: the presidency.

It would be difficult to argue that Obama was not a liberal while in the U.S. Senate. Many voting scorecards designed by media organizations and academics showed him to be decidedly left-of-center. The *National Journal* labeled him the most liberal senator in 2007.[78] Political scientists Jeff Lewis and Keith Poole found Obama progressive, but not quite so liberal: he was the twenty-first most liberal in 2005–2006, and he was tied for the tenth most liberal in 2007–2008.[79]

Obama has consistently resisted efforts to be ideologically pigeonholed. According to him, it is the precise instant in time (not literally, but perhaps a time period in between political eras) the United States is in that makes ideological warfare unproductive for progressives. He claimed that the most effective way to fight for the interests and values he believes in (that tend to be liberal and help out society's underdogs) was to *deemphasize* the ideological component of public policies. As he wrote in 2006, "Ultimately...I believe any attempt to pursue a more sharply partisan and ideological strategy misapprehends the moment we're in. I am convinced whenever we exaggerate or demonize, oversimplify or overstate our case, we lose. Whenever we dumb down the political debate, we lose."[80]

An atmosphere of hyper-partisanship and mean and unsophisticated political discourse serves the interests of conservatives. As Obama wrote in 2006, "A polarized electorate—or one that easily dismisses both parties because of the nasty, dishonest tone of the debate—works perfectly well for those who seek to chip away at the very idea of government. After all, a cynical electorate is a self-centered electorate."[81] A self-centered electorate is not hospitable to public policies that seek to redistribute economic resources and political power to the struggling, the suffering, the discriminated against, and the people most likely to lose: the underdogs.

The Struggle for the 2008 Democratic Presidential Nomination

Race and Gender

In late 2006, Obama thought that maybe the time was right for him to reach for the highest political prize available: the U.S. presidency. Obama officially announced his bid for the 2008 Democratic presidential nomination on February 10, 2007.[82]

Could a black actually win the presidential nomination of a major American political party? Was it possible? It depended on emphasis and nuance. Pollster Cornell Belcher described the challenges and opportunity that Obama had: "a *black man* can't be president of America, given the racial aversion and history that's still out there...However, an extraordinary, gifted, and talented young man who happens to be black can be president."[83]

How did Obama make this distinction? He played his race both ways by ignoring, or minimizing it, in front of white audiences while utilizing the traditional political support structure available to black politicians. Journalist Gwen Ifill called it a "racial straddle."[84] Parts of his speech to the 2004 Democratic National Convention illustrated his approach before predominantly white audiences: "There's not a black America and white America and Latino America and Asian America; there's the United States of America."[85] That was the set-up, the introduction to national politics that would help create his political image as a nonthreatening (to many whites, at least) black man. Obama did not emphasize race in his announcement speech. Instead, he talked about Lincoln, generational change, and various critical public policy challenges.[86]

Not emphasizing race had another important advantage, as Ifill points out: "Since white opinion leaders rarely engaged in race-specific conversations and largely found them uncomfortable, color blindness was considered a good thing. They were willing to embrace a black man who did not make them feel guilty about race."[87]

Obama tapped into resources that traditional black politicians used. For example, he talked to prominent black disc jockeys Steve Harvey, Michael Baisden, and Tom Joyner. They, in turn, promoted his candidacy.[88] According to Rep. Jesse Jackson, Jr., black radio is "probably the most central vehicle for communicating with the masses of African-Americans."[89]

Another resource that Obama used to appeal to blacks was *how* he talked. According to sociologist Michael Eric Dyson, Obama's speeches can charm blacks while simultaneously leaving many whites clueless. In January 2008, while campaigning in South Carolina, he spoke to a largely black audience about how some of his recent comments about Ronald Reagan were being distorted. "They're trying to bamboozle you...It's the same old okie-dokie. Y'all know about okie dokie, right?...They try to bamboozle you. Hoodwink ya. Try to hoodwink ya." Obama also addressed the issue whether he was really a Muslim in the speech: "I've been a member of the same church for almost 20 years, prayin' to Jesus—*wit'* my Bible."[90]

Dyson interprets Obama's speech in the following way: "Ironically, in style and substance, Obama's flight of rhetoric echoed...Malcolm X—or at least the one portrayed in Spike Lee's biopic...Obama was making a risky move that played to inside-group understanding even as he campaigned in the white mainstream: While denying that he was Muslim, he fastened onto the rhetoric of the most revered Black Muslim, mimicking his tone and rhythm beat for beat....But if you weren't familiar with black culture, most of what he said and how he said it went right over your head—and beyond your ears."[91]

To some people, however, Obama was not authentically black. For example, political pollster Gerald Goldhaber wrote that "Some blacks are saying, 'This guy is not one of us,' that he has not experienced discrimination or poverty."[92] Writer Stanley Crouch penned a famous newspaper column in 2006 titled *What Obama Isn't: Black Like Me.* In it, he declared that "Obama did not—does not—share a heritage with the majority of black Americans, who are descendents of plantation slaves....While he has experienced some light versions of typical racial stereotypes, he cannot claim those problems as his own—nor has he lived the life of a black American."[93]

The hullabaloo over his racial identity went to the very core of his status as an underdog. If he really was not black, then he was not as pure of an underdog as blacks who were descended from plantation slaves. This, in turn, implies that he has not suffered as much, and does not deserve as much sympathy and empathy associated with traditional black underdogs.

Even if he was not descended from plantation slaves, the critical choices he made in his personal and professional life revealed his commitment to American blacks. Political scientist Carol Swain commented that "Barack Obama says he's black. He's married to a black woman and he has black children. That makes him black enough for me and I believe most of the people."[94]

Obama did not have the overwhelming support of the majority of the black Democratic political establishment when he started his presidential bid. After all, frontrunner Hillary Clinton was married to Bill Clinton, "the first black president."[95] Many blacks were split between their support for Hillary Clinton and Obama. A June 2007 poll of black Democrats found 43 percent favored Clinton while 42 percent preferred Obama. According to Mark Mallory, the black mayor of Cincinnati, "Hillary is sort of a political institution and Barrack is a new face on the scene."[96]

One reason why black Democrats were divided was that many did not believe Obama could actually become president. There was simply too much prejudice for him to overcome to win in 2008.[97] As law professor Richard Thompson Ford observed, "Better not to get one's hopes up; in the end, racist white America will always disappoint."[98] In this way, he had another characteristic of an underdog: he was expected to lose.

To many, his victory in the Iowa caucus changed all of that. Whites had overwhelmingly voted for him in Middle America. All of sudden (or at least seemingly for some) maybe his race would not cripple his chances for the ultimate political victory. *If* that was the case, then maybe he was not so much of an underdog after all.

Another obstacle to Obama winning was the symbolic component of Hillary Clinton's candidacy. If she won, she would become the first woman U.S. president. The core question for many progressives was this: who represented the biggest underdog group? Was it blacks or women? It was this implicit narrative that helped drive the fierceness of their rivalry.

There was one person who helped complicate this narrative: Oprah Winfrey, the most famous black woman in the United States. Winfrey knew Obama personally and both were from Chicago. She plugged his potential candidacy in 2006 and officially endorsed his presidential bid in 2007.[99] Her support was critical for potential women voters for Obama because of her popularity among women; in 2007, Winfrey was the most admired woman by American women. Hillary Clinton was second.[100]

Writing in December 2007, political analyst Dick Morris predicted the importance of Oprah's endorsement: "She is iconic to women of all races; to them she's a woman who is black, not a black who is female. So her refusal to endorse a fellow female seeking the presidency is tremendously significant to women voters."[101]

Was Oprah's endorsement a sell-out for women? To many, it was. She received numerous negative comments on her Web site. For example, one writer claimed she was picking her race over the fact she was a woman.[102] A writer to a *Los Angeles Times* blog thought that Oprah forgot who had made her rich and famous: "Why I was upset with Oprah is that she [got] her billion dollars because she had her show for WOMEN—men did not cause her rise to fame. Women backed her...She knows better than anyone the struggles women have to be treated equally and fairly and she jumped right into Obama's arms telling us he could walk on water."[103]

Another *Los Angeles Times* blogger displayed his anger over this line of thinking: "It's annoying to hear progressive women complain that to be a feminist obligates one to vote for a woman. That's ridiculous. In fact, no single demographic group has it harder in the U.S. then black men—incarceration rates, disenfranchisement, lack of education, HIV."[104] Translated: black men are the biggest underdogs.

Oprah Winfrey was a symbol of the power of women. When one of the most powerful women in the United States urged her core audience (women) to vote for a man over a woman, then that was sure to have an effect on the nomination race. According to economists Craig Garthwaite and Tim Moore, it was a decisive factor.[105] Their research suggested that her "endorsement...had statistically and politically significant effects on Obama's political outcomes. Winfrey's involvement increased the share of the vote and the campaign contributions received by Obama, as well as the overall level of voter participation."[106]

On the day of the 2008 New Hampshire primary campaign, publisher and activist Gloria Steinem penned an op-ed in the *New York Times* that directly addressed the gender-race battle. Titled "Women Are Never Front-Runners," she wrote that the racial barrier in politics is taken more seriously than the sex barrier. She listed specific reasons why this was so, including the (mistaken) association between human nature and sexism and how men react to women who are powerful. She also said, "I'm not advocating a competition for who have it toughest. The caste systems of sex and race are interdependent and can only be uprooted together.... Both [Obama and Clinton] will need a coalition of outsiders to win a general election."[107]

Although Steinem denied that she was pushing a battle between who was the greatest underdog, it certainly seemed that way to some. For example, Richard Slotkin responded angrily to her op-ed in this way: "for Steinem to indulge in competitive victimology is inane and self-defeating—the sort of academic exercise that divides progressives who have fought against both racism and sexism."[108] Rachael Noguera wrote, "This is an old argument to pit the ism of gender versus race. Sadly white feminists are still stuck in this debate from the 70s."[109]

The generational divide was vital in understanding how the gender-race battle played out, ultimately to Obama's advantage. Author Gwen

Ifill recounted the observations of Dianne Bystrom, the director of the Women and Politics Center at Iowa State University:[110] She "noticed that young women, in particular, did not necessarily consider it a test of sisterhood to embrace sixty-year-old Hillary Clinton."[111] It was women who propelled Obama to victory in Iowa, the state that made him the candidate to catch. Obama won 35 percent of the women Democratic caucus participants to Clinton's 30 percent. This was significant because 57 percent of the participants were women.[112]

Could Obama be considered the underdog after his Iowa victory? National polling from January until late February 2008 found Clinton and Obama relatively close to each other during this time. However, from late February until late May 2008, Obama led Clinton in most national polls.[113] Thus from late February on, Obama could no longer be considered the national underdog to win the nomination.

The date when Obama turned into the clear frontrunner was February 5 or Super Tuesday. He won thirteen states to Clinton's ten.[114] Although the contests that day were split almost evenly, the momentum had swung to Obama. As liberal blogger Markos Moulitsas Zúñiga stated on February 6: "it should be obvious that the race has shifted and the Clinton campaign is reeling and Obama is now the front-runner. Obama is going to lead in pledged delegates after Super Tuesday."[115]

It was around this time where Hillary's campaign experimented with portraying her as the underdog. For example, right *before* the Super Tuesday Kansas caucus, Dan Lykins, the Kansas Democratic Party treasurer (and Clinton supporter), brought up the David and Goliath analogy. Guess who was David? Hillary Clinton.[116]

After Super Tuesday, however, Hillary Clinton's campaign tried to embrace the underdog image in a more programmatic fashion. On February 6, the Clinton campaign made a conference call to reporters where they tried to pin the label of establishment candidate on Obama. Was this a tactical move, or did it reflect the reality of the campaign as it stood then? Both. Clinton wanted to lower the expectations of how she would do over the next few contests. As Brian Montopoli blogged, "If Clinton the 'underdog' loses those races, it's a lesser blow than if Clinton the 'frontrunner' does."[117] Later that day, however, she also revealed that she had lent her campaign $5 million in late January.[118] That could indicate that she was expecting to lose, *unless* she infused her campaign with money.

While acknowledging his better position as a result of the Super Tuesday results, the Obama campaign would not cede the underdog image to Hillary: "Two weeks ago we were a big underdog...Now we are a slight underdog."[119] The remarkable success of Obama's fundraising would seem to contradict Obama's claim that he was *still* the underdog. Obama raised $32 million in January alone. He also raised $5.8 million within 24 hours after Super Tuesday. By contrast, Hillary Clinton raised just $13 million in January.[120]

The most difficult moment of the nomination campaign for Obama was in March, when controversial videos of his pastor Reverend Wright appeared on ABC News and the Internet. One of the most inflammatory was the following:

> The United States of America government, when it came to treating her citizens of Indian descent fairly, she failed. She put them on reservations. When it came to treating her citizens of Japanese descent fairly, she failed. She put them in internment prison camps. When it came to treating her citizens of African descent fairly, America failed. She put them in chains, the government put them on slave quarters, put them on auction blocks, put them in cotton field, put them in inferior schools, put them in substandard housing, put them in scientific experiments, put them in the lowest paying jobs, put them outside the equal protection of the law, kept them out of their racist bastions of higher education and locked them into positions of hopelessness and helplessness. The government gives them the drugs, builds bigger prisons, passes a three-strike law and then wants us to sing "God Bless America." No, no, no, not God Bless America. God damn America—that's in the Bible—for killing innocent people. God damn America, for treating our citizens as less than human.[121]

Those words stung. It cut to the core of white guilt—that the United States was hypocritical in practicing its ideals and had not lived up to the self-image that is taught to its schoolchildren. The media pounced on Wright's remarks and suddenly the rising young star was in trouble. What would Obama do?

Obama decided to tackle the controversy directly, with a speech he made in Philadelphia on March 18. Obama called Wright's contentious comments divisive and wrong. He also sought to place the political storm that had been created in historical context. He talked about moving forward, acknowledging the righteousness of black anger and the need to relate the grievances associated with it to the broader American community: "For the African-American community, that path means embracing the burdens of our past without becoming victims of our past. It means continuing to insist on a full measure of justice in every aspect of American life. But it also means binding our particular grievances—for better health care, and better schools, and better jobs—to the larger aspirations of all Americans—the white woman struggling to break the glass ceiling, the white man whose been laid off, the immigrant trying to feed his family."[122]

Obama also spoke to white anger: "a similar anger exists within segments of the white community. Most working- and middle-class white Americans don't feel that they have been particularly privileged by their race. Their experience is the immigrant experience—as far as they're concerned, no one's handed them anything, they've built it from scratch. They've worked hard all their lives, many times only to see their jobs shipped overseas or their pension dumped after a lifetime of labor."[123]

Obama empathized with blacks *and* whites. Writer Robert Creamer labeled his speech a political home run. In particular, he "made it clear to all who listened that he was absolutely 'on their side.' He demonstrated a knowledge and empathy for both sides of the racial equation."[124] Empathy is a core part of the underdog appeal. Obama demonstrated both the width and the depth of his empathy with this speech.

Obama also rhetorically joined the plight of blacks as underdogs to the need for national unity:

> In the white community, the path to a more perfect union means acknowledging that what ails the African-American community does not just exist in the minds of black people; that the legacy of discrimination—and current incidents of discrimination, while less overt than in the past—are real and must be addressed. Not just with words, but with deeds—by investing in our schools and our communities; by enforcing our civil rights laws and ensuring fairness in our criminal justice system; by providing this generation with ladders of opportunity that were unavailable for previous generations.[125]

A more perfect union would not only tangibly help the conditions of black economic underdogs, but it would also strengthen the American political creed. Some political scientists thought that, no matter how brilliant the speech was, Obama still might not get past the divisiveness of race. Stephen Schneck: "The Philly speech was strong, but one wondered if it is enough.... nothing in American politics is more divisive or more volatile than race: not political parties, not ideology, not abortion, not gun rights, not war and peace." Susan B. Hansen: "I'm afraid the dilemma for Obama is that the more he talks about race being unimportant or transcended, the more important it will become to the media and voters' perceptions."[126]

Obama was forced to talk about race again in late April when Reverend Wright made some new controversial comments. Wright claimed his sermons were being distorted and that the black church was being attacked.[127] To make matters worse, in late May a guest pastor at Trinity United Church of Christ made additional controversial statements. Rev. Michael Pfleger claimed Hillary Clinton was crying (right before the New Hampshire primary) because "a black man [was] stealing my show." Later that month, Obama and his wife Michelle formally withdrew their membership from the church where Wright had preached, Trinity United Church of Christ.[128]

Hillary and Obama fought an extraordinarily close battle throughout the spring of 2008. It was not until early June when Obama clinched the nomination.[129] How did he win? Perhaps the most significant reason was his early opposition to the Iraq War. The boldness and clarity of his position provided a sharp contrast with Hillary Clinton.

Iraq

In October 2002, Obama made his famous speech where he came out against the looming invasion of Iraq. He thought the upcoming war was unintelligent and ideological: "I am opposed to a dumb war . . . I am opposed to . . . the cynical attempt by Richard Perle and Paul Wolfowitz and other armchair, weekend warriors . . . to shove their own ideological agendas down our throats." He also believed the upcoming war was partisan: "I am opposed to . . . the attempt by political hacks like Karl Rove to distract us from a rise in the uninsured, a rise in the poverty rate . . . [and] a drop in the median income."[130] Later that month, U.S. Senator Hillary Clinton voted for the war.[131]

The Iraq War became a major issue during the nomination battle. Clinton refused to unambiguously admit that she made a mistake in voting for the war.[132] This was not a casual decision by her; it was made because of her belief in executive leadership and political calculations.[133] The political angle was obvious as Democratic consultant Bob Shrum explains, "I think there's this tremendous desire in her campaign not to get into a position where you're identified with traditional Democratic views."[134] Translation: the 2008 Democratic Presidential nominee cannot be seen as weak on national security.

In what ways was Obama's opposition to the Iraq war an underdog position? Was it a stance that could contribute to an electoral defeat? To a key part of the electorate, his initial antiwar speech was *not* an underdog position. According to Michael Crowley of the *New Republic*, his stance was a popular one with liberals in the 2004 Democratic primary for the Illinois U.S. Senate seat. Obama was eyeing that nomination. Liberals were part of the coalition that Obama was trying to put together.[135] Obama's stance was not even an underdog position *within* Illinois: state-wide polling in 2002 found that only 17 percent believed the United States should attack Iraq regardless of support from allies. Approximately 69 percent were against any attack, or believed an attack should be started only with allied support.[136]

His October 2002 position on the Iraq War matched the mood of the nation in this way: even though there was substantial support for using force on Iraq, there was no national majority support for a unilateral invasion of Iraq.[137] It did not correlate with the national mood in another way: Obama's choice of words and his presence at an antiwar rally did not complement the "rally around the flag" syndrome that the Bush Administration was trying to create within the country.

Fundamentally, Obama's initial stand on the Iraq War was core underdog. A politician who wore a lapel pin that said, *"war is not an option,"* and attended a rally that featured a marching skeleton[138] is usually not thought of as presidential timber. How did those images harmonize with the public perception of what a commander in chief looks like? If one planed to limit their political career to a safely liberal congressional district, or *perhaps* to a U.S. Senate seat, then these images were not a major concern. But could a future president speak out against a looming war with the following words? "We may have occasion in our lifetime to once again rise up in defense of our freedom, and pay the wages of war. But we ought not—we will not—travel down that hellish path blindly. Nor should we allow those who would march off and pay the ultimate sacrifice, who would prove the full measure of devotion with their blood, to make such an awful sacrifice in vain."[139]

Isn't he inferring that future U.S. casualties of an Iraq War *could* be in vain? That sounds similar to George McGovern in 1972 or Howard Dean in 2003. It is also potentially explosive, as political philosopher Michael Walzer wrote in *Just and Unjust Wars*: it "seems important to say of those who die in war *that they did not die in vain*. And when we can't say that, or think we can't, we mix our mourning with anger."[140]

In February 2007, Obama was more direct; he told an Iowa audience, "We ended up launching a war that should have never been authorized, and should never been waged, and on which we have now spent $400 billion, and have seen over 3,000 lives of the bravest young Americans wasted."[141] He later said his statement was a "slip of the tongue."[142] At a

July 2007 debate in Charleston, South Carolina, he said that American troops were not dying in vain in Iraq.[143]

Obama would have jeopardized his presidential candidacy by stating that Americans were dying in vain in Iraq. Why? Because that would have been too raw, a cut too close to the bone for many Americans. How does one publicly admit the futility of thousands of military deaths and *simultaneously* get elected as commander in chief of the military? That's a mission impossible. In this way, he chose not to start a fight that he would lose. In this respect, he did not embrace the underdog position.

Some believe that his anti-Iraq War stand was the biggest factor in his party nomination victory. Author Justin Raimondo wrote in February 2008 that "This is the real source of Obama's streak of solid victories...It's all about his opposition to the Iraq War."[144] Political analyst Chuck Todd believed that Obama's position on Iraq is what "gave him his initial presidential credibility" and that Iraq could have drove him to his nomination victory.[145] Stephen Zunes, professor of politics at the University of San Francisco, viewed the results of the race from another angle: "The most significant reason Clinton lost...was Iraq....If Clinton had apologized for her vote or come out against the war earlier...she would have probably won the nomination."[146]

Nomination Campaign Strategy

Another key part of his success was the resources he put into caucus states. Hillary Clinton paid comparatively little attention to them.[147] Many of these caucus states were states that were either toss-ups in the general election or trended Republican ("red" states).

The campaign's deliberate targeting of Democratic voters in "red" states was critical to his win. These are the true underdogs of the Democratic Party *as a party*; voters who usually see their candidates lose and are mostly forgotten by their party's presidential campaigns. Many of them are Democrats who reside in states that are sparsely populated and usually vote Republican in November. Like Idaho Democrats. Or Kansas Democrats.

Consider Idaho. The recent atmosphere for Democrats there has been bleak. Writing in 2005, James B. Weatherly and Randy Stapilus detected a negative feedback loop: "Democrats...have suffered from diminishing expectations as losses have led to expectations of loss—and a resulting diminished ability to field quality candidates, raise money and find volunteer help. News media reports, not only opinion columns but also news articles in Idaho, often describe Democratic candidates, even many months ahead of the election, as longshots or underdogs. That further undercuts Democrats' ability to compete."[148]

Nevertheless, Obama had twenty paid staff members in the state while it has been speculated that Hillary Clinton had none.[149] Obama came to Boise right before the caucus and drew almost 15,000 people to an arena.[150] Kathie Brack was at the arena and was surprised that Obama had come to the state: "It never happens...Everybody just gives up on Idaho."[151] Everybody, that is, except for candidates who are attracted to underdogs.

Obama won the February 5 caucus with 79 percent of the vote and 15 (out of 18) delegates.[152] The last time Idaho voted for a Democrat for president was 1964.[153] The recollections of Kootenai County caucus attendee Logan Stoodley reflect the enthusiasm and idealism that makes underdogs attractive to so many people: "I listened as Obama won 1015 votes (81%) in Kootenai County...in this room full of pasty white people, Barack Obama kicked ass....In a staunchly Republican area, over 1000 people came in support of a Democratic candidate...I think that Obama can win Idaho. I honestly do, and with Clinton off on the 'caucus states don't matter and that the small red states don't matter' diatribe, I am proud that my candidate of choice sees that this is wrong."[154]

Kansas had not voted Republican for president since 1964 either. Before that, the last time the state voted for a Democrat president was in 1936.[155] In late January, Obama came to El Dorado, Kansas, the home of his maternal grandmother. He spoke to a crowd at Butler County Community College, where he was endorsed by Democratic Governor Kathleen Sebelius. A young African American college student who attended the rally spoke about the importance of Obama's appearance and campaign: "This is something this community wouldn't usually get during an election year...We've all lived in Kansas our whole lives, so we know what the whole 'red state' thing is about. This is the first time someone from the Democrats is really trying to do something for the state of Kansas. It's about time."[156]

Obama devoted more resources to Kansas than Clinton did. In January 2008, the Clinton campaign had three organizers in Kansas while Obama had 18.[157] Obama handily defeated Clinton in the February 5 caucus 74 to 16 percent.[158]

Obama's plan to win "red" states was not a dreamy attempt to equalize the importance of Democratic voters in the party's nomination process. Instead, it was part of a well-thought out, and highly pragmatic, strategy to win. He successfully tapped into the feelings of isolation and unimportance that many red state Democrats experience, vis-à-vis their party's presidential candidates. Many red state Democrats just wanted to be acknowledged; Obama did just that by personally campaigning in many of these states.

Was he "using" the feelings of perceived discrimination by red state Democrats to further his own goal of winning the nomination? Absolutely. However, this is not as Machiavellian as it might seem. It is evident that empathy is an important part of what makes him who he is. Moreover, his biography provided numerous instances in which he acted on his empathy. He seemed to have satisfied the need for recognition by these underdogs just by his very presence.

In this way, Obama can be seen as Rorschach test. As writer Roger L. Simon puts it, "You get to project on him what you *think* he is or what you want him to be."[159] Many Democrats in Idaho and Kansas wanted to see him as their hero; finally a Democratic presidential

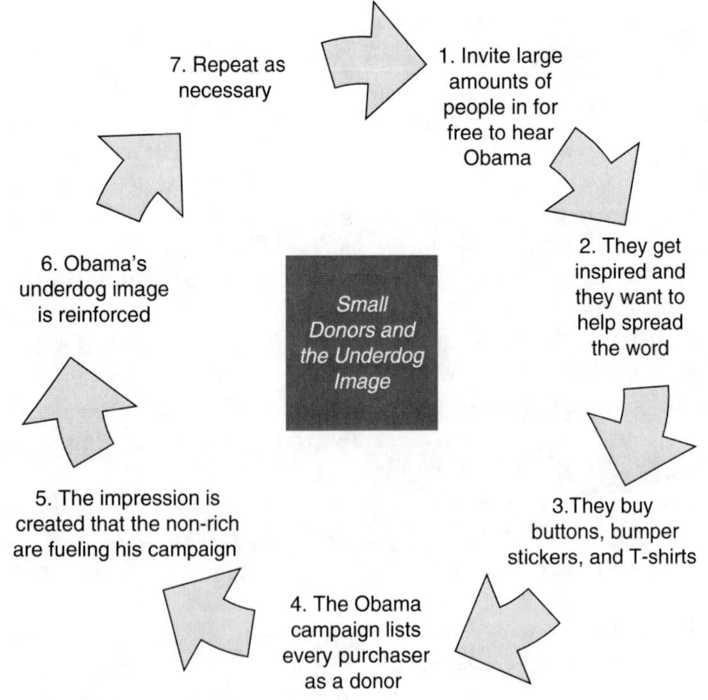

Figure 8.1   Small donors and the underdog image

candidate who acknowledged their existence. In terms of recognition, there was at least a *little* less inequality for the forgotten, red state Democrats.

Obama attracted a lot of small donors to his campaign. The numbers were startling. In the second quarter of 2007, Obama raised approximately $11 million in small donations of less than $200. This contrasted with Hillary Clinton's $2.3 million from small donors in the same quarter.[160] This helped energize his underdog image as a Democratic presidential candidate who was attracting the support of people who could only afford to pay $10, $25, or $50. If he got elected, maybe he might pay more attention, and more important act upon, the concerns of the nonrich. Perhaps equality and fairness would make their way into more public policies should Obama get elected.

These numbers impressed his competitors and dazzled the media. *How* they were created is instructive in understanding how his underdog image was created. Obama attracted large crowds throughout 2007. On one occasion, he spoke to 10,000 people in Oakland, California. $40,000 was spent that day on buttons, baseball caps, and other paraphernalia. Every person who bought an item that day was listed as a contributor.[161] See figure 8.1 for the formula.

Fundraising and the Internet

Another way that the Obama campaign bolstered his underdog image was through his use of the Internet. His campaign hired talented people who were instrumental in harnessing it for political support and donations. For example, the staff included Facebook cofounder Chris Hughes, and Joe Rospars, who had worked for Howard Dean's 2004 presidential race. Writing in October 2008, journalist Mark Hennessey described how the campaign Web site empowered supporters: "its real genius has been to involve supporters as fund-raisers themselves. They can set up their own page, set a fund-raising target for themselves and then approach friends via e-mail, again and again if necessary, to get them to contribute."[162]

The Obama online campaign, known as Triple O, was hugely successful. The numbers were staggering. In excess of $500 million was raised in this campaign. This was made up of $6.5 million in donations and three million individual contributors, with $80 as the average gift.[163] Online social networking sites were also used extensively; Obama had 2,379,102 Facebook supporters and 833,161 Myspace friends. This compares to John McCain's 620,359 Facebook supporters and 217,811

Myspace friends. Obama also had many more Twitter followers than McCain: 112,474 to 4,603.[164]

The use of the Internet can be interpreted as a great equalizing force in politics. All you needed was access to a personal computer to build support for your candidate. This was power exercised by millions of people who did not necessarily need to leave their home. Although the campaign also had its share of large donors who contributed through the traditional high-priced dinners, supporters did not need to attend them in order to make a difference. Small donors were not at such a great disadvantage, vis-à-vis political power, as they might have been before the widespread use of online political contributions.

The link between underdogs and contributors to Obama's campaign was centered on quantity and method. Obama's campaign represented a noticeable shift for recent Democratic presidential candidates in both the sheer number of contributors and how people contributed. As Obama fundraiser Mark Gorenberg observed in 2008: "If the typical Gore event was 20 people in a living room writing six-figure checks...and the Kerry event was 2,000 people in a hotel ballroom writing four-figure checks, this year for Obama we have stadium rallies of 20,000 people who pay absolutely nothing, and then go home and contribute a few dollars online."[165]

Although the image of Obama's donors was that of the "ordinary guy,"[166] the reality was more complicated. The conceptual link with political equality is, of course, contingent upon the availability of computer use to people with limited financial resources, such as economic underdogs. In addition, a report by the Campaign Finance Institute found that only about 25 percent of his contributions "came from donors whose total contributions *aggregated* to $200 or less." Moreover, contributions from large donors to his campaign outpaced small donations by 80 percent.[167] Some of Obama's most important contributors were "bundlers," whose job was to put together a large amount of money in one place from individual small donations. As of August 2008, $63.2 million (at a minimum) was raised by 561 of them for Obama.[168]

In what way does this fund-raising represent the interests of the economically disadvantaged? Aren't these people the functional equivalent of George W. Bush's "Pioneers," "Rangers," and "Super Rangers," an elite group of Republican fundraisers who helped in his 2000 and 2004 presidential elections?[169]

Furthermore, Obama also decided to not accept public financing for the general election campaign.[170] Although he never stated that he would actually use the system, he did say he would "aggressively pursue an agreement with the Republican nominee to preserve a publicly financed general election."[171] He was harshly criticized by some, including journalist Liz Sidoti: "Barack Obama chose winning over his word.... The chance to financially swamp John McCain—and maneuver for an enormous general election advantage—proved too great an allure."[172] The philosophy behind public financing of presidential elections was pure reform; it was set up (at least in part) in response to Richard Nixon's actions in his 1972 reelection campaign. It was designed to lessen the influence of money on elections, a goal that would, by definition, help economic underdogs.

From another perspective, however, his quest for the White House did remodel campaign finance—just not in the way that many liberal reformers envisioned. Writing in June 2008, Joshua Green observed, "In a sense, Obama represents a triumph of campaign-finance reform. He has not, of course, gotten the money out of politics...But he has realized the reformers' big goal of ending the system whereby a handful of rich donors control the political process. He has not done this by limiting money but by adding much, much more of it—democratizing the system by flooding it with so many new contributors that their combined effect dilutes the old guard to the point that it scarcely poses any threat."[173]

It is difficult to show a *consistent* analytical link between how the Obama campaign was financed and the concept of the underdog. There is evidence to suggest both the embrace of the underdog spirit and a pull back from it. The crux of the analytical inconsistency is centered on money. Can underdog interests be successfully fought for if one gets to office via huge sums of private money, even if that money is raised in small amounts and by means of decentralization?

Nonetheless, the importance of the Internet to his operation cannot be overstated. After the campaign was over, Chris Hughes commented on the transformational potential of the Internet on politics: "What we've learned...is that there's huge potential for people that haven't been involved in politics to discover that, yes, this is something that impacts me. Even before I joined the campaign, the fundamental premise was to help put the political process into people's own hands. That was the value from the start of the campaign, that was the value at the end of the campaign, and it's not going away."[174]

Showing citizens that politics does affect them and taking away (slowly and incompletely) the power that traditional elites have on the political process are significant political developments. They are underdog concepts, in that they are expected to be ultimately unsuccessful. They may be high ideals that conform to the American political creed, but many believe they just do not work.

There are powerful forces that operate to obfuscate the link between politics and people. They may be

- **Ignorance:** people do not want to become educated to learn about issues and controversies.
- **Fear:** people do not *want* to see how politics affects them. Why? Because if they perceive the links, they might find it more difficult to rationalize their own political inaction.
- **Laziness:** it is easier to let other people make decisions for the country.

Fighting to weaken the link between economic elites and their disproportionate influence on the political process is another sure loser. Fear is at play here as well: many people are afraid that control of the political process, even if dislodged from forces that work to maintain the status quo, will not last. They do not want to be habitually set up for disappointment. So they refuse to believe that genuine change is ever possible. As the British rock band The Who sang in 1971, we "Won't Get Fooled Again."[175]

Cynicism

Another powerful force that conceals the link between politics and people is cynicism. The following laments from the politically disappointed are commonplaces: "The game is rigged." "Eventually, they find a way to maintain their power." "They change the rules whenever they want." English professor David Mazella wrote in *The Making of Modern Cynicism*, that "cynicism...provokes suspicion, anger, disillusion, and distrust among those who care about politics."[176]

Cynicism can also threaten democracy, or at least British democracy, according to a 2008 Study from the London School of Economics. Their Syntony (equilibrium and harmony[177]) research team was in the process of creating an index of cynicism. This index would use socioeconomic backgrounds, gender, race, religion, and age categories to classify the measurement of their emotional responses. A recent survey involving the Royal Society of Arts found that the average cynicism level for politics came in at 51 percent—higher than for the media (37 percent), life (31 percent), and business (30 percent).[178]

Researcher Dr. Alain Samson stated that "our most important finding suggested that people who did not vote were more likely to be cynical about the government than distrusting." He believes that the price for this can be political disengagement. It could also lead to direct action and violence.[179]

Can the British study be analytically linked to American democracy? There is not a direct link because British culture, history, and politics are obviously distinct from that of the United States. It is not unreasonable to suggest their research may have some important correlations with the impact of cynicism on American democracy. After all, as author Duncan Watts writes in *Understanding American Politics: A Comparative Guide*: "the countries are linked by . . . a number of common ideals and values . . . there has been continuity of free and representative government, a preference for gradual rather than revolutionary change and a commitment to individual freedom."[180]

Obama spoke about the power of cynicism at a meeting of the Democratic National Committee (DNC) meeting in February 2007:

> Our rivals won't be one another, and I would assert it won't even be the other party. It's going to be cynicism that we're fighting against. It's the cynicism that's borne from decades of disappointment, amplified by talk radio and twenty-four-hour news cycles, reinforced by the relentless pounding of negative ads that have become the staple of modern politics. It's a cynicism that asks us to believe that our opponents are never just wrong, but they're bad; that our motives in politics can never be pure, that they're only driven by power and by greed; that the challenges today aren't just daunting, but they're impossible.[181]

The most corrosive component of cynicism is how it can affect people. It can generate, and perpetuate, a political discourse that is based on frightened self-censorship. As Obama said, "Too often, this cynicism makes us afraid to say what we believe. It makes us afraid. We don't trust the truth."[182]

If politicians do not trust themselves enough to tell the public the truth (as they see it), then on what basis can citizens make decisions as to whom to elect? A common saying is "In war, truth is the first causality." "In politics, too," a cynic may add. In this way, Obama is fighting for a core underdog concept; a belief that the majority of the voting public are ready to hear politicians speak their truth. Not only that, but that both election results and public policies will be affected by a discourse made up of contending truths, at least to a *greater extent* than it has recently been.

Critics contend that this is bound to fail. It is a complete and fundamental misunderstanding of politics. Most people do not want to hear this; it would require the public to consciously set priorities and make difficult tradeoffs. It could also make visible the unstated assumptions that so much of politics is based on. It is easier for politicians to rule using deliberate exaggeration and needless complexity.

It is also easier for citizens to take the easy way out by using the utilitarian "they" as a way to generically describe the actions of politicians and government. In that way, individuals do not have to make distinctions between policies, candidates, or parties. It is a method to avoid responsibility.

This fight against cynicism is bound to fall short and disappoint. Then why does Obama fight against cynicism? Because that is what underdogs do.

General Election

According to national polls, Obama was the front-runner for most of the general election campaign.[183] McCain really was the underdog. He tried to communicate that image during the last few months of the campaign. Several headlines illustrate this point.

- *USA Today* on August 22: "McCain casts himself as the 'underdog' in '08"[184]
- The *Guardian* on October 14: "McCain plays valiant underdog as once-loyal south looks uncertain"[185]
- *The Independent* on October 22: "'Underdog' McCain slams 'confident' rival"[186]

The tactic did not work. McCain never came back to win. Obama was elected president on November 4 with 52.9 percent of the popular vote and 67.8 percent of the Electoral College vote.[187]

In a television interview that aired in October 2008, Michelle Obama observed, "when he first decided to announce, no one thought he had any shot at winning this thing."[188] The truth was that the Obama campaign represented, and appealed to, deeper elements of the underdog concept than John McCain did.

Obama's election was an event that strengthened the story of America, at least the story that most people want to believe. British historian Tristram Hunt described what had occurred as a result of Obama: he "brings the narrative that everyone wants to return to—that America is the land of extraordinary opportunity and possibility, where miracles happen."[189] The underdog had made history.

As President (So Far)

When he entered office (even during the transition), Barack Obama was faced with trying to manage a severe economic crisis. In the winter of 2008–2009, the United States was experiencing a sharp economic down-town that was traumatizing the nation. The most significant action that Obama took to help jumpstart the economy was his stimulus bill. Signed into law on February 17, 2009, the $787 billion package contained numerous provisions designed to help the economy.[190] According to the White House Council of Economic Advisors, they included "increased spending on programs like unemployment insurance and Food Stamps; checks to state and local governments...and direct government spending on infrastructure, education...[and] energy efficiency."[191] Many of these provisions helped the economically disadvantaged, most notably the unemployed and people who qualify for food stamps.

Obama also signed legislation that helped additional children get health insurance, a bill that made pay discrimination litigation easier to start, and one that greatly expanded the Americorps program.[192]

Perhaps the most explicit support of life's underdogs came after Supreme Court Justice David Souter announced his retirement in the spring of 2009. President Obama talked about what characteristics he wanted to see in a new justice:

> I will seek somebody with a sharp and independent mind and a record of excellence and integrity. I will seek someone who understands that justice isn't about some abstract legal theory or footnote in a case book. It is also about how our laws affect the daily realities of people's lives— whether they can make a living and care for their families; whether they feel safe in their homes and welcome in their own nation. I view that quality of empathy, of understanding and identifying with people's hopes and struggles as an essential ingredient for arriving at just decisions and outcomes.[193]

There, he said it. Empathy. The E word. His use of the word set off an initial ideological panic among some conservatives. For example, Republican U.S. Senator Orrin Hatch was ostensibly confused about what Obama meant with the word: "What does that mean? Usually that's a code word for an activist judge."[194] Conservatives also pointed to Obama's July 2007 talk to Planned Parenthood as evidence of his dangerous disposition in viewing law within the prism of social class and power: "I think the Constitution can be interpreted in so many ways.... (including one) that says that the courts are the refuge of the powerless, because oftentimes they may lose in the democratic back-and-forth. They may be locked out and prevented from fully participating in the democratic process."[195]

Then he mentioned empathy again to describe how law applies to different types of people: "we need somebody who's got...the empathy to recognize what it's like to be a young, teenaged mom; the empathy to understand what it's like to be poor or African-American or gay or disabled or old. And that's the criteria by which I'm going to be selecting my judges."[196]

Orange County Register editorial writer Alan Brock does not like empathy being accentuated: "The goddess Justitia is depicted as blindfolded to remind us that the law is supposed to be no respecter of persons, that it shouldn't matter whether a litigant is black, white, male, female, straight, gay, rich, poor, powerful, powerless. Justice consists of dispensing legal opinions impartially."[197]

Republican National Committee Chairman Michael Steele was also troubled by Obama's use of empathy: "Sounds like the president's been watching *Dr. Phil* too much."[198] *Meet the Press* host David Gregory prodded Steele and DNC Chairman Tim Kaine into a debate on the controversy on May 17, 2009. Their back and forth is instructive in learning how each party views this core ingredient of the underdog concept:

> *Mr. Steele:* You know, the, party of no is no to judges that are going to sit there and try to come up with some feel-good legislation, effectively, to feel sorry for me, a judge is there to look at the facts and apply the law and come up with the appropriate resolution. through their opinion. That's not the role of a judge. A judge is not there He's—I don't have time for the judge to feel good or bad about an issue.
>
> *Gov. Kaine:* But that's not what the president ever said. He's, he's not...
>
> *Mr. Steele:* He said he's empathetic. Go look up the definition.
>
> *Gov. Kaine:* Right. I, I, I have. And...
>
> *Mr. Steele:* The definition is empathetic is, like, concerned about one's feelings.
>
> *Mr. Gregory:* All right.
>
> *Mr. Steele:* I don't want a judge to be concerned about my feelings.
>
> *Gov. Kaine:* Well, if you guys are against empathy, just stand on that platform.
>
> *Mr. Steele:* I'm not—it's not—look, it's not about...
>
> *Gov. Kaine:* Empathy is something we think's a great value.

> *Mr. Steele:* Come on, Chairman, you know it's not about being against empathy, it's about applying the rule of law and having jurisprudence that you can trust, not a judge who may have had a bad day or be overly sensitive to my condition."[199]

On May 26, 2009, Obama nominated Federal Appeals Court Judge Sonia Sotomayor to replace David Souter on the Supreme Court. Sotomayor's personal story is classic underdog: she grew up in the Bronx and was raised in public housing. Her father died when she was nine and her mother worked as a nurse. She did well in school and received scholarships to Princeton and Yale.[200]

Sotomayor's nomination was praised by many people for different reasons. One reason was her empathy. Law professor Doug Kmiec: "In terms of legal training, the opposition will find it difficult to find any omission in preparation... [as] a trial judge for six years showing a meticulous attention—and yes empathy—for the factual record as it affects real human lives." Law professor Charles Ogletree: "I think she has all the characteristics that he talked about: empathy, experience, judgment."[201]

Explicitly framed as a core issue for the party, empathy is all around for Democrats. The chair of the national party defended it and the Democratic president made his Supreme Court choice based partly on it. The proper role of empathy for a judge came up in Sotomayor's senate conformation hearings. Republican Jeff Sessions of Alabama said, "Empathy for one party is always prejudice against another." Empathy and bias could not be equated, according to Democratic defenders of Sotomayor. Democrat Herb Kohl of Wisconsin said, "Compassion does not mean bias or lack of impartiality. It is meant to remind us that the law is more than an intellectual game, and more than a mental exercise."[202] In early August, 2009, Sotomayor was confirmed by the U.S. Senate and was sworn into the Supreme Court shortly afterward.[203]

Could embracing empathy for underdogs ever have a political downside? Absolutely—when support for them becomes viewed as accepting their identity as victims. That has been, and continues to be, the trap for Democrats. There is another trap for Democrats, when the pull of memory eclipses the necessity of reform.

Conclusion

Balancing the Relationship between Sympathy and Victimization

A potential drawback in sympathizing with the underdog is that one can too easily fall into the trap of becoming a victim. Victims and government do not go well together. Victims look to the government for support, money, apologies, and programs. Victims create more victims. Interest-group liberalism is a key factor in this vicious circle, according to law professor Patrick M. Garry: "Interest-group liberalism has allowed, or at least tolerated, certain groups to define themselves as 'victims.' Such a definition . . . keeps the group in a perpetual state of self-righteous anger and self-pity. Groups have found that, within interest-group liberalism, political power lies in proving that they are indeed victims. Yet the maintenance of this power requires that the victims continue celebrating their victimization, which in turn leads other groups . . . to compete for power by defining themselves as victims."[204]

Because Democrats are associated with interest-group liberalism, any harm it may have brought to the country is blamed on the party. People who do not *see* themselves as victims quite naturally begin to resent government when they see their tax dollars increasingly being spent on programs meant to answer the needs of victims.

This brings us to the core ideological quandary for Democrats: how does the party champion the cause of the underdog without allowing their emotional identification with them to overshadow the need to promote individual empowerment? The key is moderation. The famous line of former U.S. Federal Reserve System Chairman William McChesney Martin concerning the Federal Reserve's role is appropriate: "to take away the punch bowl just when the party gets going."[205] According to economist Martin Feldstein, the object of taking away the punch bowl was "to slow the economy down to prevent inflation."[206]

Democrats need to watch how much they drink from the punch bowl of sympathy. If they drink *too* much, their heartfelt empathy with the people who have been discriminated against can turn into a drunken wallowing. The object of taking away the punch bowl is to not allow the public expression of grievances to create societal compassion fatigue.

Balancing the Relationship between Memory and Reform

A lot of Democrats are political romantics; they look to the past for their ideological inspiration and guidance. Some conservatives have noticed this link and find it immoral. In 2000, writer Michael Beran noted, "The civil union between a Romantic exaltation of public power and the policies of the Democratic party—a union over which FDR presided-continues to exercise a corrupting influence on the hearts of the party's tribunes. Not even the most fervent New Democrat rhetoric has succeeded in exorcising the Democrats' Romantic ghosts."[207]

Beran is insightful; Democrats *are* attracted to supporting a romantic hero for President. FDR's four elections and expansion of governmental power was unprecedented in American political history. It is quite natural for Democrats to be drawn back to past successes. It is just that liberal Democrats do not see a union between their party and public power as corrupt. In addition, there are no romantic ghosts, just guiding spirits.

The party, however, can remember *too much*. If reform is the core goal for liberals in the Democratic Party, the power of memory must be disciplined. Excessively looking back to "the good old days" of past electoral and legislative victories, can blind the party to what needs reform *now*.

Nonetheless, Democrats cannot turn their back on the underdog. Fighting for underdog causes is what helps define the party. President Obama defended the need for health care reform with a bipartisan spin in a speech to a joint session of Congress on September 9, 2009: "concern and regard for the plight of others—is not a partisan feeling. It is not a Republican or a Democratic feeling. It...is part of the American character. Our ability to stand in other people's shoes."[208] He is talking about empathy. While empathy is not partisan, it is Democrats who have most consistently fought to act upon its impulses. This was shown again in the fall and early winter of 2009, as the debate on health care reform intensified. Exactly one Republican voted for the final House and Senate bills that were passed in late 2009.

The core issue that President Obama and the Democrats face over this issue is the societal toleration of inequality in health care.[209] In early November 2009, retired physician Larry Donohue recognized the challenge that our nation faced: "we have a historic opportunity to clarify where we will draw the line on tolerance for health care access inequality. Should the line be where inequality crosses into inequity?"[210]

Most Democrats would answer yes; that is where the line should be drawn. But when, precisely, does inequality turn into inequity? That is a difficult question that is at the root of many issues. Nonetheless, Democrats should not shy away from trying to answer it. And underdogs can be thankful that they keep trying.

Notes

1 Introduction

1. David B. Guralnik, ed., *Webster's New World Dictionary, Second College Edition* (New York: Simon and Schuster, 1984), 1546.
2. *Scholastic Pocket Dictionary* (New York: Scholastic, 2005), 567.
3. "Underdog (Competition)," Wikipedia, http://en.wikipedia.org/wiki/Underdog_(competition) (accessed July 26, 2007).
4. "The Mavens' Word of the Day: March 9, 2000," Random House, http://www.randomhouse.com/wotd/index.pperl?date=20000309 (accessed August 2, 2007).
5. William Shepard Walsh, *Handy-book of Literary Curiosities* (Philadelphia: J.B. Lippincott, 1892), 243. Google Book Search. Web. (accessed August 15, 2007).

2 Culture and Underdogs: The Endearing Appeal

1. Stanley K. Schultz, "Foreword," in *Homer Simpson Goes to Washington*, ed. Joseph J. Foy (Lexington: University Press of Kentucky, 2008), viii. Google Book Search. Web. (accessed July 15, 2009).
2. R. T. France, *Jesus the Radical: A Portrait of the Man They Crucified* (Vancouver: Regent College, 1989), 96. Google Book Search. Web. (accessed November 15, 2007).
3. "Deuteronomy 15:11," BiBlos.com, http://bible.cc/deuteronomy/15–11.htm (accessed June 2, 2009).
4. *Holy Bible* Contemporary English Version (New York: American Bible Society, 1995), 640–641.
5. Phillip Yancy, *The Jesus I Never Knew* (Zondervan: Grand Rapids, 1995), 40–41. Google Book Search. Web. (accessed August 16, 2007).
6. Jim Dinn, "What's This 'Preferential Option for the Poor'?" beliefnet, http://www.beliefnet.com/Faiths/Christianity/Catholic/2001/12/Whats-This-Preferential-Option-For-The-Poor.aspx?p=2 (accessed July 30, 2009).
7. Jason Rowe, "Liberation Theology Lives On," Foreign Policy in Focus, November 15, 2007, http://www.fpif.org/fpiftxt/4729 (accessed July 30, 2009).

8. "Liberation Theology," Wikipedia, http://en.wikipedia.org/wiki/Liberation_theology (accessed July 30, 2009) and Joseph Cardinal Ratzinger, "Instruction on Certain Aspects of the 'Theology of Liberation,'" August 6, 1984, Congregation for the Doctrine of the Faith, http://www.vatican.va/roman_curia/congregations/cfaith/documents/rc_con_cfaith_doc_19840806_theology-liberation_en.html (accessed July 30, 2009).

9. Leo G. Perdue, *Reconstructing Old Testament Theology* (Minneapolis, MN: Fortress, 2005), 77–78. Google Book Search. Web. (accessed September 15, 2009).

10. Ratzinger and Ray Hundley, "The Dangers of Liberation Theology," The Mountain Retreat Center for Biblical Theology and Eschatology, http://www.mountainretreatorg.net/articles/dangers_of_liberation_theology.shtml (accessed July 30, 2009).

11. John L. Allen, "With Diaz Nomination, Obama Passes First Major Catholic Test," *National Catholic Reporter,* May 28, 2009, http://ncronline.org/blogs/all-things-catholic/diaz-nomination-obama-passes-major-catholic-test (accessed July 30, 2009).

12. "Obama Picks Cuban Liberation Theologian as U.S. Ambassador to the Holy See," *Catholic News Agency,* May 28, 2009, http://www.catholicnewsagency.com/new.php?n=16129 (accessed July 30, 2009).

13. "Christian Socialism," Wikipedia, http://en.wikipedia.org/wiki/Christian_socialism (accessed December 9, 2008).

14. "Norman Thomas," Wikipedia, http://en.wikipedia.org/wiki/Norman_Thomas#cite_note-quotes-6 (accessed December 8, 2008).

15. "Frank P. Zeidler," Wikipedia, http://en.wikipedia.org/wiki/Frank_P._Zeidler (accessed December 9, 2008).

16. William Ebenstein, *Great Political Thinkers: Plato to the Present,* Sixth Edition (Belmont, CA: Thomson, 2000), 174–175.

17. Susan Nidtich, *A Prelude to Biblical Folklore: Underdogs and Tricksters* (Urbana and Chicago: University of Illinois Press, 2000), xv. Google Book Search. Web. (accessed September 15, 2007).

18. Alain Finkielkraut, *The Imaginary Jew* (Lincoln: University of Nebraska Press, 1984), 9. Google Book Search. Web. (accessed September 16, 2009).

19. "Attitudes toward World Religions," Religious Studies Online, http://www.rsrevision.com/GCSE/shortcourse/equality/religions.htm (accessed December 5, 2008).

20. Harold E. Quinley and Charles Y. Glock, *Anti-Semitism in America* (Edison, NJ: Transaction, 1983), 2–7. Google Book Search. Web. (accessed October 4, 2007).

21. Elizabeth Feinsilber and Mike Webber, *Merriam-Webster's Dictionary of Allusions* (Springfield, MA: Merriam-Webster, 1999), 143. Google Book Search. Web. (accessed October 5, 2007).

22. Chris Matthews, *American: Beyond Our Grandest Notions* (New York: Free Press, 2002), 136.

23. Thomas Paine, *Common Sense*, Forgotten Books, 1776, http:// forgottenbooks.org/info/Common_Sense, 27. Google Book Search. Web. (accessed March 15, 2009).

24. Ibid., 30.

25. "The Last Puritan," Sam Adams Heritage Society, http://www.samuel-adams-heritage.com/ (accessed August 3, 2007).

26. Matthews, 129.

27. Robert M. Cassidy, *Counterinsurgency and the Global War on Terror: Military Culture and Irregular War* (Westport, CT: Greenwood, 2006), 24. Google Book Search. Web. (accessed March 15, 2009).

28. Robert Yates, "Essays of Brutus, I," in *The Complete Anti-Federalist*, ed. Herbert J. Storing (Chicago: University of Chicago Press, 1981), II, 363–372, in *The Dilemma of American Thought,* ed. Jeffrey L. Prewitt (Upper Saddle River, NJ: Prentice-Hall, 1996), 73.

29. "A Republic, if You Can Keep It," Ron Paul's Speeches and Statements, January 31 and February 2, 2000, http://www.house.gov/paul/congrec/congrec2000/cr020200.htm (accessed September 29, 2007).

30. See Howard Zinn, *A People's History of the United States, 1492–Present* (New York: Harper Collins, 2003), Chapters 1 and 7. Google Book Search. Web. (accessed September 25, 2007). Also see Patrick Minges, "Beneath the Underdog," *American Indian Quarterly,* Vol. 25, Issue 3, 2001, 453.

31. Cornel West, *The Cornel West Reader* (New York: Basic, 1999), 104. Google Book Search. Web. (accessed September 28, 2007).

32. Peter Collier and David Horowitz, *The Rockefellers* (New York: Holt, Rinehart and Winston, 1976), 34.

33. Daniel Yergin, *The Prize* (New York: Simon and Schuster, 1991), 102.

34. Ibid., 105.

35. "The Real Facts about WalMart," Wake Up Wal-Mart, http://www.wakeupwalmart.com/facts/#community (accessed October 26, 2007).

36. Michael Barbaro, "Wal-Mart Offers Aid to Rivals," *New York Times*, April 5, 2006, http://www.nytimes.com/2006/04/05/business/05walmart.html (accessed August 25, 2009).

37. Jim Gilliam, "Wal-Mart Admits It Destroys Small Business," April 5, 2006, http://www.jimgilliam.com/2006/04/walmart_admits_it_destroys_small_business.php (accessed September 16, 2009).

38. Thomas Wailgum Framingham, "How Wal-Mart Lost Its Technology Edge" *Computer World*, October 22, 2007, http://computerworld.co.nz/news.nsf/spec/3DBB8E6CADBA8905CC2573780078E067 (accessed August 25, 2009).

39. David Morey and Scott Miller, *The Underdog Advantage* (New York: McGraw-Hill, 2004), 69. Google Book Search. Web. (accessed September 16, 2007).

40. Liza Featherstone, *Selling Women Short: The Landmark Battle for Women's Rights at Wal-Mart* (New York: Basic, 2004), 56–57. Google Book Search. Web. (accessed October 4, 2007).

41. Constance E. Beaumont, "Bucking the Establishment," in *How Superstore Sprawl Can Harm Communities* in *The New Populist Reader,* ed. Karl Trautman (Westport, CT: Praeger, 1994).

42. "Lorain, OH Measure (2005)," Wal-Mart Watch, http://walmartwatch. com/battlemart/resources/lorain_oh_measure_2005/ (accessed October 30, 2007).

43. Bruce Bostick, "Lorain Voters Defeat Wal-Mart," *People's Weekly World*, November 17, 2005, http://www.pww.org/article/view/8112/1/295/ (accessed September 16, 2009).

44. Ibid.

45. Jimmy A. Frazier and Eldon E. Snyder, "The Underdog Concept in Sport," *Sociology of Sport Journal* 8, 1991, 382.

46. Ibid.

47. "World Series History: Championships by Club," http://www.mlb.com/ mlb/history/postseason/mlb_ws.jsp?feature=club_champs (accessed November 27, 2007).

48. Jack Curry, "Red Sox Finally Spend, but the Sum Is Modest," *New York Times,* December 29, 2008, http://www.nytimes.com/2008/12/30/sports/ baseball/30base.html?scp=3&sq=yankees&st=cse (accessed January 1, 2009).

49. Frederic J. Frommer and Harvey Frommer, *Red Sox vs. Yankees: The Great Rivalry* (Champaign, IL: Sports Publishing LLC, 2005). Google Book Search. Web. (accessed March 15, 2008).

50. "2004 American League Championship Series," Wikipedia, http:// en.wikipedia.org/wiki/2004_American_League_Championship_Series (accessed November 29, 2007).

51. "USA Today Salaries Databases," *USA Today,* http://content.usatoday.com/ sports/baseball/salaries/totalpayroll.aspx?year=2009 (accessed August 22, 2009).

52. "The Business of Baseball," *Forbes,* April 22, 2009, http://www.forbes. com/lists/2009/33/baseball-values-09_The-Business-Of-Baseball_Rank. html (accessed August 22, 2009).

53. "The Business of Baseball: #3 Boston Red Sox," *Forbes,* April 19, 2007, http://www.forbes.com/lists/2007/33/07mlb_Boston-Red-Sox_330700. html (accessed August 22, 2009).

54. "The Business of Baseball: #22 Colorado Rockies," *Forbes,* April 19, 2007, http://www.forbes.com/lists/2007/33/07mlb_Colorado-Rockies_336931. html (accessed November 29, 2007).

55. "The Business of Baseball," Forbes, April 2, 2009, http://www.forbes.com/ lists/2009/33/baseball-values-09_The-Business-Of-Baseball_Rank.html (accessed August 22, 2009).

56. Alan Schwarz, "The Surprising Rise of the Rays," *New York Times*, December 27, 2008, http://www.nytimes.com/2008/12/28/sports/ baseball/28rays.html?partner=rss&emc=rss (accessed January 1, 2009).

57. Ibid.

58. Mike Lopresti, "Tampa Bay Goes from Underdog to the World Series," *USA Today,* October 19, 2008, http://www.usatoday.com/sports/columnist/lopresti/2008–10-19-rays-alcs-game-7_N.htm (accessed January 1, 2009).

59. "Philadelphia Phillies," Wikipedia, http://en.wikipedia.org/wiki/Philadelphia_Phillies (accessed November 29, 2007).

60. "Chicago Cubs," Wikipedia, http://en.wikipedia.org/wiki/Chicago_cubs (accessed November 29, 2007).

61. Dan Kois, "Six Great Underdog Movies John McCain Should Probably Watch," October 16, 2008, http://nymag.com/daily/entertainment/2008/10/six_great_underdog_movies_joh.html#photo=1 (accessed December 14, 2008) and "Best Underdog Movies," Flixster, http://www.flixster.com/movie-list/best-underdog-movies (accessed December 14, 2008).

62. Lance Morrow, *The Best Years of Their Lives, Kennedy, Johnson and Nixon in 1948 Learning the Secrets of Power* (New York: Basic, 2006), xxv. Google Book Search. Web. (accessed August 12, 2009).

63. "Mr. Deeds Goes to Town," Wikipedia, http://en.wikipedia.org/wiki/Mr._Deeds_Goes_to_Town (accessed November 30, 2007), and Tim Dirks (reviewer), "Mr. Deeds Goes to Town (1936)," http://www.filmsite.org/mrde3.html (accessed December 1, 2007).

64. Dirks.

65. Frank Capra, *The Name above the Title: An Autobiography* (Cambridge, MA: Da Capo Press, 1997), 186. Google Book Search. Web. (accessed September 15, 2007).

66. "Mr. Smith Goes to Washington," Wikipedia, http://en.wikipedia.org/wiki/Mr._Smith_Goes_to_Washington (accessed December 1, 2007), and Tim Dirks (reviewer), "Mr. Smith Goes to Washington," http://www.filmsite.org/mrsm3.html (accessed December 1, 2007).

67. Dirks.

68. Tim Dirks (reviewer), "Meet John Doe," http://www.filmsite.org/meet.html (accessed December 1, 2007).

69. Ibid.

70. Ibid.

71. Ibid. Brackets in the original.

3   The Political Culture and Core Ideals of Democrats

1. Jo Freeman, "The Political Culture of the Democratic and Republican Parties," *Political Science Quarterly*, Vol. 101, No. 3, 1986, 328.

2. Ibid., 347.

3. Daniel, J. Elazar, "Globalization Meets the World's Political Cultures," Jerusalem Center for Public Affairs Table 7, January 1990, http://www.jcpa.org/JCPA/Templates/ShowPage.asp?DBID=1&LNGID=1&TMID=111&FID=386&PID=849&IID=1318 (accessed August 26, 2009).

4. Ibid. However, in traditionalistic and individualistic political cultures, these feelings about participation differ.

5. Don Gonyea, "Clinton, Obama Unite in Unity, N.H.," National Public Radio, June 28, 2008, http://www.npr.org/templates/story/story.php?storyId=91993782 (accessed January 2, 2009).

6. Carla Marinucci, "Obama, Clinton Finally Take to Stage Together," June 28, 2008, http://www.sfgate.com/cgi-bin/article.cgi?f=/c/a/2008/06/28/MNB911GCEN.DTL&type=politics (accessed January 2, 2009).

7. Freeman, 336–337. Italics in the original.

8. Garrison Keillor, *Homegrown Democrat* (New York: Viking, 2004), 166–167.

9. "Democrats and Country Music," Music Row Democrats, http://musicrowdemocrats.com/index.php?option=com_magazine&func=show_article&id=1 (accessed on April 17, 2008, through the Democratic Party Blog, http://www.democrats.org/a/2006/08/the_dixie_chick.php).

10. Ibid., and "Cut by Cut: About the Artists and the Songs," Music Row Democrats, http://www.musicrowdemocrats.com/index.php?option=com_content&task=view&id=29&Itemid=67 (accessed April 18, 2008), and "Music Row Democrats," Wikipedia http://en.wikipedia.org/wiki/Music_Row_Democrats (accessed April 18, 2008).

11. Betty Clarke, "The Dixie Chicks," *Guardian*, March 12, 2003.

12. "Dixies dropped over Bush remark," *BBC News*, March 20, 2003. http://news.bbc.co.uk/2/hi/entertainment/2867221.stm (accessed September 17, 2009). It should be noted that the controversy sparked a boycott and death threats against the band. Three years later, the band tackled the controversy by releasing the song "Not Ready to Make Nice." "Dixie Chicks," Wikipedia, http://en.wikipedia.org/wiki/Dixie_Chicks_political_controversy#cite_note-49 (accessed, December 26, 2009).

13. Jason Pareles, "Underdog Anthems on a Patriotic Theme," *New York Times*, October 2, 2004.

14. "Rock on the Campaign Trail," *Rolling Stone,* http://www.rollingstone.com/photos/gallery/19316835/rock_on_the_campaign_trail/photo/6 (accessed June 8, 2009).

15. Ibid. See photo at http://www.rollingstone.com/photos/gallery/19316835/rock_on_the_campaign_trail/photo/5 (accessed June 8, 2009).

16. Ibid. See photo at http://www.rollingstone.com/photos/gallery/19316835/rock_on_the_campaign_trail/photo/12 (accessed June 8, 2009).

17. Ibid. See photo at http://www.rollingstone.com/photos/gallery/19316835/rock_on_the_campaign_trail/photo/16 (accessed June 8, 2009).

18. Betty H. Zisk, "Tensions between Individualistic and Communitarian Strands of American Liberal Thought: Novels, Drama, and Folksingers, 1930–1975," paper presented at the annual meeting of the American Political Science Association, Chicago, September 1995, 18.

19. Ibid. Italics is in the original.

20. "The Freewheelin' Bob Dylan," Wikipedia, http://en.wikipedia.org/wiki/The_Freewheelin%27_Bob_Dylan#cite_note-24 (accessed August 23, 2009).

21. Diane Ravitch, *The American Reader: Words That Moved a Nation* (New York: Harper Collins, 2000), 586. Google Book Search. Web. (accessed August 23, 2009).

22. Susan R. Heffner, "Labor and Industrial Folksongs: A Select Bibliography," The Library of Congress, The American Folklife Center, June 23, 1978, http://www.loc.gov/folklife/guides/BibLabor.html (accessed August 23, 2009).

23. "This Land Is Your Land," Wikipedia, http://en.wikipedia.org/wiki/This_Land_Is_Your_Land (accessed June 8, 2009).

24. Richard Leiby and DeNeen L. Brown, "The Stars Align, with Egos in Check," *Washington Post*, January 19, 2009.

25. Peter Yarrow, "The Role of Song in Advancing Health Care Reform," *Huffington Post,* http://www.huffingtonpost.com/peter-yarrow/the-role-of-song-in-advan_b_275426.html (accessed September 17, 2009).

26. William Martin, ed., *What Liberals Believe* (New York: Skyhorse, 2008), 162.

27. Todd Leopold, "*Slumdog* Makes History, Sweeps Oscars," CNN, http://www.cnn.com/2009/SHOWBIZ/Movies/02/23/oscar.night/index.html (accessed August 23, 2009).

28. "Controversial Issues Surrounding *Slumdog Millionaire*," Wikipedia http://en.wikipedia.org/wiki/Controversial_issues_surrounding_Slumdog_Millionaire (accessed August 23, 2009).

29. Fareed Zakaria, "Slum Voyeurism?" *Newsweek,* January 30, 2009, http://www.newsweek.com/id/182341 (accessed August 23, 2009). Brackets in the original.

30. George Lakoff, *Moral Politics: How Liberals and Conservatives Think* (Chicago: University of Chicago Press, 2002), 21.

31. William Safire, *Safire's Political Dictionary* (Oxford: Oxford University Press, 2008), 388, and Eric Alterman, *Why We're Liberals* (New York: Viking, 2008), 24–25.

32. Arthur M. Schlesinger, Jr., *The Cycles of American History* (Boston: Houghton Mifflin Harcourt, 1999), 240. Google Book Search. Web. (accessed June 1, 2009).

33. Joseph Losco and Ralph Baker, *AMGOV 2009* (New York: McGraw-Hill, 2009), 141.

34. Jeff Taylor, *Where Did the Party Go?* (Columbia: University of Missouri Press, 2006), 5.

35. Daniel M. Shea, Joanne Connor Green, and Christopher E. Smith, *Living Democracy Brief National Edition* (Upper Saddle River, NJ: Pearson Prentice Hall, 2007), 360.

36. Paul Krugman, *The Conscience of a Liberal* (New York: Norton, 2007), 268.

37. William Safire, *Safire's Political Dictionary* (Oxford: Oxford University Press, 2008), 45.

38. Alterman, 21.

39. Ibid., 26.

40. Arthur Meier Schlesinger, Jr. and Sean Wilentz, *The Politics of Hope and the Bitter Heritage* (Princeton, NJ: Princeton University Press, 2007), 89. Google Book Search. Web. (accessed June 1, 2009).

41. Gary Hart, *The Good Fight: The Education of an American Reformer* (New York: Random House, 1993), xxvi–xxvii.

42. Niccoli Machiavelli, *The Prince*, trans. Luigi Ricci (Fort Worth: RDMc, 2008), 22. Google Book Search. Web. (accessed June 1, 2009).

43. Lester Frank Ward, *Outlines of Sociology* (New York: Macmillan, 1913), 74. Google Book Search. Web. (accessed May 31, 2009).

44. "Sympathy," The Free Dictionary, http://www.thefreedictionary.com/sympathy (accessed May 31, 2009).

45. Charles A. Ellwood, *An Introduction to Social Psychology* (New York: D. Appleton, 1917), 259. Google Book Search. Web. (accessed May 31, 2009).

46. Ibid., 260. My emphasis.

47. George Lakoff, *Moral Politics: How Liberals and Conservatives Think*, Second Edition (Chicago: University of Chicago Press, 2002), 12.

48. Ibid., 109–110.

49. Ibid., 111.

50. Ibid., 112.

51. Erik Asard and W. Lance Bennett, *Democracy and the Marketplace of Ideas: Communications and Government in Sweden and the United States* (Cambridge: Cambridge University Press, 1997), 93. Google Book Search. Web. (accessed June 1, 2009).

52. Garrison Keillor, *Homegrown Democrat* (New York: Viking, 2004), 1.

53. "Ethic of Reciprocity," Wikipedia, http://en.wikipedia.org/wiki/Ethic_of_reciprocity (accessed June 1, 2009).

54. Keillor, 1.

55. John Gerring, *Party Ideologies in America, 1828–1996* (Cambridge: Cambridge University Press, 1996), 17. Google Book Search. Web. (accessed July 15, 2009).

56. Mario Matthew Cuomo, "1984 Democratic National Convention Keynote Address," American Rhetoric Top 100 Speeches, delivered July 16, 1984, http://www.americanrhetoric.com/speeches/mariocuomo1984dnc.htm (accessed June 1, 2009).

57. Robert Kuttner, *The Life of the Party* (New York: Viking, 1987), 16–17.

58. Keillor, 137.

59. Lakoff, 60–61.

60. Ibid.

61. Ibid.

62. Karl Marx, "Critique of the Gotha Programme," Marxists Internet Archive, 1875, http://www.marxists.org/archive/marx/works/1875/gotha/ch01.htm (accessed May 30, 2009).

63. "From Each According to His Abilities, to Each According to His Needs," Wikipedia, http://en.wikipedia.org/wiki/From_each_according_to_his_ability,_to_each_according_to_his_need (accessed May 27, 2009).

64. Theodore D. Woolsey, *Communism and Socialism in Their Theory and History* (New York: Charles Scribner, 1880), 100. Google Book Search. Web. (accessed June 1, 2009).

65. Lakoff, 61.

66. Matt Moon, "How Do Americans Feel about Taxes Today?" *Tax Foundation*, April 2009, No. 166, 7.

67. Ibid., 8–9.

68. Dennis Jacobe, "Americans Oppose Wealth Redistribution to Fix the Economy," Gallup, June 27, 2008, http://www.gallup.com/poll/108445/Americans-Oppose-Income-Redistribution-Fix-Economy.aspx (accessed June 1, 2009).

69. Kuttner, 13–14.

70. Benjamin I. Page and Lawrence R. Jacobs, *Class War? What Americans Really Think about Economic Inequality* (Chicago and London: University of Chicago Press, 2009), 268–269. My emphasis. Sony ebook.

71. Ibid., 139. Sony ebook.

72. Samuel Huntington, *American Politics the Promise of Disharmony* (Cambridge, MA: Belknap Press of Harvard University Press, 1981), 38.

73. "Distributive Justice," Stanford Encyclopedia of Philosophy, March 5, 2007, http://plato.stanford.edu/entries/justice-distributive/ (accessed May 28, 2009).

74. Ibid.

75. Ibid.

76. John Rawls, *Political Liberalism: Expanded Edition* (New York: Columbia University Press, 1993), 6. Google Book Search. Web. (accessed June 1, 2009).

77. Stanford Encyclopedia of Philosophy.

78. Peter Wenz, *Political Philosophies in Moral Conflict* (Boston: McGraw-Hill, 2007), 193. Google Book Search. Web. (accessed June 2, 2009).

79. Stanford Encyclopedia of Philosophy.

80. Conrad P. Waligorski, *The Political Theory of Conservative Economists* (Lawrence: University Press of Kansas, 1990), 76.

81. Keillor, 171.

82. "Trends in Political Values and Core Attitudes: 1987–2009," Pew Research Center for the People & the Press, May 21, 2009, http://people-press.org/reports/pdf/517.pdf (accessed June 2, 2009), 43.

83. Ibid., 34–35.

84. Lowell Bergman and Orlana Zill, "The Government's Criminal Case against the Tobacco Industry," *Frontline* Online: Inside the Tobacco Deal, http://www.pbs.org/wgbh/pages/frontline/shows/settlement/case/ (accessed June 2, 2009).

85. Lowell Bergman, "Interviews: Michael Moore," *Frontline* Online: Inside the Tobacco Deal, http://www.pbs.org/wgbh/pages/frontline/shows/settlement/interviews/moore.html (accessed June 2, 2009) and "Mike Moore (U.S. Politician)," Wikipedia, http://en.wikipedia.org/wiki/Mike_Moore_(Mississippi_politician) (accessed June 2, 2009).

86. Bergman.

87. Ibid.

88. Ibid.

4   The Founders and the Great Commoner: Jefferson, Jackson, and Bryan

1. Fawn Brodie, *Thomas Jefferson: An Intimate Portrait* (New York: Norton, 1974), 116. Emphasis in the original.

2. "Jefferson" in John P. Foley, ed., *The Jefferson Cyclopedia* (New York and London: Funk & Wagnalls, 1900), 964. Google Book Search. Web. (accessed April 3, 2008).

3. Henry Childs Merwin, *Thomas Jefferson* (New York: Houghton, Mifflin, 1901), 39.

4. Daniel M. Shea, Joanne Connor Green, and Christopher E. Smith, *Living Democracy, Brief National Edition* (Upper Saddle River, NJ: Pearson Prentice Hall, 2007), A1.

5. John Dunn, *Democracy: A History* (New York: Open City Books, 2006), 71. Google Book Search. Web. (accessed May 1, 2009).

6. David G. McCullough, *John Adams* (New York: Simon and Schuster, 2008), 334. Google Book Search. Web. (accessed May 2, 2009).

7. Shea, A2.

8. Ibid., A4.

9. Ibid., A3.

10. Ted Nance, *Gangs of America: The Rise of Corporate Power and the Disabling of Democracy* (San Francisco: Berrett-Koehler, 2005), 41. Emphasis in the original. Google Book Search. Web. (accessed September 10, 2007).

11. "Primary Documents in American History: Alien and Sedition Acts," The Library of Congress, http://www.loc.gov/rr/program/bib/ourdocs/Alien.html (accessed May 23, 2009).

12. Noble Cunningham, *Jefferson vs. Hamilton: Confrontations That Shaped a Nation* (New York: Palgrave Macmillan, 2000), 115. Google Book Search. Web. (accessed May 20, 2009).

13. Jeff Taylor, *Where Did the Party Go?* (Columbia: University of Missouri Press, 2006), 23.

14. Gordon T. Belt, "Sedition Act of 1798: A Brief History of Arrests, Indictments, Mistreatment & Abuse," First Amendment Center, http://www.firstamendmentcenter.org/PDF/Sedition_Act_cases.pdf (accessed May 23, 2009).

15. Ibid.

16. Ibid.

17. Ibid.

18. Edward John Larson, *A Magnificent Catastrophe* (New York: Simon and Schuster, 2008), 135. Google Book Search. Web. (accessed May 23, 2009).

19. Joseph J. Ellis, *Founding Brothers* (New York: Alfred A. Knopf, 2001), 210.

20. "United States Presidential Election Results," Dave Leip's Atlas of U.S. Presidential Elections, http://uselectionatlas.org/RESULTS/ (accessed May 24, 2009).

21. James Horn, "Thomas Jefferson and the Revolution of 1800," *Monticello Newsletter*, Vol. 11, No. 1, Spring 2000. http://www.monticello.org/press/newsletter/2000/rev1800.pdf (accessed June 9, 2009).

22. Brodie, 438.

23. Merwin, 118.

24. Jules Witcover, *Party of the People* (New York: Random House, 2003), 79.

25. "Albert Gallatin," Conservapedia, http://www.conservapedia.com/Albert_Gallatin (accessed June 10, 2009).

26. Larson, 260.

27. Ibid.

28. Brodie, 440.

29. "Twelfth Amendment to the United States Constitution," Wikipedia, http://en.wikipedia.org/wiki/Twelfth_amendment (accessed June 10, 2009).

30. Thomas Jefferson, "The Letters of Thomas Jefferson: 1743–1826, to Dr. Joseph Priestly," From Revolution to Reconstruction, March 21, 1801, http://www.let.rug.nl/usa/P/tj3/writings/brf/jefl137.htm (accessed June 10, 2009).

31. "Thomas Jefferson to Spencer Roane, 1819," Thomas Jefferson on Politics and Government, Section 5: The Sovereignty of the People, University of Virginia Library, http://etext.virginia.edu/jefferson/quotations/jeff0300.htm (accessed September 1, 2009).

32. Taylor, 10.

33. R. B. Bernstein, *Thomas Jefferson* (New York: Oxford University Press, 2005), 75. Google Book Search. Web. (accessed April 2, 2009).

34. Gary Hart, *The Good Fight: The Education of an American Reformer* (New York: Random House, 1993), 47.

35. Andrew Burstein, *Jefferson's Secrets* (New York: Basic Books, 2005), 54. Google Book Search. Web. (accessed September 10, 2009).

36. John Gerring, *Party Ideologies in America: 1828–1996* (Cambridge: Cambridge University Press, 1996), 262. Google Book Search. Web. (accessed September 10, 2009).

37. Robert V. Remini, *The Life of Andrew Jackson* (New York: Harper Perennial Modern Classics, 1988), 5–9.

38. Ibid., 9.

39. "Battle of New Orleans," Wikipedia, http://en.wikipedia.org/wiki/Battle_ of_new_orleans (accessed January 23, 2009), and Donald R. Hickey, *Don't Give Up the Ship! Myths of the War of 1812* (Urbana and Chicago: University of Illinois Press, 2006), 278.

40. Hickey, 287.

41. "1959 in Music," Wikipedia, http://en.wikipedia.org/wiki/1959_in_music (accessed February 1, 2009).

42. "United States Presidential Election Results."

43. "23d. The 1824 Election and the 'Corrupt Bargain,'" U.S. History, http:// www.ushistory.org/us/23d.asp (accessed February 1, 2009).

44. Jon Meacham, *American Lion* (New York: Random House, 2008), 45. Google Book Search. Web.(accessed April 3, 2009).

45. H. W. Brands, *Andrew Jackson His Life and Times* (New York: Doubleday, 2005), 458. Emphasis in the original. Google Book Search. Web. (accessed April 3, 2009).

46. "United States Presidential Election, 1828," Wikipedia, http://en.wikipedia. org/wiki/U.S._presidential_election,_1828 (accessed May 24, 2009).

47. Kenneth T. Walsh, "The Most Consequential Elections in History: Andrew Jackson and the Election of 1828," *U.S. News & World Report*, August 20, 2008, http://www.usnews.com/articles/news/politics/2008/08/20/ the-most-consequential-elections-in-history-andrew-jackson-and-the- election-of-1828.html (accessed May 24, 2009).

48. Brands, 414.

49. Sean Wilentz, *Andrew Jackson* (New York: Palgrave Macmillan, 2005), 54. Google Book Search. Web. (accessed August 20, 2008).

50. "Second Bank of the United States," Wikipedia, http://en.wikipedia.org/ wiki/Second_Bank_of_the_United_States (accessed February 2, 2009).

51. Brands, 470–471. My emphasis.

52. Joseph White, "The Political Divide and Its History," prepared remarks for Junior State of America ORV Great Lakes Region Spring One-Day Conference, March 18, 2007, http://policy.case.edu/juniorstatemarch18. pdf (accessed June 11, 2009).

53. David S. Reynolds, *Waking Giant* (New York: Harper, 2008), 96–97. Google Book Search. Web. (accessed June 11, 2009).

54. "Indian Removal Act," Wikipedia, http://en.wikipedia.org/wiki/Indian_ Removal_Act (accessed January 23, 2009).

55. "Indian Removal Act," Encyclopedia.com, http://www.encyclopedia.com/ doc/10119-IndianRemovalAct.html (accessed February 22, 2009).

56. "Indian Treaties and the Removal Act of 1830," U.S. Department of State, http://www.state.gov/r/pa/ho/time/dwe/16338.htm (accessed February 22, 2009).

57. Robert V. Remini, *Andrew Jackson and the Course of American Democracy, 1833–1845,* Volume III (New York: Harper and Row, 1984), 314.

58. Ibid.

59. S. E. Ruckman, "The 'Great White Father' Laid to Rest," Native American Times, http://nativetimes.com/index.php?option=com_content&task=view&id=955&Itemid=&Itemid=33 (accessed January 29, 2009).

60. "President Andrew Jackson's Case for the Removal Act: First Annual Message to Congress, December 8, 1830," Mount Holyoke, http://www.mtholyoke.edu/acad/intrel/andrew.htm (accessed May 24, 2009).

61. Meacham, 96.

62. Gerring, 164–165.

63. "United States Presidential Election Results," (accessed June 8, 2009).

64. Richard Norton Smith, "William Jennings Bryan: Father of the Modern Democratic Party," The Online NewsHour, produced by Anna Shoup on August 26, 2008, http://www.pbs.org/newshour/vote2008/reportersblog/2008/08/william_jennings_bryan_father.html (accessed August 3, 2009).

65. Mary Baird Bryan, *The Memoirs of William Jennings Bryan* (Chicago: John C. Winston, 1925), 463. Google Book Search. Web. (accessed August 3, 2009).

66. Milton Friedman, *Money Mischief: Episodes in Monetary History* (New York: Mariner Books, 1994), 53. Google Book Search. Web. (accessed August 3, 2009).

67. "Coinage Act of 1873," Wikipedia. http://en.wikipedia.org/wiki/Coinage_Act_of_1873 (accessed August 4, 2009).

68. "Panic of 1873," Wikipedia, http://en.wikipedia.org/wiki/Panic_of_1873 (accessed August 4, 2009).

69. "Bland-Allison Act," Wikipedia, http://en.wikipedia.org/wiki/Bland-Allison_Act (accessed August 4, 2009).

70. "Bland-Allison Act," U.S. History, http://www.u-s-history.com/pages/h718.html (accessed August 4, 2009).

71. Charles R. Geisst, *Wall Street: A History* (New York: Oxford University Press, 1999), 110. Google Book Search. Web. (accessed August 4, 2009).

72. Jerry W. Markham, *A Financial History of the United States,* Volume I (Armonk, NY: M.E. Sharpe, 2001), 331–332. Google Book Search. Web. (accessed August 4, 2009).

73. Michael Kazin, *A Godly Hero: The Life of William Jennings Bryan* (New York: Random House, 2006), 50.

74. Ibid., 46.

75. James L. Sundquist, *Dynamics of the Party System Revised Edition* (Washington: Brookings Institution, 1983), 137–138.

76. "Bryan's 'Cross of Gold' Speech: Mesmerizing the Masses," History Matters, http://historymatters.gmu.edu/d/5354/ (accessed August 5, 2009).

77. Ibid.

78. Ibid.

79. Sundquist, 139.

80. David M. Kennedy, *The Brief American Pageant,* Fifth Edition (Boston: Houghton Mifflin, 2000), 394.

81. Kazin, 36.

82. Rebecca Edwards, "1896: The Populist Party," Vassar College, 2000, http://projects.vassar.edu/1896/populists.html (accessed August 6, 2009), and "United States Presidential Election Results," (accessed August 6, 2009).

83. "Population of the 100 Largest Urban Places: 1890," U.S. Bureau of the Census http://www.census.gov/population/www/documentation/twps0027/tab12.txt (accessed August 6, 2009).

84. Michael Kazin, *The Populist Persuasion* (New York: Basic, 1995), 42.

85. "Senators Who Changed Parties during Senate Service (Since 1890)," United States Senate, http://www.senate.gov/artandhistory/history/common/briefing/senators_changed_parties.htm#1 (accessed August 6, 2009).

86. Sundquist, 164. Italics in the original.

87. Kazin, *A Godly Hero,* 69.

88. David Burner, *The Politics of Provincialism* (New York: W.W. Norton, 1975), 7. Contained within Elizabeth Sanders, *Roots of Reform: Farmers, Workers and the American State, 1877–1917* (Chicago: University of Chicago Press, 1999), 447. Google Book Search. Web. (accessed August 6, 2009).

89. "1896 Presidential Election Results," Dave Leip's Atlas of U.S. Presidential Elections. http://uselectionatlas.org/RESULTS/ (accessed August 5, 2009).

90. Kazin, *A Godly Hero,* 54.

91. Ibid., 67.

92. William D. Harpine, *From the Front Porch to the Front Page* (College Station, TX: A&M University Press, 2006), 156. Google Book Search. Web. (accessed August 8, 2009).

93. Kazin, *The Populist Persuasion*, 43–44.

94. Ibid., 43.

95. "United States Presidential Election Results," (accessed August 11, 2009).

96. "Philippine-American War," Wikipedia, http://en.wikipedia.org/wiki/Philippine%E2%80%93American_War (accessed August 11, 2009).

97. "The World of 1898: The Spanish-American War," Hispanic Division: The Library of Congress, http://www.loc.gov/rr/hispanic/1898/intro.html (accessed August 12, 2009).

98. "Second Boer War," Wikipedia, http://en.wikipedia.org/wiki/Second_Boer_War (accessed August 12, 2009).

99. "Speeches of William Jennings Bryan: Imperialism," Humanities Web, http://www.humanitiesweb.org/human.php?s=h&p=c&a=p&ID=23090 (accessed August 11, 2009).

100. Kazin, *A Godly Hero*, 99–100.

101. Ibid., 98.

102. "Bryan's 'Cross of Gold' Speech."

103. Taylor, 169.

104. "Public Policy Inquiry Campaign Finance History," Hoover Institution, http://www.campaignfinancesite.org/history/reform1.html (accessed August 12, 2009 from www.opensecrets.org).

105. Kazin, *A Godly Hero*, 93–94.

106. Robert W. Cherney, *A Righteous Cause: The Life of William Jennings Bryan* (Norman: University of Okalahoma Press, 1994), 199. Google Book Search. Web. (accessed August 12, 2009).

107. Ibid.

108. Herbert David Croly, *The Promise of American Life* (New York: Macmillan, 1911), 156. Google Book Search. Web. (accessed August 12, 2009).

5   The Glory Days: FDR to Humphrey

1. "Groton's Beginnings," Groton School, http://www.groton.org/home/content.asp?id=1 (accessed August 16, 2009).

2. Geoffrey C. Ward, *Before the Trumpet: Young Franklin Roosevelt 1882–2005* (New York: Ward Press, 2007), 192.Google Book Search. Web. (accessed August 13, 2009).

3. James Chowning Davies, "Abraham and Mary, Franklin and Eleanor: Their Growth from Private to Public Comprehension," in *Franklin D. Roosevelt and Abraham Lincoln: Competing Perspectives on Two Great Presidencies* ed. William D. Pederson and Frank J. Williams (Armonk, NY: M.E. Sharpe, 2002), 91. Google Book Search. Web. (accessed August 17, 2009).

4. "Franklin D. Roosevelt," Wikipedia, http://en.wikipedia.org/wiki/Franklin_D._Roosevelt#cite_note-navyreward-19 (accessed August 17, 2009).

5. Conrad Black, *Franklin Delano Roosevelt Champion of Freedom* (New York: Public Affairs, 2003), 53.

6. H. W. Brands, *Traitor to His Class* (New York: Doubleday, 2008), 54–60.

7. Ibid., 60.

8. Jean Edward Smith, *FDR* (New York: Random House, 2008), 80. Google Book Search. Web. (accessed August 17, 2009).

9. "The Triangle Factory Fire: Introduction," Cornell University ILR School, http://www.ilr.cornell.edu/trianglefire/narrative1.html (accessed August 17, 2009).

10. Black, 59.

11. Ibid.

12. Armond S. Goldman, Elizabeth J Schmalstieg, Daniel H Freeman, Daniel A Goldman, and Frank C Schmalstieg, "What Was the Cause of Franklin Delano Roosevelt's Paralytic Illness?" *Journal of Medical Biography* 2003; 11: 232–240, http://web.archive.org/web/20080307005449/http://www.rsmpress.co.uk/jmb_2003_v11_p232–240.pdf (accessed August 14, 2009).

13. Ibid.

14. Hugh Gregory Gallagher, *FDR's Splendid Deception* (New York: Dead, Modd, 1985), 23–24.

15. Ibid., 34–35.

16. "Birthday Balls: Franklin D. Roosevelt and the March of Dimes," Franklin D. Roosevelt Presidential Library and Museum, http://docs.fdrlibrary.marist.edu/bdtext.html (accessed September 17, 2009).

17. Gallagher, 43 and 45.

18. William B. Rhoads, "Franklin D. Roosevelt and the Architecture of Warm Springs," *Georgia Historical Quarterly,* Vol. LXVII, No. 1 (Spring 1983), via *GeorgiaInfo* http://georgiainfo.galileo.usg.edu/FDRarticle3.htm (accessed August 15, 2009).

19. "History," Roosevelt Warm Springs, http://www.rooseveltrehab.org/history.php (accessed August 15, 2009).

20. Gallagher, 29.

21. Ibid., 49.

22. Ibid., 51.

23. Black, 169.

24. Gallagher, 214.

25. Christopher N. Breiseth, "Warm Springs and the Emergence of Franklin Roosevelt as a Political Leader," The Franklin and Eleanor Roosevelt Institute (speech), April 12, 2006: 6, http://livingnewdeal.berkeley.edu/pdf/Breiseth06.pdf (accessed August 16, 2009).

26. Adam Cohen, *Nothing to Fear: FDR's Inner Circle and the Hundred Days that Created Modern America* (New York: Penguin, 2009), 22. Google Book Search. Web. (accessed August 16, 2009).

27. Gallagher, 95.

28. Brands, 182.

29. David Wallechinsky and Irving Wallace, "President Franklin D. Roosevelt: Political Career and Road to the White House," Trivia-Library.com, http://www.trivia-library.com/a/president-franklin-d-roosevelt-political-career-and-road-to-the-white-house.htm (accessed January 13, 2008).

30. "Albert Ottinger," Wikipedia, http://en.wikipedia.org/wiki/Albert_Ottinger (accessed August 18, 2009).

31. Black, 184–186.

32. Ibid., 190–192.

33. Nicolas Spulber, *Managing the American Economy, from Roosevelt to Reagan* (Bloomington: Indiana University Press, 1989), 1–2. Google Book Search. Web. (accessed May 3, 2009).

34. Black, 203.

35. Ibid.

36. Ibid., 216.

37. Quoted in June Hopkins, *Harry Hopkins: Sudden Hero, Brash Reformer* (New York: Palgrave Macmillan, 1999), 156. Parenthesis in the original. Google Book Search. Web. (accessed September 4, 2009).

38. Alan R. Lawson, *A Commonwealth of Hope* (Baltimore: Johns Hopkins University Press, 2006), 119.Google Book Search. Web. (accessed September 4, 2009).

39. Franklin D. Roosevelt, "The Forgotten Man," New Deal Network, April 7, 1932, http://newdeal.feri.org/speeches/1932c.htm (accessed January 25, 2008).

40. Black, 251.

41. Nick Taylor, *American-Made: The Enduring Legacy of the WPA—When FDR Put the Nation to Work* (New York: Bantam Books, 2008), 7.

42. Alan Brinkley, *Liberalism and Its Discontents* (Cambridge, MA and London, England: Harvard University Press, 1998), 18.

43. Jules Witcover, *Party of the People* (New York: Random House, 2003), 362–363.

44. William E. Leuchtenburg, *Franklin D. Roosevelt and the New Deal* (New York: Harper and Row, 1963), 119. Google Book Search. Web. (accessed September 7, 2009).

45. "Franklin D. Roosevelt First Inaugural Address," Bartleby.com, March 4, 1933, http://www.bartleby.com/124/pres49.html (accessed January 13, 2008).

46. "Address of the President Delivered by Radio from the White House," Mid-Hudson Regional Information Center, May 7, 1933 http://www.mhric.org/fdr/chat2.html (accessed September 7, 2009).

47. Ibid.

48. Ibid.

49. "History of Rural Electric Coops," Coop Litigation News, http://coop-litigation.com/rechistory.aspx#_ftn1 (accessed September 9, 2009).

50. "TVA: Electricity for All—Rural Electrification," New Deal Network, http://newdeal.feri.org/tva/tva10.htm (accessed September 9, 2009).

51. Ibid.

52. Leuchtenburg, 157–158.

53. "TVA: Electricity for All—Rural Electrification."

54. John Varrasi, "Lighting the Countryside," *Mechanical Engineering*, June 2005, http://www.memagazine.org/backissues/membersonly/june05/features/lightingc/lightingc.html (accessed September 9, 2009).

55. "Electrification," Virginia History, http://www.vahistory.org/electrification. html#1 (accessed September 9, 2009).

56. JoAnne Sears Rife, "How Women Brought Rural Electrification to Benton County Arkansas," RootsWeb, http://freepages.genealogy.rootsweb. ancestry.com/~dmccamey/stories/REA.htm (accessed on September 16, 2009). Underlining in the original.

57. "32: Franklin D. Roosevelt 1933–1945," The White House, http://www. whitehouse.gov/about/presidents/franklindroosevelt/ (accessed September 7, 2009).

58. "Second Inaugural Address of Franklin D. Roosevelt" January 20, 1937 http://avalon.law.yale.edu/20th_century/froos2.asp (accessed September 17, 2009).

59. Dexter Perkins, *The New Age of Franklin Roosevelt, 1932–1945* (Chicago: University of Chicago Press, 1967), 73. Google Book Search. Web. (accessed September 4, 2009).

60. William Howard Leuchtenburg, *The FDR Years: On Roosevelt and His Legacy* (New York: Columbia University Press, 1995), 238. Google Book Search. Web. (accessed September 4, 2009).

61. Brands, 658–659.

62. Black, 723.

63. Brian Masuri Hayashi, *Democratizing the Enemy: The Japanese American Internment* (Princeton, NJ and Oxford: Princeton University Press, 2004), 77.

64. Ibid.

65. Ibid., 78.

66. Ibid.

67. Robert N. Rosen, *Saving the Jews: Franklin D. Roosevelt and the Holocaust* (New York: Thunder's Mouth Press, 2006), 210–211. Google Book Search. Web. (accessed September 5, 2009).

68. "'Suffering under a Great Injustice': Ansel Adam's Photographs of Japanese-American Internment at Manzanarm," Library of Congress, http://www. loc.gov/teachers/classroommaterials/connections/manzanar/history.html (accessed September 8, 2009).

69. Brands, 656.

70. Hayashi, 214.

71. Ibid.

72. Doris Kearns Goodwin, *No Ordinary Time* (New York: Simon and Schuster Paperbacks, 1994), 322.

73. Ibid., 323.

74. Allida M. Black, *Casting Her Own Shadow: Eleanor Roosevelt and the Shaping of Postwar Liberalism* (Irvington, NY: Columbia University Press, 1997), 143. Google Book Search. Web. (accessed September 8, 2009).

75. Goodwin, 323.

76. Darlene Clark Hine, William C. Hine, and Stanley Harrold, *The African-American Odyssey Volume II,* Fourth Edition (Upper Saddle River, NJ: Pearson Prentice Hall, 2008), 357–358.

77. Ibid., and Brinkley, 34.

78. "Lynchings: By Year and Race," Statistics provided by the Archives at Tuskegee, Institute, University of Missouri-Kansas City School of Law, http://www.law.umkc.edu/faculty/projects/ftrials/shipp/lynchingyear. html (accessed September 9, 2009).

79. Robert A. Gibson, "The Negro Holocaust: Lynching and Race Riots in the United States, 1880–1950," Yale-New Haven Teachers Institute, http://www.yale.edu/ynhti/curriculum/units/1979/2/79.02.04.x.html (accessed September 9, 2009).

80. Ibid.

81. Conrad Black, *Franklin Delano Roosevelt Champion of Freedom,* 438.

82. James MacGregor Burns and Susan Dunn, *The Three Roosevelts: Patrician Leaders Who Transformed America* (New York: Grove Press, 2001), 394. Google Book Search. Web. (accessed December 30, 2009).

83. Ibid., 393–394.

84. Jerome Brunner (reply), "Lynching," *New York Review of Books,* September 25, 2003, http://www.nybooks.com/articles/16808 (accessed September 9, 2009).

85. Smith, 375; and R. W. Apple, Jr., "G.O.P Tries Hard to Win Black Votes, but Recent History Works against It," *New York Times,* September 19, 1996, http://www.nytimes.com/1996/09/19/us/gop-tries-hard-to-win-black-votes-but-recent-history-works-against-it.html (accessed September 9, 2009).

86. "Franklin Delano Roosevelt (1982–1945): Campaigns and Elections," Miller Center of Public Affairs, University of Virginia, http://millercenter. org/academic/americanpresident/fdroosevelt/essays/biography/3 (accessed September 9, 2009).

87. Brinkley, 76.

88. Jay Cost, "Race, Realignment, and the Election of 1948," Real Clear Politics, April 22, 2009, http://www.realclearpolitics.com/horseraceblog/2009/04/race_realignment_and_the_elect.html (accessed September 9, 2009).

89. David McCullough, *Truman* (New York, Touchstone, 1992), 234.

90. Raymond H. Geselbracht ed., *The Civil Rights Legacy of Harry S. Truman* (Kirksville, MO: Truman State University Press, 2007), 189. Appendix C. Google Book Search. Web. (accessed September 9, 2009).

91. "Harry S. Truman (1884–1972): Domestic Affairs," Miller Center of Public Affairs, University of Virginia, http://millercenter.org/academic/americanpresident/truman/essays/biography/4 (accessed September 9, 2009).

92. "Desegregation of the Armed Forces," Harry S. Truman Library & Museum, http://www.trumanlibrary.org/whistlestop/study_collections/

desegregation/large/index.php?action=chronology (accessed September 10, 2009).

93. "To Secure These Rights: The Report of the President's Committee on Civil Rights: XII." Harry S. Truman Library & Museum, http://www.trumanlibrary.org/civilrights/srights1.htm#VII (accessed September 10, 2009).

94. Ibid., 20–30.

95. Ibid., 36.

96. Ibid., 63–64.

97. Ibid. http://www.trumanlibrary.org/civilrights/srights1.htm#contents (whole document). (accessed September 10, 2009).

98. "Creating the Commission on Civil Rights," Civilrights.org, March 2009, http://www.civilrights.org/publications/reports/commission/creating-the-commission.html (accessed September 10, 2009).

99. Harry S. Truman, "State of the Union Address," TeachingAmericanHistory.org, January 7, 1948, http://teachingamericanhistory.org/library/index.asp?document=1361 (accessed January 25, 2008).

100. Ibid.

101. McCullough, 586–587.

102. "Creating the Commission on Civil Rights."

103. Lawrence J. Korb and Laura Conley, "It's Time for Obama to Follow Truman's Example," Center for American Progress, July 27, 2009, http://www.americanprogress.org/issues/2009/07/trumans_example.html (accessed September 10, 2009).

104. Colin Powell, "Truman, Desegregation of the Armed Forces and a Kid from the South Bronx," in Geselbracht, 121.

105. Romney Wheeler, "Georgia Governor Opposes Revolt, Sticks by Demos," Associated Press, *St. Petersburg Times,* February 7, 1948.

106. Ibid., 588.

107. Zachary Karabell, *The Last Campaign* (New York: Alfred A. Knopf, 2000), 24. Google Book Search. Web. (accessed September 12, 2009).

108. Michael R. Garner, *Harry Truman and Civil Rights: Moral Courage and Civil Rights* (Carbondale and Edwardsvillle: Southern Illinois University Press, 2002), 80. Google Book Search. Web. (accessed September 12, 2009).

109. Gary A. Donaldson, *Truman Defeats Dewey* (Lexington: University Press of Kentucky, 1998), 111. Google Book Search. Web. (accessed September 13, 2009).

110. "2008 Presidential General Election Results," Dave Leip's Atlas of U.S. Presidential Elections, http://uselectionatlas.org/RESULTS/ (accessed February 2, 2008); and Michael Streich, "The States' Rights Party in the 1948 Election," suite101.com, March 25, 2009, http://modern-us-history.suite101.com/article.cfm/the_states_rights_party_in_the_1948_election (accessed September 11, 2009).

111. Alexander Heard in Kari A. Frederickson, *The Dixiecrat Revolt and the End of the Solid South, 1932–1968* (Chapel Hill: University of North Carolina Press, 2001), 5. Google Book Search. Web. (accessed September 12, 2009).

112. Merle Miller, *Plain Speaking: An Oral Biography of Harry S. Truman* (New York: Berkley, 1974), 269.

113. Ibid., 235.

114. William Yale at the State Department thought Israel's survival chances were minimal. For an example, see Michael T. Benson, *Harry S. Truman and the Founding of Israel* (Westport, CT: Praeger 1997), 80. Google Book Search. Web. (accessed September 13, 2009).

115. Frank Cocozzelli, "Universal Health Care: Harry S. Truman and the Throne of God," Street Prophets, August 22, 2009, http://www.streetprophets.com/storyonly/2009/8/22/16580/8833 (accessed September 12, 2009).

116. Brian Hamel, "Harry Truman's Reluctance in Going Public for National Health Insurance," paper presented at the annual meeting of the International Communication Association, New Orleans, LA, May 27, 2004, pg. 26, All Academic Research, http://www.allacademic.com/meta/p113371_index.html (accessed September 12, 2009).

117. Karabell, 244.

118. Richard D. Brown and Jack Tagger, *Massachusetts: A Concise History* (Amherst: University of Massachusetts Press, 2000), 178–179. Google Book Search. Web (accessed September 12, 2009).

119. Margaret Irene Laing, *The Next Kennedy: A Woman's View of Robert F. Kennedy as a Prospective President* (New York: Coward-McCann, 1968), 172. Google Book Search. Web. (accessed September 12, 2009).

120. Charles Kenney, *John F. Kennedy: The Presidential Portfolio—History as Told through the Collection of the John F. Kennedy Library and Museum* (New York: Public Affairs, 2000), 40. Google Book Search. Web. (accessed September 12, 2009).

121. Allida Black, June Hopkins, John Sears, Christopher Alhambra, Mary Jo Binker, Christopher Brick, John S. Emrich, Eugenia Gusev, Kristen E. Gwinn, and Bryan D. Peery, ed., "The West Virginia Primary," in *Eleanor Roosevelt, John Kennedy, and the Election of 1960: A Project of The Eleanor Roosevelt Papers* (Columbia, SC: Model Editions Partnership, 2003). Electronic version based on unpublished letters. http://adh.sc.edu (accessed September 12, 2009).

122. Kenney, 41.

123. "The West Virginia Primary."

124. Carl Solberg, *Hubert Humphrey: A Biography* (Saint Paul: Minnesota Historical Society Press, 2003), 209. Google Book Search. Web. (accessed September 13, 2009).

125. Kenneth P. O'Donnell, David F. Powers, and Joe McCarthy, *Johnny, We Hardly Knew Ye* (New York: Pocket, 1973), 191.

126. David Pietrusza, *1960—LBJ vs. JFK vs. Nixon: The Epic Campaign That Forged Three Presidencies* (New York: Sterling, 2008), 117. Google Book Search. Web. (accessed September 12, 2009).

127. "The West Virginia Primary."

128. Theodore H. White, *In Search of History* (New York: Warner Books, 1978), 466.

129. Sandy Grady, "Another Epic West Virginia Battle," *USA Today,* May 13, 2008, http://blogs.usatoday.com/oped/2008/05/another-epic-we.html (accessed September 12, 2009).

130. White, 465.

131. John Hellmann, *The Kennedy Obsession: The American Myth of JFK* (New York: Columbia University Press, 1997), 126. Google Book Search. Web. (accessed September 12, 2009).

132. Contained within Sidney Kraus, *Televised Presidential Debates and Public Policy,* Second Edition (Mahwah, NJ: Lawrence Erlbaum Associates, 2000), 228. Google Book Search. Web. (accessed September 13, 2009).

133. Michael O'Brien, *John F. Kennedy: A Biography* (New York: Thomas Dune, 2005), 393–394. Google Book Search. Web. (accessed September 13, 2009).

134. Ibid., 394.

135. Sean J. Savage, *JFK, LBJ and the Democratic Party* (Albany: SUNY Press, 2004), 18.

136. Savage, 19 and Arthur Meier Schlesinger, *Robert Kennedy and His Times* (Boston: Houghton-Mifflin, 2002), 214. Google Book Search. Web. (accessed June 13, 2008).

137. Savage, 91–92.

138. Martin Kelly, *About.com* http://americanhistory.about.com/od/johnfkennedy/p/pkennedy.htm (accessed September 18, 2009).

139. Sean Wilentz, "What if Kennedy Had Lived?" *New York Times,* November 21, 2003, http://www.nytimes.com/2003/11/21/opinion/what-if-kennedy-had-lived.html (accessed September 13, 2009).

140. Robert B. Semple, Jr. ed., *Four Days in November* (New York: St. Martin's Press, 2003), 101, 103–104, 107.

141. "Early Career: Lyndon B. Johnson, 36th President," PBS American Experience, http://www.pbs.org/wgbh/amex/presidents/36_l_johnson/l_johnson_early.html (accessed September 13, 2009).

142. Henry Graff, "Lyndon B. Johnson: Early Years," Profiles of U.S. Presidents, http://www.presidentprofiles.com/Kennedy-Bush/Lyndon-B-Johnson-Early-years.html (accessed September 13, 2009).

143. Robert Dallek, *Flawed Giant* (New York: Oxford University Press, 1998), 4. Google Book Search. Web. (accessed September 13, 2009).

144. "Lyndon Baines Johnson's Biography," Lyndon Baines Johnson Library and Museum, http://www.lbjlib.utexas.edu/johnson/archives.hom/biographys.hom/lbj_bio.asp (accessed September 13, 2009).

145. Gene B. Preuss, "Public Schools Come of Age," in *Twentieth-Century Texas: A Social and Cultural History*, ed. John W. Storey and Mary L. Kelley (Denton; University of North Texas Press, 2008), 375. Google Book Search. Web. (accessed September 13, 2009).

146. William E. Leuchtenburg, *The White House Looks South* (Baton Rouge: Louisiana State University Press, 2005), 246. Google Book Search. Web. (accessed September 13, 2009).

147. "Lyndon B. Johnson's Address before a Joint Session of Congress, November 27, 1963," Lyndon Baines Johnson Library and Museum, http:// www.lbjlib.utexas.edu/johnson/archives.hom/speeches.hom/631127.asp (accessed September 13, 2009).

148. Wilentz.

149. "Transcript of President Johnson's Thanksgiving Day Address to the Nation Urging 'New Dedication,'" *New York Times,* November 29, 1963, http://www.nytimes.com/books/98/04/12/specials/johnson-thankadd. html (accessed September 13, 2009).

150. "Civil Rights Act of 1964," Wikipedia http://en.wikipedia.org/wiki/ Civil_Rights_Act_of_1964 (accessed December 27, 2009).

151. Rob Langenderfer, "Perspectives in History, Northern Kentucky University History/Geography Department, President Lyndon Johnson and Domestic Politics: Conflicting Historical Viewpoints since 1985," *Journal of the Alpha Beta Phi Chapter of Phi Alpha Theta* (Highland Heights, KY: 2000), 52.

152. Contained within Dallek, 120.

153. Dallek, 161–162.

154. Letter to Hon. Hebner Ladner, Secretary of State, State of Mississippi from Annie Devine, Secretary and Temporary State Executive Committee, July 20, 1964 (copy—personal possession of author).

155. "Mississippi Freedom Democratic Party," The University of Southern Mississippi, http://www.usm.edu/crdp/html/cd/mfdp.htm (accessed September 13, 2009).

156. Kay Mills, *This Little Light of Mine: The Life of Fannie Lou Hamer* (Lexington: University Press of Kentucky, 2007), 105. Google Book Search. Web. (accessed September 13, 2009).

157. "Three Murdered Workers Found" and "Mississippi Harassment," *The Student Voice* (Atlanta, GA), August 12, 1964.

158. "Say It Plain," American Radio Works, http://americanradioworks. publicradio.org/features/sayitplain/flhamer.html (accessed September 13, 2009).

159. "Mississippi Freedom Democratic Party."

160. Dallek, 164.

161. "Mississippi Freedom Democratic Party."

162. Ibid., and Mills, 131.

163. Mills, 132.

164. Nick Kotz, *Judgment Days: Lyndon Baines Johnson, Martin Luther King, Jr., and the Laws That Changed America* (Boston: Houghton-Mifflin, 2005), 94. Google Book Search. Web. (accessed September 15, 2009).

165. Jack Bass and Walter De Vries, *The Transformation of Southern Politics Social Change and Political Consequence since 1945* (Athens: University of Georgia Press, 1995), 9. Google Book Search. Web. (accessed September 15, 2008).

166. "Lyndon B. Johnson's Annual Message to the Congress on the State of the Union, January 8, 1964," Lyndon Baines Johnson Library and Museum http://www.lbjlib.utexas.edu/johnson/archives.hom/speeches.hom/640108.asp (accessed September 18, 2009).

167. "LBJ for Kids! Weapons against Poverty," Lyndon Baines Johnson Library and Museum, http://www.lbjlib.utexas.edu/Johnson/lbjforkids/pov_weapons.shtm (accessed September 13, 2009).

168. "The Great Society," PBS, http://www.pbs.org/johngardner/chapters/4c.html (accessed September 13, 2009).

169. "Landmark Laws of the Lyndon B. Johnson Administration," Lyndon Baines Johnson Library and Museum, http://www.lbjlib.utexas.edu/johnson/civilrights/PDF/PresidentJohnson'sLandmarkLaws.pdf (accessed September 13, 2009).

170. "A Timeline of Sen. Eugene McCarthy's Life and Political Career," Minnesota Public Radio, December 10, 2005, http://news.minnesota.publicradio.org/features/2005/06/15_newsroom_mccarthytimeline/ (accessed February 29, 2008).

171. Walter LaFeber, *The Deadly Bet: LBJ, Vietnam, and the 1968 Election* (Lanham, MD: Rowman and Littlefield, 2005), 41. Google Book Search. Web. (accessed March 14, 2008).

172. "A Timeline of Sen. Eugene McCarthy's Life and Political Career."

173. Eugene J. McCarthy, *The Year of the People* (Garden City, NY: Doubleday, 1969), 292.

174. Joseph J. Thorndike, "Tax History Project Historical Perspective: Sacrifice and Surcharge," Tax History Project, December 5, 2005, http://www.taxhistory.org/thp/readings.nsf/cf7c9c870b600b9585256df80075b9dd/6b24abb33fe1996c852570d200756a5d?OpenDocument (accessed March 26, 2008).

175. Ibid.

176. "Episode 13: Make Love, Not War (the Sixties)," *The Cold War*, The George Washington University, http://www.gwu.edu/~nsarchiv/coldwar/interviews/episode-13/mccarthy1.html (accessed February 29, 2008).

177. Ibid.

178. C. David Heymann, *RFK* (New York: Dutton, 1998), 445. Google Book Search. Web. (accessed March 14, 2008).

179. Spartacus Educational, http://www.spartacus.schoolnet.co.uk/USAkennedyR.htm (accessed April 20, 2008).

180. Heymann, 445 and 447.

181. Ibid., Schlesinger, *Robert Kennedy and His Times* (Boston: Houghton-Mifflin, 2002), 416. The author implies this is how his friend, David Hackett, saw Kennedy. Google Book Search. Web. (accessed March 14, 2008).

182. Ronald Gottesman, ed., *Violence in America: An Encyclopedia*, Volume 2 (New York: Charles Scribner, 1999), 215. Google Book Search. Web. (accessed March 15, 2008).

183. Heymann, 356–357.

184. "Remarks of Robert F. Kennedy at the University of Kansas, March 18, 1968," John F Kennedy Presidential Library and Museum Historical Resources, http://www.jfklibrary.org/Historical+Resources/Archives/Reference+Desk/Speeches/RFK/RFKSpeech68Mar18UKansas.htm (accessed March 19, 2008).

185. Joseph A. Palermo, "Here's What RFK Did in California in 1968," *The Huffington Post,* January 10, 2008, http://www.huffingtonpost.com/joseph-a-palermo/heres-what-rfk-did-in-ca_b_80931.html (accessed March 19, 2008). Excerpt from Palermo's *In His Own Right: The Political Odyssey of Senator Robert F. Kennedy* (Irvington, NY: Columbia University Press: 2001).

186. Jessica Nevarez Laura Jasso, Tania Ugarte, and Oscar Estrada, "Cesar Chávez: Simple Man, People's Hero," Borderlands, El Paso Community College, http://epcc.edu/nwlibrary/borderlands/15_cesar_chavez.htm (accessed March 19, 2008). Also see The United Farm Workers Web site, and in particular the veterans of historic Delano Grape Strike mark 40th anniversary with two-day reunion in Delano and La Paz, http://www.ufw.org/_page.php?menu=research&inc=history/05.html (accessed September 16, 2009).

187. Palermo.

188. Hubert H. Humphrey, "1948 Democratic National Convention Address," American Rhetoric Top 100 Speeches, http://www.americanrhetoric.com/speeches/huberthumphey1948dnc.html (accessed February 2, 2008).

189. Hubert H. Humphrey, *The Education of a Public Man* (Garden City, NY: Doubleday, 1976), 112.

190. Solberg, 11–12.

191. "Hubert Humphrey," Wikipedia, http://en.wikipedia.org/wiki/Hubert_Humphrey (accessed September 13, 2009).

192. Josh Gottheimer, *Ripples of Hope: Great American Civil Rights Speeches* (New York: Basic Civitas Books, 2003), 197. Google Book Search. Web. (accessed September 15, 2008).

193. "Hubert H. Humphrey, 38th Vice President (1965–1969)," United States Senate, http://www.senate.gov/artandhistory/history/common/generic/VP_Hubert_Humphrey.htm (accessed September 13, 2009).

194. "Hubert Humphrey." Wikipedia (accessed September 13, 2009).

195. "Hubert Horatio Humphrey Vice President 1965–1969," Lyndon Baines Johnson Library and Museum http://www.lbjlib.utexas.edu/johnson/

archives.hom/FAQs/humphrey/HHH_home.asp (accessed September 13, 2009).

196. "Hubert H. Humphrey, 38th Vice President (1965–1969)."
197. "THE CAMPAIGN: The Liberal Flame," *Time,* February 1, 1960, http://www.time.com/time/magazine/article/0,9171,826037,00.html (accessed September 13, 2009).
198. Humphrey, *Education of a Public Man*, 267–287.
199. Ibid., 283. Italics in the original.
200. "Hubert Humphrey," Wikipedia (accessed February 8, 2008).
201. Charles Lloyd Garrettson, *Hubert H. Humphrey: The Politics of Joy* (New Brunswick: Transaction, 1993), 16. Google Book Search. Web. (accessed September 15, 2009).
202. "1968 Presidential General Election Results," Dave Leip's Atlas of U.S. Presidential Elections, http://uselectionatlas.org/RESULTS/ (accessed September 13, 2009).
203. "Hubert Humphrey," Wikipedia (accessed September 13, 2009).
204. "Hubert H. Humphrey Quote Page," http://home.att.net/~howington/hhh.html (accessed September 13, 2009).

6 The 1970s and 1980s: McGovern, Carter, Hart, and Jackson

1. Bruce Miroff, *The Liberals' Moment* (Lawrence: University Press of Kansas, 2007), 27.
2. "The Senator George S. McGovern Collection," Dakota Wesleyan University, http://www.dwu.edu/library/mcgovern_finding_aid.htm (accessed March 20, 2008).
3. "George McGovern," Wikipedia, http://en.wikipedia.org/wiki/George_McGovern (accessed August 31, 2009).
4. "A History of the Colorado Coal Field War," Colorado Coal Field History Project http://www.du.edu/ludlow/cfhist.html (accessed August 31, 2009).
5. Miroff, 28.
6. "George McGovern," McGovern Center for Leadership and Public Service, http://www.mcgoverncenter.com/george.htm (accessed August 31, 2009).
7. R. Shep Melnick, *Between the Lines: Interpreting Welfare Rights* (Baltimore: Brookings Institution, 1994), 201. Google Book Search. Web. (accessed September 3, 2009).
8. "Nixon's Beginning to Feel Pressure for More Aid for Hungry Americans," *The Bulletin* May 7, 1969.
9. George McGovern, *The Essential America: Our Founders and the Liberal Tradition* (New York: Simon and Schuster, 2004), 115. Google Book Search. Web. (accessed September 3, 2009).

10. "Conference Archives," McGovern Center for Leadership and Public Service, http://www.mcgoverncenter.com/conference_past.htm (accessed September 3, 2009).

11. George McGovern, "The Lessons of 1968," *Harper's Magazine*, January 1970: 43.

12. Andrew Busch, *Outsiders and Openness in the Presidential Nominating System* (Pittsburgh: University of Pittsburgh Press, 1997), 134. Google Book Search. Web. (accessed September 3, 2009).

13. Ibid., 44.

14. McGovern, "The Lessons of 1968," 45.

15. Andrea Louise Campbell, "Parties, Electoral Participation, and Shifting Voting Blocs" in *The Transformation of American Politics: Activist Government and the Rise of Conservatism,* ed. Paul Pierson and Theda Skocpol (Princeton, NJ: Princeton University Press, 2007), 71–72. Google Book Search. Web. (accessed September 3, 2009).

16. Campbell, 71, and Marty Cohen, David Karol, Hans Noel, and John Zaller, "The Invisible Primary in Presidential Nominations, 1980–2004" in *The Making of the Presidential Candidates 2008,* ed. William G. Mayer (Lanham, MD: Rowman and Littlefield, 2008), 3. Google Book Search. Web. (accessed September 4, 2009).

17. Miroff, 130.

18. Ibid., 43.

19. Ibid., 45.

20. "Statement by Senator George McGovern (D.-S.D.) Announcing Candidacy for the 1972 Democratic Presidential Nomination, Sioux Falls, South Dakota, January 18, 1971," 4President.org, http://www.4president.org/speeches/mcgovern1972announcement.htm (accessed March 20, 2008).

21. James Joyner, "Iraq Versus Vietnam: A Comparison of Public Opinion," Outside the Beltway, August 24, 2005, http://www.outsidethebeltway.com/archives/2005/08/iraq_versus_vietnam_a_comparison_of_public_opinion (accessed March 21, 2008).

22. Miroff, 38.

23. Ibid., 120.

24. "The Nation: How Voters Assess George McGovern v. Richard Nixon" *Time,* July 17, 1972, http://www.time.com/time/magazine/article/0,9171,877865,00.html (accessed September 10, 2009).

25. Ibid., Miroff, 178.

26. Miroff, 177.

27. Ibid.

28. Ibid., 177–179.

29. Ibid., 179.

30. R. Hal Williams, *The Democratic Party and California Politics, 1880–1896* (Palo Alto: Stanford University Press, 1993), 246. Google Book Search. Web. (accessed September 4, 2009).

31. Miroff, 119.

32. Ibid., 125.

33. Hunter S. Thompson, *Fear and Loathing: On the Campaign Trial '72* (New York: Warner, 1973), 82.

34. Miroff, 128.

35. David Usbourne, "Nixon Wanted to Drop Nuclear Bomb on Vietnam," *The Independent*, March 2, 2002, http://www.independent.co.uk/news/world/americas/nixon-wanted-to-drop-nuclear-bomb-on-vietnam-654499.html (accessed March 22, 2008).

36. Ray Smith, "Casualties—U.S. vs NVA/VC," April 4, 1995, information, Ray's Web Server, http://www.rjsmith.com/kia_tbl.html (accessed March 22, 2008).

37. Aner Govrin, "When the Underdog Scheme Dominates the We-ness Schema," *The Psychoanalytic Review,* 93(4), August 2006: 624.

38. Ibid.

39. Ibid., 631.

40. George McGovern, *Grassroots* (New York: Random House, 1977), 204.

41. Miroff, 92.

42. Ibid.

43. "Angela Davis," Wikipedia, http://en.wikipedia.org/wiki/Angela_Davis (accessed April 9, 2008).

44. Richard Dougherty, *Goodbye, Mr. Christian* (Garden City, NY: Doubleday, 1973), 66.

45. "Front and Center for George McGovern," *Time*, May 8, 1972, http://www.time.com/time/magazine/article/0,9171,943431–6,00.html (accessed April 9, 2008).

46. Ibid.

47. Jimmy Carter, *A Government as Good as Its People* (New York: Pocket, 1977), 88.

48. Martin Schram, *Running for President* (New York: Kangaroo, 1977), 46. Brackets in the original.

49. Ibid., 53–54.

50. Carter, 37.

51. Ibid., 65–66. My emphasis.

52. Kenneth Earl Morris, *Jimmy Carter: American Moralist* (Athens: University of Georgia Press, 1996), 152. Google Book Search. Web. (accessed April 13, 2008).

53. Burt I. Kaufman, *The Presidency of James Earl Carter, Jr.* (Lawrence: University Press of Kansas, 1993), 9.

54. Schram, 56.

55. A. Leon Higginbotham, "The Case of the Missing Judges," *New York Times*, July 29, 1992, http://query.nytimes.com/gst/fullpage.html?res=9E0CE0DC123BF93AA15754C0A964958260 (accessed April 14, 2008).

56. Kaufman, 110.

57. Jody Powell, *The Other Side of the Story* (New York: William Morrow, 1984), 186.

58. Frances X. Clines, "A Dump Carter Movement?" About New York, *New York Times,* February 24, 1979, 23.

59. "ADA Is Urged to Shun Carter in 1980 Election," *New York Times*, section 1, June 24, 1979.

60. Elizabeth Drew, *Portrait of an Election* (New York: Simon and Shuster, 1981), 15.

61. Powell, 189.

62. Daniel Horowitz, *Jimmy Carter and the Energy Crisis of the 1970s* (Boston: Bedford/St.Martin's, 2005), 5.

63. Kaufman, 99–101.

64. Edwin C. Hargrove, *Jimmy Carter as President: Leadership and the Politics of the Public Good* (Baton Rouge: Louisiana State University Press, 1988), 79. Google Book Search. Web. (accessed April 13, 2008).

65. W. Carl Biven, *Jimmy Carter's Economy: Policy in an Age of Limits* (Chapel Hill: University of North Carolina Press, 2002), 260. Google Book Search. Web. (accessed April 13, 2008).

66. Powell, 247.

67. Drew, 247.

68. Ibid., 248.

69. "Ted Kennedy: 1980 Democratic National Convention Address, Delivered 12 August 1980, New York, NY," American Rhetoric, http://www.americanrhetoric.com/speeches/tedkennedy1980dnc.htm (accessed April 16, 2008). My emphasis.

70. Peter S. Canellos, ed., *Last Lion: The Fall and Rise of Ted Kennedy* (New York: Simon and Schuster, 2009), 231.

71. Jeff Cohen and Norman Solomon, "Jimmy Carter and Human Rights: Behind the Media Myth," FAIR: Fairness and Accuracy in Reporting, September 21, 1994, http://www.fair.org/index.php?page=2263 (accessed April 16, 2008).

72. David Beetham, ed., *Politics and Human Rights* (Oxford and Cambridge, MA: Blackwell, 1995), 117. Google Book Search. Web. (accessed April 15, 2008).

73. Jimmy Carter, "Human Rights and Foreign Policy," Speech at Notre Dame University, May 22, 1977, American Information Web, http://usinfo.org/facts/speech/55.htm (accessed April 16, 2008).

74. Jimmy Carter, *Keeping Faith* (New York: Bantam Books, 1982), 144.

75. Tamar Jacoby, "Did Carter Fail on Human Rights? Jimmy Carter," *Washington Monthly*, June 1986, http://findarticles.com/p/articles/mi_m1316/is_v18/ai_4262005/pg_2/?tag=content;col1 (accessed August 9, 2009).

76. Douglas Brinkley, *The Unfinished Presidency* (New York: Penguin, 1999), 19.

77. "Tough Negotiation Expected," *Eugene (Oregon) Register-Guard,* March 27, 1977. http://news.google.com/newspapers?id=3HkRAAAAIBAJ&sjid=JO ADAAAAIBAJ&pg=6282,6376182&dq=tough+negotiation+expected&hl =en (accessed September 4, 2009).

78. Associated Press, "Carter Reaffirms 'Rights Crusade,'" *Kingman Daily Miner,* March 31, 1977. http://news.google.com/newspapers?id=MrUOA AAAIBAJ&sjid=6YIDAAAAIBAJ&pg=4334,6494837&dq=carter+reaffir ms+rights+crusades&hl=en (accessed September 4, 2009).

79. Carter, *Keeping Faith,* 146–147.

80. James Chance, "U.S. Foreign Policy and Human Rights," *The Ledger,* May 29, 1977.

81. Rosalyn Carter, *First Lady from Plains* (Fayetteville: University of Arkansas Press, 1994), 218. Google Book Search. Web. (accessed September 4, 2009).

82. "Remembering the Iran Hostage Crisis," *BBC News,* November 4, 2004, http://news.bbc.co.uk/2/hi/middle_east/3978523.stm (accessed August 9, 2009).

83. "Iran Hostage's Diary: Robert C. Ode," Jimmy Carter Library and Museum, January 8 through November 23, 1980: 69, http://www.jimmycarterlibrary. org/documents/r_ode/Ode_pages51thru100.pdf (accessed August 9, 2009).

84. Jimmy Carter, *Keeping Faith,* 459.

85. "The Hostage Crisis in Iran," Jimmy Carter Library & Museum http:// www.jimmycarterlibrary.gov/documents/hostages.phtml (accessed August 9, 2009).

86. Brinkley, 10.

87. Gary Sick, *October Surprise* (New York, Times Books, 1991), 177.

88. Mark Bowden, *Guests of the Ayatollah* (New York: Grove Press, 2006), 608.

89. Athan G. Theoharis and Richard H. Immerman, *The Central Intelligence Agency* (Santa Barbara: Greenwood Press, 2005), 60. Google Book Search. Web. (accessed September 4, 2009).

90. "The Religious Affiliation of President Jimmy Carter," adherents. com, http://www.adherents.com/people/pc/Jimmy_Carter.html (accessed August 7, 2009).

91. Eval J. Naveth, "Beyond Illusion and Despair: Niebuhr's Liberal Legacy in a Divided American Culture" in *Rheinhold Niebuhr Revisited: Engagements with an American Original,* ed. Daniel Rice (Grand Rapids: Wm. B. Erdman's, 2009), 263. Google Book Search. Web. (accessed September 4, 2009).

92. "Rheinhold Niebuhr," Wikipedia, http://en.wikipedia.org/wiki/Reinhold_ Niebuhr (accessed August 7, 2009).

93. Hugh Sidey, "The Presidency by Hugh Sidey: A Man among Old Friends," *Time,* September 6, 1976, http://www.time.com/time/magazine/ article/0,9171,918293,00.html (accessed August 9, 2009).

94. Jimmy Carter, "Letter to Ursula M. Niebuhr," *Rheinhold Niebuhr Papers: Library of Congress, Manuscript Reading Room,* Speaking of Faith, August1, 1976, http://speakingoffaith.publicradio.org/programs/niebuhr-rediscovered/c78.shtml (accessed August 9, 2009).

95. "Our Nation's Past and Future: Address Accepting the Presidential Nomination at the Democratic National Convention in New York City," *The American Presidency Project,* July 15, 1976, http://www.presidency.ucsb.edu/ws/index.php?pid=25953 (accessed September 18, 2009.)

96. Carl Cannon, "Obama's Favorite Theologian? A Short Course on Rheinhold Niebuhr," Transcript, May 4, 2009, The Pew Forum on Religion & Public Life, http://pewforum.org/events/?EventID=219#14 (accessed. August 9, 2009).

97. Naveth, 264.

98. Jimmy Carter, "President Jimmy Carter's Farewell Address," Selected Speeches of Jimmy Carter, January 14, 1981, http://www.jimmycarterlibrary.org/documents/speeches/farewell.phtml (accessed April 16, 2008).

99. Joe Hallett, "Up Close in Iowa: Democrats Get It Going," *Toledo Blade,* February 19, 1984.

100. "United States Presidential Election, 1984," Wikipedia, http://en.wikipedia.org/wiki/United_States_presidential_election,_1984 (accessed July 8, 2008).

101. "Restoring Economic Growth," Policy statement by Senator Gary Hart, June 1982, campaign pamphlet: 1.

102. Ibid.

103. Norman C. Miller, "Senator Gary Hart: A New Breed of Democrat?" *Wall Street Journal,* May 6, 1982.

104. Dinesh D'Souza, "What Ever Happened to Neoliberalism?" *National Review,* June 2, 1989.

105. Jack Germond and Jules Witcover, *Wake Us When It's Over* (New York: Palgrave Macmillan, 1985), 178.

106. Ibid., 177.

107. Ibid.

108. "The Man Who Wears No Label," *Time,* March 12, 1984, http://www.cnn.com/ALLPOLITICS/1996/analysis/back.time/9603/08/index.shtml (accessed July 10, 2008).

109. "Yuppie," Wikipedia, http://en.wikipedia.org/wiki/Yuppie (accessed July 13, 2008), and Walter Shapiro, "The Birth and—Maybe—Death of Yuppiedom," *Time,* April 8, 1991, http://www.time.com/time/magazine/article/0,9171,972695–1,00.html (accessed July 12, 2008).

110. Jason Manning, "Yuppie Culture," http://eightiesclub.tripod.com/id295.htm (accessed September 18, 2009).

111. Jonathan Moore, ed., *Campaign for President: The Managers Look at '84* (Santa Barbara: Greenwood, 1986), 119. Google Book Search. Web. (accessed July 13, 2008).

112. John E. Chubb and Paul E. Peterson, "The New Two-Party System," in *The New Direction in American Politics,* ed. Thomas E. Cavanagh and James L. Sundquist (Washington: Brookings Institution, 1985), 63. Google Book Search. Web. (accessed July 14, 2008).

113. Susan Berry Casey, *Hart and Soul* (Concord, NH: NHI Press, 1986), 1.

114. Jules Witcover, *Party of the People* (New York: Random House, 2003), 622.

115. Ibid.

116. Casey, 208.

117. Germond and Witcover, 622.

118. http://www.time.com/time/magazine/0,9263,7601840312,00.html (accessed June 4, 2009).

119. Germond and Witcover, 195.

120. Ibid., 200.

121. Ibid., 204.

122. Jack Germond, Jules Witcover, Peter Goldman, Tony Fuller, and William A. Henry, III, "Why Gary Hart Lost," *Washington Monthly*, October 1985, http://findarticles.com/p/articles/mi_m1316/is_v17/ai_3959886 (accessed July 6, 2008).

123. "United States Presidential Election Results," Dave Leip's Atlas of U.S. Presidential Elections, http://uselectionatlas.org/RESULTS/ (accessed August 13, 2009).

124. "Gary Hart Presidential Campaign 1998," Wikipedia, http://en.wikipedia.org/wiki/Gary_Hart_presidential_campaign_1988 (accessed July 14, 2008).

125. Ibid.

126. Walter Shapiro, "The Ghost of Gary Past," *Time*, December 18, 1987, http://www.time.com/time/magazine/article/0,9171,966328–1,00.html (accessed July 14, 2008).

127. Ibid. My emphasis.

128. "Gary Hart Presidential Campaign 1998."

129. Elizabeth O. Colton, *The Jackson Phenomenon* (New York: Doubleday, 1989), 12.

130. Marshall Frady, *Jesse: The Life and Pilgrimage of Jesse Jackson* (New York: Random House, 1996), 33. Google Book Search. Web. (accessed July 17, 2008).

131. "Jesse Jackson," Wikipedia, http://en.wikipedia.org/wiki/Jesse_Jackson (accessed July 17, 2008).

132. Frady, 332.

133. Germond and Witcover, 277.

134. Frady, 335–336, and Kerstin Fischer and Antje Cordes, "Intercultural Communication: Winter Semester, 2005–2006, 17.01.2006," http://nats-www.informatik.uni-hamburg.de/pub/User/InterculturalCommunication/Penningtonhandout.doc (accessed July 18, 2008).

135. Frady, 336.

136. Alessandra Stanley, Bruce Van Voorst, and Jack E. White et al., "An Office and a Gentleman Comes Home: Lieut. Robert O. Goodman," *Time*, January 16, 1984 http://www.time.com/time/magazine/article/0,9171,921482–1,00.html (accessed September 18, 2009).

137. Ibid., Frady 341 and Kurt Andersen, Christopher Ogden, and Hays Corey, "Going for a Knockout," *Time*, March 5, 1984 http://www.time.com/time/magazine/article/0,9171,952336–4,00.html (accessed September 18, 2009).

138. Ibid., 350.

139. "Jesse Jackson Disavows Black Muslims Comments," *Spokane Chronicle*, June 29, 1984: 7.

140. Ibid. Frady, 348.

141. Ibid., 347. Emphasis in the original.

142. Ibid., Germond and Witcover, 282.

143. Katherine Tate, "Symposium II: African-American Politics in the 1990s: The Impact of Jesse Jackson's Presidential Bids on Blacks' Relationship with the Democratic Party," Ethnic Politics & Civil Liberties, *National Political Science Review,* 1992: 193.

144. Michael B. Preston, "The 1984 Presidential Primary Campaign: Who Voted for Jesse Jackson and Why?" in *Jesse Jackson's 1984 Presidential Campaign: Challenge and Change in American Politics,* ed. Lucius J. Barker and Ronald W. Walters (Champaign: University of Illinois Press, 1989), 136. Google Book Search. Web. (accessed July 12, 2008).

145. Germond and Witcover, 287.

146. Frady: 358–359.

147. Ibid., 359. Emphasis in the original.

148. Ibid., 360.

149. Lucius J. Barker, *Our Time Has Come: A Delegate's Diary of Jesse Jackson's 1984 Presidential Campaign* (Champaign: University of Illinois Press, 1988), 107–108. Google Book Search. Web. (accessed July 16, 2008).

150. Frady, 389.

151. Frady, 391, and Jack Germond and Jules Witcover, *Whose Broad Stripes and Bright Stars?* (New York: Warner, 1989), 279.

152. Frady, 391.

153. Jesse Jackson, Frank Clemente, and Frank Watkins, *Keep Hope Alive: Jesse Jackson's 1988 Presidential Campaign* (Cambridge, MA: South End Press, 1990), 7. Google Book Search. Web. (accessed July 19, 2008).

154. Germond and Witcover, *Whose Broad Stripes and Bright Stars?* 289.

155. Colton, 93–94.

156. Ibid., 100.

157. Jane Gross, "A Campaign Stirs Conflicts among Gay Voters," *New York Times*, April 13, 1988. http://query.nytimes.com/gst/fullpage.html?res=9 40DEFD9103BF930A25757C0A96E948260 (accessed July 20, 2008).

158. Colton, 102.
159. Frady, 391–392.
160. Colton, 179–181.
161. E. J. Dionne, Jr., *Why Americans Hate Politics* (New York: Touchstone, 1991), 306.
162. Ibid.
163. Ron Daniels, "Racism Looking Forward, Looking Back" in *Race and Resistance African-Americans in the Twenty-First Century,* Herb Boyd, ed. (Cambridge, MA: South End Press: 2002), 1–2. Google Book Search. Web. (accessed July 20, 2008).
164. Jesse Jackson, "1988 Democratic National Convention Address," American Rhetoric, http://www.americanrhetoric.com/speeches/jesse-jackson1988dnc.htm (accessed July 20, 2008).
165. Frady, 388–389.
166. Colton, 10.

7 The 1990s to 2004: Bill Clinton, Al Gore, and Howard Dean

1. David Maraniss, *First in His Class* (New York: Simon and Schuster, 1995), 39–41.
2. Ibid., 38.
3. Ibid.
4. Bill Clinton, *My Life* (New York: Alfred A. Knopf, 2004), 52.
5. Charles F. Allen and Jonathan Portis, *The Comeback Kid* (New York: Birch Lane, 1992), 17.
6. Clinton, 44.
7. Maraniss, 11–18.
8. Ibid., 17.
9. Ibid., 16.
10. Allen and Portis, 51, and David S. Broder, *Changing of the Guard* (New York: Penguin, 1984), 382.
11. Allen and Portis, 55, and Maraniss, 360.
12. Maraniss, 361.
13. Ibid., 376.
14. Ibid., 377, and Melissa Nelson, "Recalling Cuban 'Bat Lift,' the Price of Freedom," The Associated Press, *Seattle Times*, April 8, 2001 (accessed via cubanet.org, http://www.cubanet.org/CNews/y01/apr01/09e7.htm on August 1, 2008).
15. Maraniss, 379.
16. Nelson.
17. Clinton, 275.
18. Lemoyne, James, "Most Who Left Mariel Sailed to New Life, a Few to Limbo," *New York Times*, April 15, 1990, http://query.nytimes.com/gst/fullpage.html?res=9C0CE3DB1630F936A25757C0A966958260 (accessed August 2, 2008).

19. Mirta Ojito, *Finding Manana* (New York: Penguin Press, 2005), 275.
20. Ibid., and "Cuban Immigration to the United States," United States Immigration Support, http://www.usimmigrationsupport.org/cubaimmigration.html (accessed September 6, 2009).
21. Allen and Portis, 71.
22. Maraniss, 400–401.
23. Ibid., 401.
24. Ibid., 403.
25. Ibid.
26. Clinton, 302.
27. Allen and Portis, 82–91.
28. Ibid., 91.
29. Clinton, 309.
30. Allen and Portis, 91.
31. Ibid. My emphasis.
32. Peter Applebome, "Clinton Record in Leading Arkansas: Successes, but Not without Criticism," *New York Times*, December 22, 1991, http://query.nytimes.com/gst/fullpage.html?res=9D0CE6DD1739F931A15751C1A967958260&sec=&spon=&pagewanted=print (accessed August 3, 2008).
33. Allen and Portis, 275.
34. Applebome.
35. B. Drummond Ayres, Jr., "The 1992 Campaign; Clinton's Record in Arkansas Is Uneven on Health Issues," *New York Times*, April 2, 1992, http://query.nytimes.com/gst/fullpage.html?res=9E0CE6DB153DF931A35757C0A964958260 (accessed August 3, 2008).
36. Maraniss, 416.
37. Ibid., 416–417.
38. John F. Harris, *The Survivor: Bill Clinton in the White House* (New York: Random House, 1995), xxiii.
39. "Announcement Speech," Bill Clinton for President, Old State House, Little Rock, Arkansas, October 3, 1991. Pamphlet: 2.
40. "The New Covenant: Responsibility and Rebuilding the American Community," Bill Clinton for President, Georgetown University, Washington, DC, October 23, 1991. Pamphlet: 3.
41. Ibid., 4.
42. See Kevin Phillips, *The Politics of Rich and Poor* (New York: Harper: 1990); Kevin Phillips, *Boiling Point* (New York: Random House, 1993); Donald L. Bartlett and James B. Steele, *America: What Went Wrong?* (Kansas City: Andrew McMeel, 1992); and Lawrence Mishel and Jared Bernstein, *The State of Working America: 1992–1993.* (Economic Policy Institute, Armonk, NY: M.E. Sharpe, 1993).
43. Bill Clinton, "Putting People First: A National Economic Strategy for America," 1992 campaign pamphlet.
44. Ibid.
45. Ibid.

46. Jules Witcover, *Party of the People* (New York: Random House, 2003), 655–656.

47. Ibid., 657–658.

48. Mary Matlin and James Carville with Peter Knobler, *All's Fair* (New York: Random House, 1994), 141.

49. Witcover, 660, and "Democratic Party (United States) Presidential Primaries, 1992," Wikipedia, http://en.wikipedia.org/wiki/Democratic_Party_%28United_States%29_presidential_primaries%2C_1992 (accessed August 6, 2008).

50. Sheila Rule, "THE 1992 CAMPAIGN: Racial Issues; Rapper, Chided by Clinton, Calls Him a Hypocrite," *New York Times*, June 17, 1992 http://www.nytimes.com/1992/06/17/us/the-1992-campaign-racial-issues-rapper-chided-by-clinton-calls-him-a-hypocrite.html (accessed September 18, 2009).

51. Ibid., Clinton, 411.

52. Christine F. Ridout, "News Coverage and Talk Shows in the 1992 Presidential Campaign," *PS: Political Science and Politics*, Vol. 26, No. 4 (December 1993): 713.

53. Gwen Ifill, "The 1992 Campaign: Political Memo; Clinton Deftly Navigates Shoals of Racial Issues," *New York Times*, June 17, 1992, http://query.nytimes.com/gst/fullpage.html?res=9E0CE3DE1F31F934A25755C0A964958260 (accessed August 6, 2008).

54. Wilson Carey McWillims, *The Politics of Disappointment* (Chatham, NJ: Chatham House, 1995), 163.

55. Anthony Lewis, "Abroad at Home; Black and White," *New York Times*, June 18, 1992, http://query.nytimes.com/gst/fullpage.html?res=9E0CE6DD1031F93BA25755C0A964958260&sec=&spon=&pagewanted=print (accessed August 6, 2008).

56. Ian Vasquez, "Doing What We Can for Haiti," Cato Institute, Policy Analysis no. 183, November 5, 1992, http://www.cato.org/pub_display.php?pub_id=1043&full=1 (accessed August 6, 2008).

57. Deborah Sontag, "Appeals Court Overturns Bush's Order on Haitians," *New York Times*, July 30, 1992, http://query.nytimes.com/gst/fullpage.html?res=9E0CE4D6103DF933A05754C0A964958260 (accessed August 6, 2008).

58. Elizabeth Drew, *On the Edge: The Clinton Presidency* (New York: Simon and Schuster, 1994), 332.

59. Howard W. French, "Haitians See a Renewal of Hope with Clinton," *New York Times*, November 23, 1992, http://query.nytimes.com/gst/fullpage.html?res=9E0CE1DC1338F930A15752C1A964958260&sec=&spon=&pagewanted=all (accessed August 6, 2008).

60. Harris, 6–7.

61. Clinton, *My Life*, 463–464.

62. Ibid., 616.

63. "History of Haiti," Wikipedia, http://en.wikipedia.org/wiki/History_of_Haiti (accessed August 7, 2008), and Paul Robyn, "The United States and Haiti (1993–1994): A Case Study in Coercive Diplomacy," http://wws.princeton.edu/research/cases/haiti.pdf (accessed September 11, 2009).
64. Clinton, *My Life,* 616.
65. Harris, 141. My emphasis.
66. Harris, 16–18, and Drew, 42–48.
67. Drew, 42.
68. Ibid., Clinton, *My Life,* 486.
69. Clinton, *My Life,* 485–486.
70. "Defense of Marriage Act," Wikipedia, http://en.wikipedia.org/wiki/Defense_of_Marriage_Act (accessed August 7, 2008).
71. Harris, 245.
72. Drew, 84.
73. Bob Woodward, *The Agenda* (New York: Simon and Schuster, 1994), 126.
74. Clinton, *My Life,* 492.
75. Drew, 84.
76. Ibid., Clinton, 497.
77. Ibid., 496–497.
78. Drew, 84.
79. Drew, 84 and 87–88.
80. Ibid., 201.
81. "Extra," FAIR, July/August 1993, http://www.fair.org/extra/best-of-extra/guinier-queen.html (accessed August 14, 2008).
82. Drew, 204.
83. "Extra."
84. Randall Kennedy, "Lani Guinier's Constitution," *American Prospect* November 30, 2002, http://www.prospect.org/cs/articles?article=lani_guiniers_constitution (accessed August 14, 2008).
85. Drew, 198–211.
86. "Extra."
87. Kennedy.
88. Barbara Ehrenreich, "Lurch to the Left? You're Kidding," *Time,* June 21, 1993, http://www.time.com/time/magazine/article/0,9171,978737,00.html (accessed August 13, 2008).
89. Drew, 53.
90. "Your Rights under the Family and Medical Leave Act of 1993," U.S. Department of Labor, U.S. Government Printing Office, 2001, http://www.dol.gov/esa/regs/compliance/posters/fmlaen.pdf (accessed August 12, 2008).
91. Drew, 303–304.
92. Ibid., 303.
93. E. J. Dionne, Jr., *They Only Look Dead* (New York: Simon and Schuster, 1996), 119.

94. Ibid., 120.

95. Clinton, *My Life*, 594–595.

96. Harris, 112.

97. United Nations Security Council, "Letter Dated 15 December from Secretary-General Addressed to the President of the Security Council," http://daccessdds.un.org/doc/UNDOC/GEN/N99/395/47/IMG/N9939547.pdf?OpenElement (accessed August 12, 2008).

98. Harris, 127.

99. Clinton, *My Life*, 593.

100. Dionne, Jr., 57.

101. "World: Europe UN Gives Figure for Kosovo Dead," BBC News, November 10, 1999, http://news.bbc.co.uk/2/hi/europe/514828.stm (accessed August 13, 2008).

102. "Focus on Kosovo: A Timeline of Tensions," CNN.com, http://www.cnn.com/SPECIALS/1998/10/kosovo/timeline/#1998 (accessed August 13, 2008); and "Kosovo," Wikipedia, http://en.wikipedia.org/wiki/Kosovo#cite_note-21 (accessed August 13, 2008).

103. Clinton, *My Life*, 850–851.

104. Drew, 339.

105. Rep. David Bonior, "The Impact of NAFTA on American Jobs (House of Representatives, July 28, 1993)," The Library of Congress, THOMAS, http://thomas.loc.gov/cgi-bin/query/F?r103:40:./temp/~r103WKqKa6:e232 (accessed August 13, 2008).

106. Clinton, *My Life*, 432.

107. Ibid., 546–547. My emphasis.

108. "NAFTA Job Retraining Program out of Money," *Northwest Labor Press*, http://www.nwlaborpress.org/2001/4-20-01NAFTA.html (accessed August 13, 2008).

109. Dionne, Jr., 138–139. Emphasis in the original.

110. Harris, 176.

111. Ibid., 177.

112. Joe Conason, and Gene Lyons, *The Hunting of the President: The Ten-Year Campaign to Destroy Bill and Hillary Clinton* (New York: Thomas Dunne Books St. Martin's Press, 2000); and David Brock, *Blinded by the Right: The Conscience of an Ex-Conservative* (New York: Three Rivers Press, 2003).

113. Dale Bumpers, "Closing Defense Arguments at the Impeachment Trial of William J. Clinton," *American Rhetoric*, January 21, 1999, http://www.americanrhetoric.com/speeches/dalebumpersdefenseofclinton.htm (accessed June 5, 2009).

114. Tracey Fessenden, Nicholas F. Radel, and Magdalena J. Zaborowska, ed., "Introduction," *The Puritan Origins of American Sex* (New York: Routledge, 2001), 1–3. Google Book Search. Web. (accessed June 5, 2009).

115. James McGregor Burns and Georgia J. Sorensen, *Dead Center* (New York: Lisa Drew Scribner, 1999), 154. Google Book Search. Web. (accessed June 5, 2009).

116. Nigel Hamilton, *Bill Clinton: Mastering the Presidency* (New York: Public Affairs, 2007), 376. Google Book Search. Web. (accessed June 6, 2009).

117. Robin Toner, "The Flutters; Adding up Concern for Bush and Doubts about Quayle, the Democrats Get Zero," *New York Times,* May 12, 1991, http://www.nytimes.com/1991/05/12/weekinreview/flutters-adding-up-concern-for-bush-doubts-about-quayle-democrats-get-zero.html (accessed September 6, 2009).

118. "Democratic Leadership Council" SourceWatch http://www.sourcewatch.org/index.php?title=Democratic_Leadership_Council (accessed September 5, 2009).

119. Al Gore, "Foreword" in *Building the Bridge: 10 Big Ideas to Transform America,* ed. Will Marshall (Lanham, MD: Rowman and Littlefield, 1997), vii. Google Book Search. Web. (accessed September 5, 2009).

120. John Micklethwart and Adrian Wooldridge, *The Right Nation* (New York: Penguin, 2004), 118.

121. Alex Isenstadt, "Bill Clinton Defends DLC Role, Legacy," Politico, http://www.politico.com/news/stories/0609/23833.html (accessed September 5, 2009).

122. Major R. Owens, "Hillary Must Rescue Herself from the DLC," *Huffington Post,* January 16, 2008, http://www.huffingtonpost.com/rep-major-r-owens/hillary-must-rescue-herse_b_81827.html (accessed September 5, 2009).

123. David Maraniss and Ellen Nakashima, *The Prince of Tennessee* (New York: Simon and Schuster, 2000).

124. James W. Ceaser and Andrew E. Busch, *The Perfect Tie* (Lanham, MD: Rowman and Littlefield, 2001), 126. Google Book Search. Web. (accessed August 27, 2008).

125. "U.S. Vice President Al Gore Delivers Acceptance Speech at Democratic National Convention August 17, 2000," CNN, http://www.cnn.com/ELECTION/2000/conventions/democratic/transcripts/gore.html (accessed August 27, 2008).

126. Ceaser and Busch, 126–127.

127. James W. Ceaser, and Andrew E. Busch, *Red Over Blue* (Lanham, MD: Rowman and Littlefield, 2005), 84. Google Book Search. Web. (accessed August 27, 2008).

128. Kathleen Hall Jamieson and Paul Waldman, *Electing the President, 2000: The Insiders View* (Philadelphia: University of Pennsylvania Press, 2000), 56. Google Book Search. Web. (accessed August 27, 2008).

129. John B. Judas and Ruy Teixeira, *The Emerging Democratic Majority* (New York: Lisa Drew/Scribner, 2004), 142. Google Book Search. Web. (accessed August 28, 2008).

130. Ceaser and Busch, *The Perfect Tie*, 159.

131. "Statement of Ralph Nader, Announcing His Candidacy for the Green Party's Nomination for President," commondreams.org, February 21, 2000, http://www.commondreams.org/views/022100–107.htm (accessed September 18, 2009).

132. Ralph Nader, *Crashing the Party* (New York: Palgrave Macmillan, 2002), 27.

133. "Liberal vs. Liberal" OnlineNewsHour, October 24, 2000, http://www. pbs.org/newshour/bb/election/july-dec00/nader_10–24.html (accessed September 5, 2008).

134. Justin Martin, *Nader: Crusader, Spoiler, Icon* (New York: Basic Books, 2002), 245. Google Book Search. Web. (accessed September 5, 2008).

135. Ibid., xiii.

136. Matt Schudel, "Gary Sellers, 71; Onetime Ally of Ralph Nader" (obituary), *Washington Post,* Section B, March 24, 2007, http://www.washingtonpost. com/wp-dyn/content/article/2007/03/23/AR2007032301746.html (accessed September 7, 2008).

137. Ibid.

138. James Dao, "The 2000 Campaign: The Green Party; Democrats Ask Nader to Back Gore in Swing States," *New York Times*, October 31, 2000, http://query.nytimes.com/gst/fullpage.html?res=9E05E2DD1230 F932A05753C1A9669C8B63&sec=&spon=&pagewanted=all (accessed September 5, 2008).

139. Martin, 268.

140. Witcover, 710.

141. Ceaser and. Busch, *The Perfect Tie*, 12.

142. Ibid.

143. Ibid., 13. My emphasis.

144. Tracy Campbell, *Deliver the Vote: A History of Election Fraud, an American Political Tradition-1742–2004* (New York: Carroll and Graf, 2005), 303. Google Book Search. Web. (accessed September 7, 2008).

145. Ceaser and Busch, *The Perfect Tie*, 183–184; and "Bush v. Gore," Wikipedia, http://en.wikipedia.org/wiki/Bush_v._Gore (accessed September 7, 2008).

146. Campbell, 308.

147. Ibid.

148. Ibid., 306.

149. Patrick Martin, "Republican Witch-Hunt over Military Ballots Incites Anti-Gore Comments from Officer Corps," World Socialist Web Site, December 1, 2000, http://www.wsws.org/articles/2000/dec2000/mili-d01_prn.shtml (accessed September 9, 2008).

150. Ceaser and Busch, *The Perfect Tie*, 202.

151. Howard Dean, *You Have the Power* (New York: Simon and Schuster, 2004), 12.

152. "Howard Dean," dKosopedia, http://dkosopedia.com/wiki/Howard_ Dean (accessed September 20, 2008).

153. Charles Lewis, *The Buying of the President 2004, Center for Public Integrity* (New York: Harper Collins, 2004), 279.

154. Howard Dean, "What I Want to Know," Speech delivered at the California State Democratic Convention on March 15, 2003, Wikisource, http://en.wikisource.org/wiki/Howard_Dean%27s_speech_of_ March_15,_2003 (accessed September 20, 2008).

155. Howard Dean, *Winning Back America* (New York: Simon and Schuster, 2003), 69–70.

156. Dean, "What I Want to Know."

157. Joel Roberts, "Democrats Clash on Iraq," Associated Press, CBS News, February 21, 2003, http://www.cbsnews.com/stories/2003/02/21/ politics/main541540.shtml?source=search_story (accessed September 21, 2008).

158. Jim Cullen, "People Oppose War. So What?" *Progressive Populist*, March 15, 2003: 12.

159. "CBS News/New York Times Poll," PollingReport.com, http://www. pollingreport.com/iraq17.htm (accessed September 21, 2008).

160. Ibid.

161. Roberts.

162. Jerome Armstrong and Markos Moulitsas Zunga, *Crashing the Gate* (White River Junction VT: Chelsea Green, 2006), 142.

163. Ibid., 143.

164. Howard Dean, "Address to California State Democratic Convention," Sacramento, California, March 15, 2003, Transcript, http://www.gwu. edu/~action/2004/cdp0303/dean031503spt.html (accessed September 23, 2006).

165. Josh Benson, "Rocking Dean," Salon.com, November 4, 2003, http:// dir.salon.com/story/news/feature/2003/11/04/rock_vote/print.html (accessed September 23, 2008).

166. "Dean Slammed over Confederate Flag Comment," Fox News, November 1, 2003, http://www.foxnews.com/story/0,2933,101935,00. html (accessed September 23, 2008).

167. Jim VandeHei, "Dean Regrets 'Pain' Caused by Confederate Flag Comments: Democratic Candidate Calls Statement 'A Clumsy Way' to Start a Discussion about Race," *Washington Post*, November 5, 2003, http://www.washingtonpost.com/ac2/wp-dyn/A3651–2003Nov5? language=printer (accessed September 23, 2008).

168. Benson.

169. Sam Smith, "Pickup Drivers for Dean," *Progressive Populist*, December 1, 2003: 8.

170. Dean, *You Have the Power*, 17.

171. Ibid., 20

172. Joanna Glasner, "It's All Dean, All of the Time," *Wired*, May 23, 2003, http://www.wired.com/techbiz/media/news/2003/05/58953 (accessed September 26, 2008).

173. "Meetup.com," Wikipedia, http://en.wikipedia.org/wiki/Meetup.com (accessed September 26, 2008).

174. Joe Trippi, *The Revolution Will Not Be Televised* (New York: HarperCollins, 2004), 84. Google Book Search. Web. (accessed September 25, 2008).

175. Howard Dean, "Cooper Union, New York: Prepared Remarks," The George Washington University, November 6, 2003, http://www.gwu.edu/~action/2004/dean/dean110603sp.html (accessed September 26, 2008).

176. Armstrong and Zunga, 144–145.

177. Ibid., 144.

178. "White House 2004: Democratic Nomination," PollingReport.com, http://www.pollingreport.com/wh04dem.htm (accessed September 21, 2008).

179. Evan Thomas, *Election 2004* (New York: Public Affairs, 2004), 21.

180. Paul Maslin, "The Front-Runner's Fall," *Atlantic Monthly*, May 2004, http://www.theatlantic.com/doc/200405/maslin (accessed July 10, 2007). My emphasis.

181. "Howard Dean," Wikipedia, http://en.wikipedia.org/wiki/Howard_Dean (accessed September 24, 2008).

182. Ibid. (accessed September 26, 2008).

183. Joe Conason, "Howard Dean, Vindicated," Salon.com, November 10, 2006, http://www.salon.com/opinion/conason/2006/11/10/dean_dems/ (accessed September 26, 2008).

184. Amy Sullivan, *The Party Faithful* (New York: Scribner, 2008), 214. Emphasis in the original.

8 Barack Obama and the Future of the Democratic Party

1. Barack Obama, *Dreams from My Father* (New York: Three Rivers Press, 2004), 9–18.

2. Ibid., 11.

3. Ibid.

4. Ibid., 18.

5. Ibid., 18 and 20.

6. David Mendell, *Obama from Promise to Power* (New York: Amistad, 2007), 24 and 26.

7. Amanda Ripley, "The Story of Barack Obama's Mother," *Time*, April 9, 2008, http://www.time.com/time/printout/0,8816,1729524,00.html (accessed April 4, 2009).

8. Ibid., Obama, 38.

9. Obama, 39.

10. Ibid.

11. Ibid., 30.

12. Ibid., 51.

13. Mendell, 43.

14. Obama, 60.

15. Sudhin Thanawala, "In Multiracial Hawaii, Obama Faced Discrimination," Thumper's Corner, May 19, 2008, http://www.thumperscorner.com/discus/messages/36043/37043.html (accessed September 17, 2009).

16. Barack Obama, "A Life's Calling to Public Service," *Punahou Bulletin*, Fall 1999 http://www.punahou.edu/uploaded/News_Content/Media/Pun_Bull_Obama_article.pdf (accessed April 5, 2009).

17. Mark Niesse, "Island Life in Multiracial Hawaii Shaped Obama," Boston.com., August 7, 2008, http://www.boston.com/news/politics/2008/articles/2008/08/07/island_life_in_multiracial_hawaii_shaped_obama (accessed September 17, 2009).

18. Obama, "A Life's Calling to Public Service."

19. Obama, *Dreams from My Father*, 133.

20. Mendell, 63.

21. "Barack Obama," Wikipedia, http://en.wikipedia.org/wiki/Barack_Obama (accessed April 5, 2009).

22. Obama, *Dreams from My Father*, 156.

23. Mendell, 66.

24. Obama, *Dreams from My Father*, 157. My emphasis.

25. Ibid., 195.

26. Barack Obama, *The Audacity of Hope* (New York: Crown, 2006), 235.

27. Ibid., 235–236.

28. Ibid., 236.

29. "Barack Obama," Wikipedia.

30. Gretchen Reynolds, "Vote of Confidence," *Chicago Magazine*, January 1993, http://www.chicagomag.com/Chicago-Magazine/January-1993/Vote-of-Confidence/ (accessed April 9, 2009).

31. Ibid.

32. "Barack Obama," Wikipedia.

33. Mike Robinson, "Obama Got Start in Civil Rights Practice," Associated Press, *Washington Post*, February 20, 2007, http://www.washingtonpost.com/wp-dyn/content/article/2007/02/20/AR2007022000045.html (accessed April 9, 2009).

34. Michael Weisskopf, "How He Learned to Win," President Obama: The Path to the White House, *Time*, Special Commemorative Edition 2008: 50.

35. Mendell, 126–127.

36. Mendell, 180–181.

37. Mendell, 189.

38. Weisskopf, 50.

39. Edward McClelland, "Is Bobby Rush in Trouble?" The Obama Reader, Chicago Reader, January 15, 2009, http://www.chicagoreader.com/obama_reader/bobby_rush/ (accessed April 11, 2009). Original article that contained this story was published on March 17, 2000.

40. Mendell, 142.

41. Weisskopf, 50.

42. McClelland.

43. Mendell, 133.

44. Monica Davey, "From Crowded Field, Democrats Choose State Legislator to Seek Senate Seat," *New York Times*, March 17, 2004, http://www.nytimes.com/2004/03/17/politics/campaign/17ILLI.html?ex=1080104400&en=bbcde46887876b70&ei=5062&partner=GOOGLE (accessed April 11, 2009); and "Daniel Hynes," Wikipedia, http://en.wikipedia.org/wiki/Dan_Hynes (accessed April 11, 2009).

45. "United States Senate Election Campaign in Illinois, 2004," Wikipedia, http://en.wikipedia.org/wiki/United_States_Senate_election_in_Illinois,_2004 (accessed April 15, 2009).

46. William Voegeli, "The Rise and Fall of Blair Hull," The Claremont Institute for the Study of Statesmanship and Political Philosophy, March 19, 2004, http://www.claremont.org/publications/pubid.339/pub_detail.asp (accessed April 17, 2009).

47. Mendell, 235.

48. Ibid., 231.

49. "United States Senate Election Campaign in Illinois, 2004."

50. "Jack Ryan (Politician)," Wikipedia, http://en.wikipedia.org/wiki/Jack_Ryan_(politician) (accessed April 17, 2009).

51. Mendell, 275–276.

52. Ibid., 276.

53. Ibid., 276.

54. Obama, *The Audacity of Hope*, 358.

55. "2004 Democratic National Convention Keynote Address," Wikipedia, http://en.wikipedia.org/wiki/2004_Democratic_National_Convention_keynote_address (accessed April 20, 2009).

56. "Barack Obama's Remarks at the Democratic Convention," The Associated Press, *USA Today*, July 27, 2004, http://www.usatoday.com/news/politicselections/nation/president/2004-07-27-obama-speech-text_x.htm (accessed April 20, 2009).

57. Robert C. Rowland and John M. Jones, "Recasting the American Dream and American Politics: Barack Obama's Keynote Address to the 2004 Democratic National Convention," *Quarterly Journal of Speech*, Vol. 93, No. 4, November 2007, 437.

58. Ibid., 438.

59. Robin Toner, "Optimistic, Democrats Debate the Party's Vision," *New York Times*, A1, May 9, 2006, http://select.nytimes.com/search/restricted/article?

res=FB0F10FB3D5A0C7A8CDDAC0894DE404482# (accessed July 28, 2007).

60. Rowland and Jones, 438. My emphasis.

61. "Barack Obama's Remarks at the Democratic Convention."

62. Rowland and Jones, 442.

63. "2004 Democratic National Convention Keynote Address," Wikipedia http://en.wikipedia.org/wiki/2004_Democratic_National_Convention_keynote_address (accessed September 19, 2009).

64. "Election 2004," CNN.com, http://www.cnn.com/ELECTION/2004/pages/results/states/IL/S/01/index.html (accessed April 26, 2009).

65. "United States Senate Election Campaign in Illinois, 2004."

66. Debbie Howlett, "Obama Extends Reach beyond Illinois Race," *USA Today*, October 14, 2004, http://www.usatoday.com/news/politicselections/nation/ussenate/2004–10-13-illinois-senate_x.htm (accessed April 26, 2009).

67. "United States Senate Career of Barack Obama," Wikipedia, http://en.wikipedia.org/wiki/United_States_Senate_career_of_Barack_Obama (accessed April 26, 2009).

68. "Family and Children's Issues," Project Vote Smart, http://www.votesmart.org/issue_rating_category.php?can_id=9490&type=category&category=31&go.x=16&go.y=11 (accessed April 27, 2009).

69. "Best & Worst Members of Congress for Children," Children's Defense Fund Action Council, http://www.cdfactioncouncil.org/cdf-action-council-congressional-votes-scorecard/2007_scorecard_bestworst.pdf (accessed April 27, 2009); and "Obama Making Less Than a Quarter of Senate Votes," CNNpolitics.com, November 2, 2007. http://www.cnn.com/2007/POLITICS/11/02/obama.missed.votes/ (accessed December 29, 2009).

70. "Barrack Obama," Sourcewatch, http://www.sourcewatch.org/index.php?title=Barack_Obama (accessed April 27, 2009).

71. "Description of Votes Scored," National Education Association, http://www.nea.org/home/19552.htm (accessed April 27, 2009).

72. "United States Senate Career of Barack Obama."

73. *ADA Today*, Vol. 62, No. 1 (February 2007): 14, 15, and 17.

74. Jodi Enda, "Great Expectations," The American Prospect, January 16, 2006, http://www.prospect.org/cs/articles?articleId=10828 (accessed April 27, 2009).

75. Ibid.

76. David Sirota, "Mr. Obama Goes to Washington," *The Nation*, June 8, 2006, http://www.thenation.com/doc/20060626/sirota/2 (accessed April 27, 2009).

77. Ibid.

78. Brian Friel, Richard E. Cohen, and Kirk Victor, "Obama: Most Liberal Senator in 2007," NationalJournal.com, January 31, 2008, http://news.nationaljournal.com/articles/voteratings/ (accessed April 27, 2009).

79. "United States Senate Career of Barack Obama" (accessed April 27, 2009); Jeff Lewis and Keith Poole, "109th Senate Rank Ordering," Voteview, December 31, 2006 http://voteview.com/sen109.htm (accessed April 27, 2009); and Jeff Lewis and Keith Poole, "110th Senate Rank Ordering," Voteview, December 22, 2008, http://voteview.com/sen110.htm (accessed April 27, 2009).

80. Obama, *The Audacity of Hope*, 39–40.

81. Ibid., 40.

82. "Barack Obama," Wikipedia.

83. Gwen Ifill, *The Breakthrough Politics and Race in the Age of Obama* (New York: Random House, 2009), 54. Emphasis in the original.

84. Ifill, 66.

85. "Barack Obama's Remarks at the Democratic Convention."

86. "Full Text of Senator Barack Obama's Announcement for President," Organizing for America, February 10, 2007, http://www.barackobama. com/2007/02/10/remarks_of_senator_barack_obam_11.php (accessed April 30, 2009).

87. Ifill, 65.

88. Ifill, 64.

89. Felicia R. Lee, "Building a Conversation, One Radio Show at a Time," *New York Times*, February 13, 2007, http://www.nytimes.com/2007/02/13/ arts/13joyn.html?pagewanted=1&_r=1 (accessed April 30, 2009).

90. Michael Eric Dyson, "His Way with Words Begins at the Pulpit," *Washington Post*, January 18, 2009, http://www.washingtonpost.com/wp-dyn/content/ article/2009/01/16/AR2009011602312.html (accessed April 30, 2009). Emphasis in the original.

91. Ibid.

92. John K. Wilson, *This Improbable Quest* (Boulder, CO: Paradigm, 2008), 58.

93. Ibid., 57.

94. Ibid., 61.

95. Toni Morrison, "Comment," *New Yorker*, October 5, 1998, http:// www.newyorker.com/archive/1998/10/05/1998_10_05_031_TNY_ LIBRY_000016504 (accessed May 1, 2009).

96. Scott Helman, "Obama, Clinton, in Tight Battle for Black Vote," *Boston Globe*, July 13, 2007, http://www.boston.com/news/nation/ articles/2007/07/13/obama_clinton_in_a_tight_battle_for_black_vote/ (accessed May 1, 2009).

97. James W. Ceaser, Andrew E. Busch, and John J. Pitney, *Epic Journey: The 2008 Elections and American Politics* (Lanham, MD: Rowman and Littlefield, 2009), 111. Google Book Search. Web. (accessed May 2, 2009).

98. Richard Thompson Ford, "Who's Afraid for Obama?" January 8, 2008, Slate http://www.slate.com/id/2181585/pagenum/all/#p2 (accessed May 1, 2009).

99. Jeff Zeleny, "Oprah Endorses Obama," May 3, 2007, http://thecaucus.

blogs.nytimes.com/2007/05/03/oprah-endorses-obama-2/ (accessed May 1, 2009); and "Oprah Winfrey's Endorsement of Barack Obama" Wikipedia, http://en.wikipedia.org/wiki/Oprah_Winfrey's_endorsement_of_Barack_Obama#cite_note-39 (accessed May 1, 2009).

100. Jeffrey M. Jones, "Hillary Edges Out Obama as Most Admired Woman in '07," Gallup, December 26, 2007, http://www.gallup.com/poll/103462/Hillary-Edges-Oprah-Most-Admired-Woman-07.aspx (accessed May 1, 2009).

101. Dick Morris, "The Oprah Factor: A Big Boost for Obama," DickMorris.com, December 12, 2007, http://www.dickmorris.com/blog/2007/12/12/the-oprah-factor-a-big-boost-for-obama/ (accessed May 1, 2009).

102. Tony Allen-Mills, "Women Turn on 'Traitor' Oprah Winfrey for Backing Barack Obama," *TimesOnLine*, January 20, 2008, http://www.timesonline.co.uk/tol/news/world/us_and_americas/us_elections/article3216586.ece (accessed May 1, 2009). Capitals in the original.

103. Andrew Malcolm, "Oprah's Ex-Fans Trash Her Support for Obama Over a Woman," Top of the Ticket, *Los Angeles Times Blogs*, April 10, 2008, http://latimesblogs.latimes.com/washington/2008/04/oprahsfansandno.html (accessed May 2, 2009).

104. Ibid.

105. "Oprah Winfrey's Endorsement of Barack Obama."

106. Craig Garthwaite and Tim Moore, "The Role of Celebrity Endorsements in Politics: Oprah, Obama, and the 2008 Democratic Primary," Paper can be accessed from The Monkey Cage, September 2008, http://econweb.umd.edu/~garthwaite/celebrityendorsements_garthwaitemoore.pdf (accessed September 19, 2009).

107. Gloria Steinem, "Women Are Never Front-Runners," *New York Times,* January 8, 2008, http://www.nytimes.com/2008/01/08/opinion/08steinem.html (accessed May 2, 2009).

108. Richard Slotkin, "Readers' Comments: Women Are Never Front-Runners," *New York Times,* January 8, 2008, http://community.nytimes.com/article/comments/2008/01/08/opinion/08steinem.html?s=4 (accessed May 2, 2009).

109. Jeff Noguera, "Readers' Comments: Women Are Never Front-Runners," *New York Times,* January 8, 2008, http://community.nytimes.com/article/comments/2008/01/08/opinion/08steinem.html?s=3&pg=2 (accessed May 2, 2009).

110. "2008 Iowa Caucuses," Iowa State University, http://www.public.iastate.edu/~nscentral/news/2007/dec/caucuses.shtml (accessed May 18, 2009).

111. Ifill, 82.

112. "ElectionCenter 2008," CNNPolitics.com, http://www.cnn.com/ELECTION/2008/primaries/results/epolls/#IADEM (accessed May 2, 2009).

113. "Nationwide Opinion Polling for the Democratic Party 2008 Presidential Candidates," Wikipedia, http://en.wikipedia.org/wiki/

Nationwide_opinion_polling_for_the_Democratic_Party_2008_ presidential_candidates (accessed May 2, 2009).

114. "Super Tuesday, 2008," Wikipedia, http://en.wikipedia.org/wiki/Super_ Tuesday,_2008 (accessed May 12, 2009).

115. Markos Moulitsas, "Not a Tie," Daily Kos, February 6, 2008, http://www. dailykos.com/storyonly/2008/2/6/142357/5631 (accessed May 12, 2009).

116. John Hanna, "Key Clinton Supporter Predicts Obama Win in Kansas Caucuses," Hutchnews.com, February 4, 2008, http://www.hutchnews. com/Todaystop/obama2008_02_04T21_59_30 (accessed May 14, 2009).

117. Brian Montopoli, "Hillary Clinton, Underdog?" CBS News, February 6, 2008, http://www.cbsnews.com/blogs/2008/02/06/politics/horserace/ entry3798877.shtml (accessed May 14, 2009).

118. Kate Phillips, "Clinton Lent Campaign $5 Million, Considers More," *New York Times,* February 6, 2008, http://thecaucus.blogs.nytimes. com/2008/02/06/clinton-considers-lending-her-campaign-money/ (accessed May 14, 2009).

119. Montopoli.

120. Julianna Goldman, "Obama Raises $5.8 million on Line after Super Tuesday (Update 2)," Bloomberg.com, February 7, 2008, http://www. bloomberg.com/apps/news?pid=20601087&sid=aWPzrc7Oc0uk (accessed May 15, 2009).

121. "Jeremiah Wright Controversy," Wikipedia, http://en.wikipedia.org/ wiki/Jeremiah_Wright_controversy (accessed May 2, 2009).

122. "Text of Obama's Speech: A Perfect Union," Washington Wire, *Wall Street Journal,* Blogs, http://blogs.wsj.com/washwire/2008/03/18/text-of- obamas-speech-a-more-perfect-union/?mod=googlenews_wsj (accessed May 2, 2009).

123. Ibid.

124. Robert Creamer, "Why Obama's Speech on Race Was Such a Political Home Run," *Huffington Post*, March 19, 2008, http://www.huffingtonpost.com/ robert-creamer/why-obamas-speech-on-rac_b_92374.html (accessed May 2, 2009).

125. "Text of Obama's Speech: A Perfect Union."

126. Jeff Newton-Small, "Reaction to the Obama Speech," *Time*, March 18, 2008, http://www.time.com/time/printout/0,8816,1723442,00.html (accessed May 2, 2009).

127. Kate Phillips, "Wright Defends Church and Blasts Media," *New York Times,* April 28, 2008, http://thecaucus.blogs.nytimes.com/2008/04/28/ rev-wright-defends-church-blasts-media/ (accessed May 11, 2009).

128. Shailagh Murray and Hamil R. Harris, "Priest Again Apologizes for Remarks in Sermon," *Washington Post*, June 2, 2008, http://www.washingtonpost. com/wp-dyn/content/article/2008/06/01/AR2008060102186. html?sid=ST2008060200033 (accessed May 11, 2009).

129. Jeff Zeleny, "First Black to Lead the Ticket for a Major Party," *New York Times*, A1, June 4, 2008.

130. Barack Obama, "Remarks of Illinois State Sen. Barack Obama against Going to War with Iraq," BarackObama.com, October 2, 2002, http://www.barackobama.com/pdf/warspeech.pdf (accessed May 20, 2009).

131. "U.S. Senate Roll Call Votes 107th Congress: 2nd Session," United States Senate, http://www.senate.gov/legislative/LIS/roll_call_lists/roll_call_vote_cfm.cfm?congress=107&session=2&vote=00237 (accessed May 20, 2009).

132. Roger Simon, "Does Hillary Have Something to Be Sorry About?" Politico, February 12, 2007, http://dyn.politico.com/printstory.cfm?uuid=B64E1E6A-3048–5C12–00551697D7973498 (accessed May 20, 2009).

133. Patrick Healy, "Clinton Gives War Critics New Answer on '02 Vote," *New York Times*, February 18, 2007, http://www.nytimes.com/2007/02/18/us/politics/18clinton.html?pagewanted=1&ref=politics (accessed May 20, 2009).

134. Ibid.

135. Michael Crowley, "Cinderella Story," *New Republic*, February 27, 2008, http://www.tnr.com/politics/story.html?id=aaad0724-dd13–4ffa-810b-d5d3220ff055&k=88887&p=2 (accessed May 20, 2009).

136. Tomas B. Edsall, "The Attempts to Discredit Obama's Iraq War Stance Has Begun," *Huffington Post*, August 8, 2007, http://www.huffingtonpost.com/2007/08/09/thomas-b-edsall-the-atte_n_59875.html (accessed May 20, 2009).

137. "Talk of War," Online NewsHour, October 7, 2002, http://www.pbs.org/newshour/bb/middle_east/july-dec02/iraqpolls_10–07-02.html (accessed May 20, 2009).

138. Crowley. Emphasis in the original.

139. Obama, "Remarks of Illinois State Sen. Barack Obama against Going to War With Iraq."

140. Michael Walzer, *Just and Unjust Wars*, Fourth edition, revised (New York: Basic Books, 2006), 110. Emphasis in the original. Google Book Search. Web. (accessed May 20, 2009).

141. Jake Tapper, "Obama Apologizes for Saying Troops' Lives 'wasted,'" February 13, 2007, *abcnews* http://abcnews.go.com/Politics/story?id=2872135&page=1 (accessed September 19, 2009).

142. "McCain Says He Misspoke in Saying U.S. lives 'Wasted,'" CNN, March 1, 2007, http://www.cnn.com/2007/POLITICS/03/01/mccain/index.html (accessed May 20, 2009).

143. Richard Adams, "Democratic Presidential Debate," *Guardian*, July 23, 2007, http://www.guardian.co.uk/world/2007/jul/23/uselections2008.usa (accessed May 20, 2009).

144. Justin Raimondo, "The War Party Targets Obama" Antiwar.com, February 16, 2008, http://www.antiwar.com/justin/?articleid=12366 (accessed December 29, 2009).

145. Chuck Todd and Sheldon Gawiser, *How Barack Obama Won* (New York: Random House, 2009), 39. Google Book Search. Web. (accessed May 20, 2009).

146. Stephen Zunes, "Why Obama Won," ZNet, June 8, 2008, http://www.zmag.org/znet/viewArticle/17867 (accessed May 20, 2009).

147. Tim Dickinson, "The Machinery of Hope," *Rolling Stone*, March 20, 2008, http://www.rollingstone.com/news/coverstory/obamamachineryofhope/page/4 (accessed May 12, 2009).

148. James B. Weatherby and Randy Stapilus, *Governing Idaho: Politics, People and Power* (Caldwell, Idaho: Caxton, 2005), 57. Google Book Search. Web. (accessed May 11, 2009).

149. Dickinson.

150. Scott Helman, "The Obama Show Comes to Boise," Political Intelligence, Boston.com, February 2, 2008, http://www.boston.com/news/politics/politicalintelligence/2008/02/boise_idaho_thi.html (accessed May 11, 2009).

151. Carrie Budoff Brown, "Obama Aims to Please in Red States," Politico, February 3, 2008, http://www.politico.com/news/stories/0208/8280.html (accessed May 12, 2009).

152. "Results: Idaho," CNNPolitics.com, February 5, 2008, http://www.cnn.com/ELECTION/2008/primaries/results/state/#ID (accessed May 11, 2009).

153. "Idaho," 270toWin.com, http://www.270towin.com/states/Idaho (accessed May 11, 2009).

154. Logan Stoodley, "The Idaho Caucus," Organizing for America, February 12, 2008, http://my.barackobama.com/page/community/post/stoodlemayer/C43z/commentary (accessed May 11, 2009).

155. "Kansas," 270toWin.com, http://www.270towin.com/states/kansas (accessed May 12, 2009).

156. Nadia Plfaum, "There's Nothing the Matter with Kansas," Salon, January 30, 2008, http://www.salon.com/news/feature/2008/01/30/obama/ (accessed May 12, 2009).

157. Peter Slevin, "Obama Mines Small, Traditionally Red States," *Washington Post*, January 29, 2008, http://www.washingtonpost.com/wp-dyn/content/article/2008/01/28/AR2008012802558.html (accessed May 12, 2009).

158. "Results: Kansas," CNNPolitics.com, http://www.cnn.com/ELECTION/2008/primaries/results/state/#KS (accessed May 12, 2009).

159. Roger L. Simon, "Obama: The Candidate as Rorschach Test," Pajamas Media, October 30, 2008, http://pajamasmedia.com/rogerlsimon/2008/10/30/obama-the-candidate-as-rorschach-test/ (accessed May 14, 2009). Emphasis in the original.

160. David D. Kirkpatrick, Mike McIntire, and Jeff Zeleny, "Obama's Camp Cultivates Crop in Small Donors," Correction Appended, *New York Times*,

July 17, 2007, http://www.nytimes.com/2007/07/17/us/politics/17obama.html?_r=1 (accessed May 16, 2009).

161. Ibid.

162. Mark Hennessy, "Counting the Cost of Campaign Communications," *Irish Times,* October 29, 2008, http://www.irishtimes.com/newspaper/world/2008/1029/1225197273865_pf.html (accessed May 16, 2009).

163. Jose Antonio Vargas, "Obama Raised Half a Billion Online," The Clickocracy, *Washington Post,* November 20, 2008, http://voices.washingtonpost.com/44/2008/11/20/obama_raised_half_a_billion_on.html (accessed May 17, 2009).

164. Elizabeth Poeschl, "How Barack Obama's Presidential Campaign Will Change Your Small Business," Scribd, March 18, 2009, http://www.scribd.com/doc/13453287/How-Barack-Obamas-Presidential-Campaign-Will-Change-Your-Small-Business (accessed June 6, 2009).

165. Joshua Green, "The Amazing Money Machine," *The Atlantic Online,* June 2008, http://www.theatlantic.com/doc/200806/obama-finance/1 (accessed June 6, 2009).

166. Hennessy.

167. Michael Malbin, "REALITY CHECK: Obama Received about the Same Percentage from Small Donors in 2008 as Bush in 2004," The Campaign Institute, November 24, 2008, http://www.cfinst.org/pr/prRelease.aspx?ReleaseID=216 (accessed May 16, 2009). Emphasis in the original. These figures are only through October 24, 2008.

168. "Bundlers," Opensecrets.org, http://www.opensecrets.org/pres08/bundlers.php?id=N00009638 (accessed May 18, 2009).

169. "Bush Pioneer," Wikipedia, http://en.wikipedia.org/wiki/Bush_pioneer (accessed May 18, 2009).

170. Sam Youngman, "Obama Won't Accept Public Financing," The Hill, June 19, 2008, http://thehill.com/campaign-2008/obama-wont-accept-public-financing-2008-06-19.html (accessed May 18, 2009).

171. David Lightman, "Obama, With Plenty of Money, Forgoes Public Financing," McClatchy, June 19, 2008, http://www.mcclatchydc.com/254/story/41562.html (accessed May 18, 2009).

172. Liz Sidoti, "Analysis: Obama Chose Winning over His Word," The Associated Press, SignOnSanDiego.com, June 19, 2008, http://www.signonsandiego.com/news/politics/20080619-1235-obama-money-analysis.html (accessed May 18, 2009).

173. Green.

174. Vargas.

175. "Won't Get Fooled Again," Wikipedia, http://en.wikipedia.org/wiki/Won't_Get_Fooled_Again (accessed May 18, 2009).

176. David Mazella, *The Making of Modern Cynicism* (Charlottesville: University of Virginia Press, 2007), 1.

177. Associated with "Syntonic," Yourdictionary.com, http://www. yourdictionary.com/syntonic (accessed May 18, 2009).

178. Caroline Davies, "Cyndex: Cynicism 'Can Damage Democracy's Health,'" *The Observer,* September 14, 2008, http://www.lrcg.co.uk/ index.php?option=com_content&task=view&id=28&Itemid=35 (accessed May 17, 2009).

179. Ibid.

180. Duncan Watts, *Understanding American Government and Politics: A Comparative Guide* (Manchester: Manchester University Press, 2003), 21. Google Book Search. Web. (accessed May 18, 2009).

181. Wilson, 17. The original quote was from another source.

182. Ibid.

183. "General Election: McCain vs. Obama," Real Clear Politics, http:// www.realclearpolitics.com/epolls/2008/president/us/general_election_ mccain_vs_obama-225.html#polls (accessed May 18, 2009).

184. David Jackson, "McCain Casts Himself as the 'Underdog' in '08," *USA Today,* August 22, 2008, http://www.usatoday.com/news/politics/ election2008/2008–08-21-mccain-cover_N.htm (accessed May 19, 2009).

185. Suzanne Goldenberg, "McCain Plays Valiant Underdog as Once-Loyal South Looks Uncertain," *Guardian,* October 14, 2008, http://www. guardian.co.uk/world/2008/oct/14/uselections2008-johnmccain1 (accessed May 19, 2009).

186. "'Underdog' McCain Slams 'Confident' Rival," *The Independent,* October 22, 2008, http://www.independent.co.uk/news/world/americas/ underdog-mccain-slams-confident-rival-969344.html (accessed May 19, 2009).

187. "2008 Presidential General Election Results," Dave Leip's Atlas of U.S. Presidential Elections, http://www.uselectionatlas.org/RESULTS/ (accessed May 18, 2009).

188. Mark Silva, "Michelle Obama: 'Underdog' til Nov. 4," The Swamp, *Chicago Tribune,* October 16, 2008, http://www.swamppolitics.com/ news/politics/blog/2008/10/michelle_obama_underdog_til_no.html (accessed March 27, 2009).

189. Ethan Bronner, "For Many Abroad, an Ideal Renewed," *New York Times,* A1, November 5, 2008.

190. Stephen Dian, "Obama Signs Massive Stimulus Bill," *Washington Times,* February 17, 2009, http://www.washingtontimes.com/news/2009/feb/17/ obama-signs-massive-economic-stimulus-bill (accessed June 6, 2009).

191. Christina D. Romer, "Fiscal Policy and Economic Recovery," Council of Economic Advisors, March 3, 2009, http://www.whitehouse. gov/administration/eop/cea/speeches_testimony/03032009/ (accessed May 20, 2009).

192. "Obama's 100 Days of Progress," Think Progress, April 29, 2009, http:// pr.thinkprogress.org/2009/04/pr20090429 (accessed September 17, 2009).

193. "The President's Remarks on Justice Souter," May 1, 2009 *whitehouse.gov* http://www.whitehouse.gov/blog/09/05/01/The-Presidents-Remarks-on-Justice-Souter/ (accessed September 19, 2009).

194. Chris Weigant, "Is the Media Misinterpreting Obama's 'Empathy' Dog Whistle?" *Huffington Post*, May 7, 2009, http://www.huffingtonpost.com/chris-weigant/is-the-media-misinterpret_b_198389.html (accessed May 20, 2009).

195. Ibid.

196. "Barack Obama before Planned Parenthood Action Fund, July 17, 2007," http://lauraetch.googlepages.com/barackobamabeforeplannedparenthoodaction (accessed, September 19, 2009).

197. Alan Brock, "Seeking Empathy on the Court," *The Orange County Register*, May 10, 2009, http://www.ocregister.com/articles/court-law-justice-2399802-supreme-obama (accessed May 20, 2009).

198. "Party Chairs Kaine and Steele Debate Pelosi, Obama & More," *Meet the Press*, Real Clear Politics, May 17, 2009, http://www.realclearpolitics.com/articles/2009/05/17/party_chairs_kaine_and_steele_debate_pelosi_obama_96536.html (accessed May 20, 2009).

199. Ibid.

200. "Remarks by the President in Nominating Judge Sonia Sotomayor to the United States Supreme Court," The White House, May 26, 2009, http://www.whitehouse.gov/the_press_office/Remarks-by-the-President-in-Nominating-Judge-Sonia-Sotomayor-to-the-United-States-Supreme-Court/ (accessed June 6, 2009).

201. Ibid.

202. Daphne Eviatar, "Sotomayor Hearing Pits 'Bias' against 'Empathy,'" *Washington Independent*, July 14, 2009, http://washingtonindependent.com/50715/sotomayor-hearing-pits-bias-against-empathy (accessed September 14, 2009).

203. "Sotomayor Sworn in as Justice," *USA Today*, August 9, 2009, http://www.usatoday.com/news/washington/judicial/2009-08-08-sotomayor-confirmation_N.htm (accessed September 14, 2009).

204. Patrick M. Garry, *Liberalism and American Identity* (Kent, OH: Kent State University Press, 1992), 182. Google Book Search. Web. (accessed September 17, 2009).

205. Melody Petersen, "William McChesney Martin, 91, Dies; Defined Fed's Role," *New York Times*, July 29, 1998, http://www.nytimes.com/1998/07/29/business/william-mcchesney-martin-91-dies-defined-fed-s-role.html (accessed September 17, 2009).

206. Martin Feldstein, "Interview Martin Feldstein," *Frontline*, http://www.pbs.org/wgbh/pages/frontline/meltdown/interviews/feldstein.html (accessed September 15, 2009).

207. Michael Knox Beran, "Incurable Romantic: Why Gore Glorifies Public Power," *National Review*, November 6, 2000, http://www.accessmylibrary.com/coms2/summary_0286-28481211_ITM?email=ktrautman@cmcc.edu&library= (accessed October 17, 2008).

208. Barack Obama, "Obama's Health Care Speech to Congress," *New York Times* September 9, 2009, http://www.nytimes.com/2009/09/10/us/politics/10obama.text.html?pagewanted=7&_r=1 (accessed September 15, 2009).

209. Attributed to T.R. Reid in *The Healing of America: A Global Quest for Better, Cheaper, and Fairer Health Care* (New York: Penguin, 2009) in Larry Donohue. "Health Care Reform- How Much Inequality Will We tolerate?" *seattlepi.com*, November 5, 2009 http://blog.seattlepi.com/larrydonohue/archives/183938.asp (accessed December 31, 2009).

210. Larry Donohue. "Health Care Reform- How Much Inequality Will We tolerate?" *seattlepi.com*, November 5, 2009 http://blog.seattlepi.com/larrydonohue/archives/183938.asp (accessed December 31, 2009).

Index